DATE DUE

Demco, Inc. 38-293

INDEX

(50音順)

SPECIAL FEATURE（特集）
【 passot 】

passot
sales front line

最善の解決方法は、販売現場にある。

会社概要

社名： passot 株式会社（パッソ 株式会社）

設立年月： 2005年5月

営業所： 東京都港区赤坂1丁目5番2号　外堀通ビル4F
tel: 03-3568-4330　fax: 03-3568-4331
www.passot.co.jp

2005年設立、国際ネットワーク企業 Marin's のネットワークに加わる。
2009年、日本国内で "Lamà" の独占ライセンシーとなる。
消費材メーカーを中心に、多くの企業にサービスを提供している passot のファブリス シンドラー社長にお話を伺いました。

---

1. What do you think about the current trends of the "SP" industry throughout the world?

The industry has changed very much in the last 10 years and we see now more and more of the impact that good SP can have on sales, market share increase and as an overall, on profitability.

Global companies driven by profit and institutional shareholders are forced to perform well but even more to meet market expectations. For those reasons companies need to manage their costs but above all they need to put all chances to plan a good ROI. The company performances are well measured and severely judged by the market. Communication budget are not always shrinking as we often hear, sometimes they are even increasing to prevent a drop in the communication efficiency toward customers.

The budget allowance is just changing, shifting from institutional media (TV, newspaper and magazines) to new media or "Great value media". Quite of a complex game, media planning becomes the key success to increase the ROI, market share and turn-over. We are in a test period, in order to communicate, which medium shall companies use for what budget and for what kind of effects??

Naturally, Sales promotion or promotion at the point of sales became the "risk free" on that complex game. Indeed, the store still remains the last place where customer might change mind before purchasing. We are leaving in the "new mass market world" where Distributors become kings and Makers servile subjects. Wall Mart has become the biggest company in the world, who would have predict it 30 years ago? You produce in the world, for the world and sell to the world. The "SP" industry and more generally global communication world is in mutation, it is then natural that we come back to basics before moving on to new horizons. The printing world is entering a critical phase.

---

1. 世界のSP業界のトレンドや流れについてどのように思われますか？

ＳＰ業界は、過去10年で大きく変化しました。現在、ＳＰは売上や市場シェア、そして、なによりも収益性を拡大しています。

利益性を追求するグローバル企業は、業績を伸ばすだけでなく、市場の期待にも答えなくてはなりません。このような理由から、企業は経費カットを断行するだけでなく、投資利益率（ROI）を高めるすべてのチャンスを逃してはいけません。企業業績は綿密に分析され、市場から厳しく評価されます。昨今、企業の宣伝費は、常に削減されているという訳ではなく、顧客に対してもっと効率的に宣伝をするためとして、その宣伝費出費を増大させている場合も多くあります。宣伝予算は、制度化されたメディア（つまり、テレビ、新聞および雑誌など）から新しいメディアやグレートバリューメディアと呼ばれる効果が確実に表れる店頭販促などのメディアにますます多く投入されるようになっています。メディアプランニングこそが、ROIや市場シェアそして回転率を拡大する大きな成功要素のカギとなりつつありますが、メディアプランニングを立てることは簡単なことではありません。今は試験段階なのです。つまり、企業は、どのようなメディアを使えば、宣伝費を効果的に使うことができ、どのように効果が得られるかを模索しているのです。

当然、一般的な販売促進活動の中で効果確実な店頭販促は、このような複雑なゲームにおいては「リスクフリー」となります。まさしく、現在でも店頭こそが、顧客が品物を購入しようと意思決定をする最後の「砦」となっているのです。現在は、近代的大量市場が世界を席巻しており、ディストリビューターがキングとなって、メーカーが召使いのような存在となっています。Wall Martが世界最大の企業ですが、このことは30年前に誰が予想したでしょう。商品は世界中で生産されており、世界中の消費者のために世界中で売られています。ＳＰ業界、さらにはコミュニケーション業界全体が突然変異の真っただ中にあり、そのような状況の中では、次の世代に移行するまで、基本に立ち返ろうとする本能が生まれるのは当然なことなのです。印刷業界はまさに危機的な段階に突入しているのです。

2. What do you think about the current trends of the "SP" industry in Japan?

The "SP" industry in Japan, in my opinion, is following international trends at a lower intensity that is to say, with a decade late. Japanese market is historically a reluctant market to change. The "SP" industry has a key role to play in the Japanese market mutation. Few years ago, Hakuhodo and Dentsu where feeling a need to create some new branchs or let's say sister companies SP specialist, with Hakuhodo product and Dentsu tech and they did have a great chance in the business, as they had the customers already. My opinion is that the real opportunity in the business is for company like Toppan, DNP or other printers alike.

They do possess the production know how and logistic power, they are learning very fast about marketing and design. We will see what they will make of this opportunity in the next 5 years.

2. 日本でのSP業界のトレンドや流れについてどのように思われますか?

日本におけるSP業界は、私に言わせれば、世界の流れにまだ追いついていません。つまり、10年は遅れていると思います。日本市場は、歴史的に見ても、変化には素早く対応できないようです。しかし、SP業界は、日本市場の「突然変異」において大きな役割を果たすでしょう。数年前、博報堂と電通は、たとえばSP専門部門と言った部門を設立しようとした動きがありました。その結果、「博報堂プロダクト」や「電通テック」といった関連会社が設立されました。そのような会社は、すでに顧客を持っているため、宣伝分野において多大な可能性を持っています。しかし、私としては、宣伝業界における真の可能性というのは、トッパン、DNPあるいは他の印刷会社にこそあるものだと思っています。それらの企業は製造ノウハウやロジスティックパワーを持っており、現在、彼らはマーケティングおよびデザインを急速に学習しています。彼らが、今後5年間でこの「チャンス」をどのように自分のものにするか見てみたいと思います。

3. What are the characteristics of LAMA (system), and what are the advantages for the customers at LAMA?

First of all Lama concept is based on a new way of thinking. It is the reason why Marins international has become so strong on the "SP" market in the last 2 decades. It is as well how they could develop such a strong and large network globally. The Lama is a system and it eventually became a product, a new medium with a fantastic line up that is being copied worldwide. Now, Marins international can boast the power of a global network strong of over 700 peoples. It is the largest adaptable and creative "SP" network worldwide. It is as well a fantastic and very powerful tool for companies. Who can provide in less than 24 hours, solutions at the point of sales in about 120 countries to his customers? WE CAN !

When you are a global company in the search of better performances and costs efficiencies, it then doesn't looks to me strategically reasonable to choose to be outside of this network by copying the product. Though it will be rather smart to me, for those companies to get into negotiation to get the best deal out of it !

Technically speaking the characteristics of the LAMA system could be summarize roughly as:

Simple
As the "Lego block" that everybody uses to manipulate and nobody ever managed to recreate in full, the Lama is using a very simple process that allows a very easy manufacturing. From design to print, from print to die cut, from Die-cut to assembly, from assembly to packing, it is just always the same process no matter the product you develop, no matter the new product you want to create or to customize.

Cost efficient
Basic parts are set and are reused from one product to another, so producing and storing parts in advance is possible, making it highly cost efficient. It is a very efficient paper consumption tool, standard die cut mold adaptable for new product developments, a standard assembly method, a very well studied packing size and method that allow production cost efficiency for all the Lama line up. As a result we can say that the linear production cost for the Lama line up helps customer on planning their communication budget. It is indeed a major competitive advantage to our few competitors that have to re-think each new product from the beginning , and have to bear new R&D and mold costs for each new product batches.

Time efficiency
Highly standardized process from the very early stage of the project development to the final delivery, we are able to shorten the production to 2weeks for almost all the line up for an average 3000 pieces.

Adaptive :
The Lama system adapts to most of the shape or usages that our customer can think of. Impossible is a word we don't like to say to our customers and while creating this Lama system Francois l'Hotel, the inventor and patent owner had always done his best to make Lama system product adaptable to many usage and customized it to all needs. Our limits are coming from the material we are using, as an example we haven't yet found a paper that can be used for outdoors (strong enough to resist rain) and that could be foldable.

Non-limitative
Our magic was to be able to provide to our customers a tool they can play with and develop by themselves. They are free to create, free to innovate, we support them, we advise them, and we work together with our customer so that they can get the best for their communication campaigns. We are not a supplier; we are a creative and comprehensive partner for their product and marketing development campaign.

Compact
As you can imagine, the direct impact of the fact that our product is compact is the space saving (cost for the ware housing) but as well the packing and the shipping cost. We will explain as well below how it impacts on sales figures.

Those "technical" or "manufacturing" concerns are very important and explain how we can reply efficiently to the buyer concerns or buying department requests.

Looking at the more marketing or sales approach, the real advantages of the product developed with Lama System are also found in the extents of:

Visibility
All our product are printed on both sides, either same visual design or different visual design, or just let say on all sides. It is then easy to imagine that at the point of sales the impact is stronger than all those one side floor display. The product is well finished and give a rather high visual impression and quality-impression, contributing to add value to customer brand-image.

Easy set-up
You should just try it on !

The marketing or the buying department might just like our products but the users, meaning the sales people or even more in Japan, the store staff, just dream of having a so easy set up display all the time. If it takes you more than 30 seconds to set it up, it might mean that the product you have in hand is not a Lama system product, there is no other explanations !

□ Eco friendly

We are eco friendly since the beginning even before it became a trend ! All our products are done with paper - recycled paper most of the time -, natural rubber band and we use as well some corrugated cardboard but in very small quantities.

Our product when not laminated is 100 % recyclable . Our product is so compact when folded that it use for packing at least half the quantity of corrugated cardboard of our competitors and can reduce up to 60% of CO_2 emissions in the transportation process.

□ Sales performances

Not only in Japan the sales representatives are going from stores to stores to pursue their duties. It is more and more difficult for small and big corporation to keep a large sales force and those sales forces have to be more efficient.Using our product they can visit more stores, the set up time for each display is no more than 30 seconds, giving each sales-man more time for negotiation with each store manager than before. As our product is at least twice more compact compared to other our competitor products they can carry at least double quantities products.

□ Planning

Strategy is vital for the marketing and sales team in the race to be the best on the market. We offer to our customer the possibility to use in the same size different product for the same price. We can develop in less that 24 hours new products and we are able to deliver mass production within 2 weeks. We have the wider range of automatic display in the world. We work with over 2.000 major companies in the world and we can share our experience with you. We can support our customer during all the very important phases of the campaign from planning to realization.

□ Accurate forecasts

When you launch a campaign what you want is to be able to apply your marketing strategy to all the different stores. This is the key of your visibility, your branding. Being automatic our product gives you the assurance that all the product you order will be set up the same way everywhere, no mistakes in building can be made.

Here are some of the key elements that we can point out easily, but there is so much more that can be pointed out and that depends also on the customer, because each customer have there own problems and own needs.

Contact us might you still be in doubts of the benefits of our products or just make a trip around the world you will see our products directly in use !

3. LAMAの特徴は何ですか？そして、顧客がLAMAを使う利点は何ですか？

まず、ＬＡＭＡコンセプトは、すべてある新しい「考え方」に基づいています。これが、Marins International社が、過去20年にもわたりＳＰ市場で圧倒的な存在を示している理由です。同社は、特に強力で広大なネットワークをグローバルに展開しています。ＬＡＭＡはシステムそのものであり、最終的に「製品」として展開されたものです。ＬＡＭＡは非常に優れたラインアップを持つ新しいメディアであり、世界中でコピーされています。現在Marins internationalは世界中で700人以上の人材を持ち、グローバルなネットワークパワーを保持していると言えます。そして、最も高度な適応性のある、クリエイティブなSPネットワークとなっています。また、ＬＡＭＡは、顧客企業にとっても非常に優れた、そして、パワフルなツールとなります。誰が、120カ国もの国で、24時間以内に店頭で「ソリューション」を提供できるでしょうか？我々だったらできるのです。

たとえば御社がグローバル企業だとして、業績の向上とコスト削減のために、我々のネットワークを利用せず、LAMA製品をコピーする会社を選ぶとすると、それは、あまり賢い選択ではありません。むしろ、そのような企業は、我々と交渉して最大限の恩恵を得るべきです。

技術的な観点からみると、ＬＡＭＡシステムは以下のように要約することができます。

□ シンプル

LAMAシステムは「レゴブロック」のように、誰でも自分の好きなように使うことができ、LAMA製品はとてもシンプルなプロセスで非常に簡単に製造することができますが、まだ完全に「復元」されたことはありません。LAMAはデザインからプリント、プリントからダイカット、ダイカットからアセンブリー、アセンブリーからパッケージングまで、どのようなプロダクトを構築しようとも、また、どのような新製品を構築したいと思っても、また、どのような製品をカスタマイズしたいと思っていても常に同じプロセスなのです。

□ 高いコスト性

基本的パーツは設定されており、1種類のプロダクトから別の種類のプロダクトへ再利用でき、同時に事前にパーツを造ったり保存したりできるため、LAMA製品製造は非常に高いコスト性を持っています。たとえば、新製品開発に適用できるスタンダードなダイカットモールド、スタンダードなアセンブリーメソッド、綿密に計算されたパッキングサイズおよび方法など、すべてのLAMA製品ラインアップでコストを抑えることができる非常に効率的な紙ツールなのです。

その結果、ＬＡＭＡラインアップに対する直線的なプロダクションコストは、顧客が宣伝費を事前に確認し確保するのに役立ちます。このことは、他社との競争上の大きな優位性となるものです。つまり、他社の製品を使うと、新しいプロダクトを展開する場合、最初からプロダクトを再構築する必要があり、結局、全体的コストは大きくなります。

□ 時間の効率性

プロジェクト展開の早い段階から最終デリバリーまで非常に標準化されたプロセスにより、ほとんどすべてのLAMA製品で例えば3000LOTの製造期間を他社製品製造期間に比べ2週間短縮することができます。

□ 適応性

ＬＡＭＡシステムは、顧客が考え付くすべての形や使用方法のほとんどに適用することができます。「不可能」という言葉は我々の顧客に対しては使いたくありません。Francois l'Hotelは、このＬＡＭＡシステムの発明者および特許保持者ですが、彼は、システム開発中において、ありとあらゆるニーズに対応するため、このシステムを多種多様な使用法に適応しカスタマイズしました。現在、システムの限界というのは、使われているマテリアルによるものです。たとえば、屋外で利用でき、かつ折りたたむことができる紙はまだ実現していません。

□ あらゆる可能性

顧客自らが工夫・展開できるツールを提供することは、我々のマジックといえるでしょう。 LAMA製品は、自由に構築したりカスタマイズすることができます。我々はそれらをサポートしたり、顧客にアドバイスをしたり、さらには、顧客のキャンペーンが最大限の効果をもたらすよう顧客と協力し合うことができます。我々はサプライヤーではなく、プロダクトやマーケティング展開キャンペーンのクリエイティブで包括的なパートナーという存在なのです。

□ コンパクト

お分かりのように、LAMA製品がコンパクトであるということは、空間が節約されるだけでなく（倉庫コストの節約）、パッケージングコストや出荷コストも節約されることを意味します。

以上のように、技術的あるいは製造面で顧客や顧客の調達部門が懸念しうる問題・疑問に我々は的確かつ迅速に対応することができます。

マーケティングや営業といった面からLAMAシステムを考えると、LAMAシステムで開発されたLAMA製品にはさらに以下のような多くの利点があります。

□ 視認性

LAMA製品は、両面同柄にしろ、片面ずつ違うデザインにしろ、全面にデザインが印刷されます。したがって、LAMA製品を店頭に置くことで、一面だけのフロアディスプレイに比べインパクトが格段と大きくなります。LAMA製品は完成度が高く、強い印象と高品質なイメージを持ち、顧客は大きなブランド性を彼らの商品に与えることができます。

□ 容易なセットアップ

とにかく試してみてください。マーケティング部門や調達部門は単に我々のLAMA製品を気に入っているだけかもしれませんが、営業担当や日本のストアスタッフといった実際の現場でのユーザーは、本当にセットアップが簡単なディスプレイを使いたいと切実に思っているでしょう。ディスプレイをセットアップするのに30秒以上もかかるとすれば、手元にあるプロダクトはLAMAシステムのプロダクトではないでしょう。そうでなければ他に説明がつきません。

□ エコ

弊社は、エコが叫ばれ始めたころからエコを第一に考えています。LAMA製品の材料は紙（ほとんどが再生紙）および天然ゴムバンドです。また、少量ですが、ある程度の段ボールも使用されています。

LAMA製品はラミネート加工されていなければ、100％リサイクル可能となっています。LAMA製品は非常にコンパクトなため、競合相手の段ボール箱の半分以下の段ボール箱に収めることができます。その結果、LAMA製品の輸送プロセスにおいては、他社製品の輸送に比べ最大で60％もの二酸化炭素排出が削減されることもあるのです

□ 営業

営業担当が営業活動をするのに何軒も店舗を回るのは日本だけではありません。大企業さえも、大きな営業部門を維持するのがますます困難になっており、そのような営業部門もさらなる効率化を余儀なくされています。

LAMA製品を使えば、営業担当はより多くの店舗を訪問することができます。それぞれのディスプレイをセットアップする時間は30秒もかからず、営業担当は他のことに時間を費やすことができるようになります。LAMA製品は他の競合プロダクトより2倍以上もコンパクトであり、したがって2倍以上の量の製品を持ち歩くことができます。

□ プラニング

市場でトップになるためには、マーケティング及び営業部門にとってはストラテジーが最も重要となります。我々は、同じサイズであれば形状などが異なるプロダクトでも、同じ価格で使用できる様、オファーをしています。また、新しいプロダクトは24時間以内に構築することができ、2週間以内に大量生産することができます。また、我々は、世界中で、各種自立式ディスプレイを提供しています。我々は、世界中で2,000社以上もの主要企業に対応しており、我々の経験を御社と共有できると思います。我々は、この厳しい経済環境の中でも顧客を支援することができます。

□ 安定性

御社がキャンペーンを展開する場合、御社のマーケティングストラテジーをすべての店舗に適用したいでしょう。このことは、御社の存在、つまり、ブランドを示す上でカギとなります。LAMA製品は「自立式」であることから、御社が注文するすべてのLAMA製品は、いかなる場所でも同じようにセットアップされることが保証されます。LAMA製品のセットアップ中にはミスは起きないのです。

これまで、主なポイントを簡単な例と共に説明してきましたが、まだまだ説明したいポイントが多くあります。しかし、各顧客で、特殊事情やニーズがあり、ポイントの説明はそれらによって異なります。もし、質問や疑問があればいつでも弊社に連絡してください。またLAMA製品は世界中で使われておりますので、ぜひ直接見てください。

4. What is your opinion about the future of the "SP" industry?

The "SP" industry is going through one of its most promising and interesting phase, the industry has probably know since years. The "SP" industry wealth will depend on its capacity to adapt, to bring creativity and to anticipate needs. The all industry has to become proactive, has to take risks, there is no choice anymore. We are in a global world; Kao, Lion and others are facing P&G, Unilever or more to say the rest of the world competition.

The "SP" industry is being more and more challenging as well. From a specialist oriented industry, it has to become a more "generalist" industry, yet made of specialists. It would be interesting to see mergers in that industry but who will take risks in this quite traditional and conservative industry. With hundreds of, thousands of small and medium players, the Japanese market is in need of "SP" companies that can help them for and on the national market, but as well, that can support eventual expansion to the other very close and promising Asian market.

4．ＳＰ業界の将来についてはどう思われますか？

現在、ＳＰ業界は、将来性のある興味深いフェーズを通り抜けようとしています。このことは、この業界がずっと前から予測していたことです。ＳＰ業界の存在価値は、その順応性、独創性、そして先行性の如何によって左右されることになるでしょう。

どのような業界でも、我々はグローバルな環境にいる限り、何事も積極的に対処し、リスクを負って競争しなければなりません。花王やライオンなどの日本企業は、P&G、Unilever、そして、さらに多くの外国企業と競争しなければならない環境にいるのです。

ＳＰ業界は、ますます多くの課題に直面しています。ＳＰ業界は元々それぞれの分野に特化した専門性の高い業界ですが、もっと顧客の要求に柔軟に対応できるよう広く適応できる業界となる必要があります。このような業界で吸収合併が起きるのを目のあたりにするのも興味深いことですが、しかし、特に伝統を重んじる保守的な業界で、誰がそのようなリスクを冒すでしょうか？

何百、何千という中小企業プレイヤーがいる日本の市場には、ＳＰカンパニーが必要なのです。そのＳＰカンパニーは彼らが全国市場に進出するのを支援することができ、さらには、彼らが、すぐ隣の大きな可能性を持つアジア市場へ進出するのも支援できるのです。

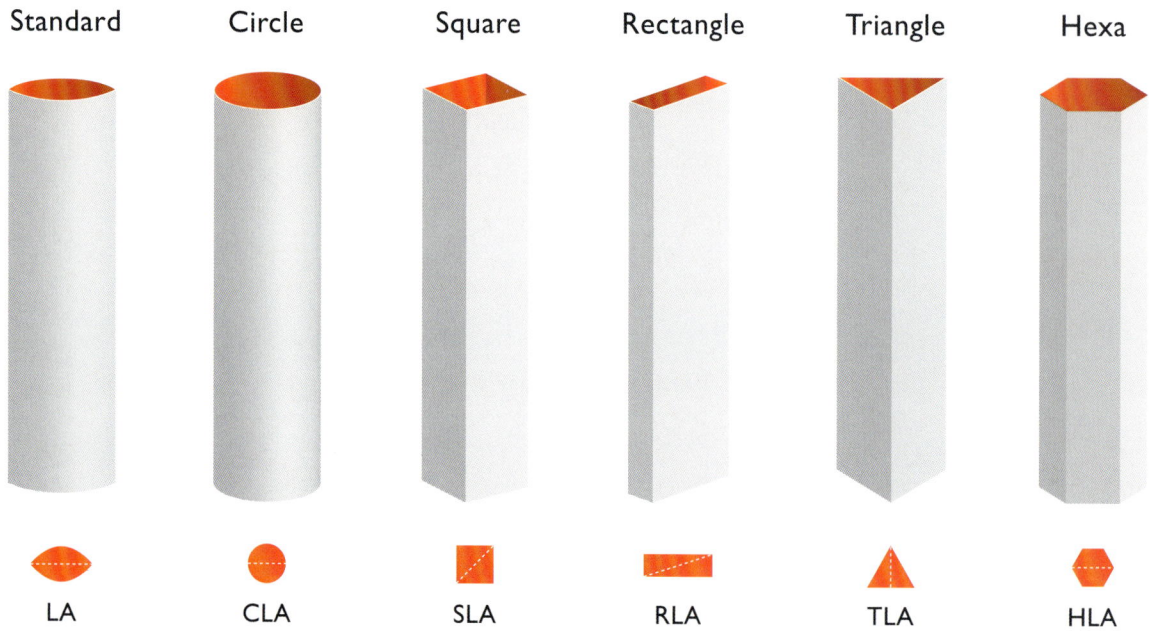

Standard	Circle	Square	Rectangle	Triangle	Hexa
LA	CLA	SLA	RLA	TLA	HLA

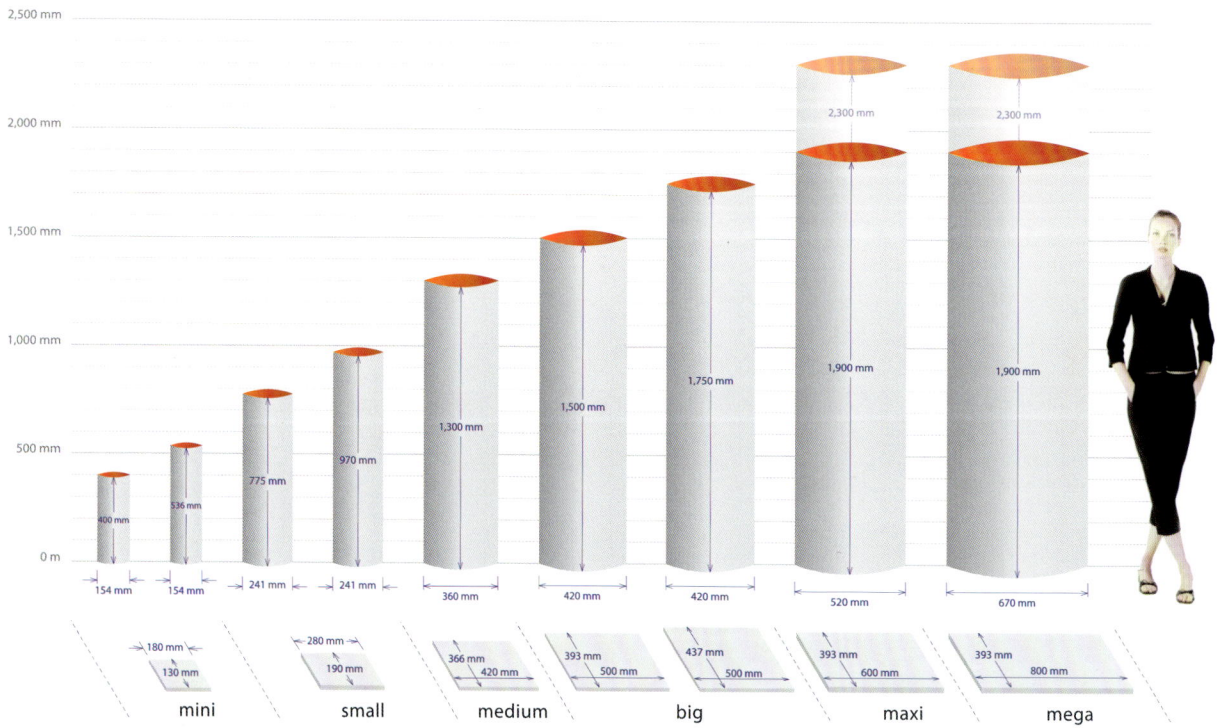

Square

Assembly :
2 sec

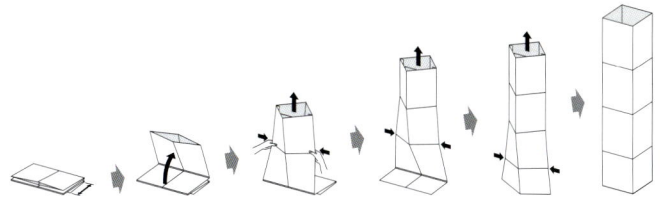

LA	CLA	SLA	RLA	TLA	HLA

Pole

Possible shapes:

Assembly : **2 sec**

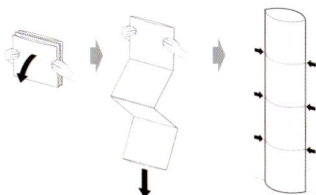

Folding :
2 sec

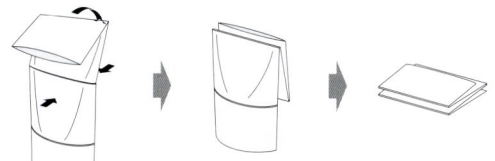

Assembly :
4 sec

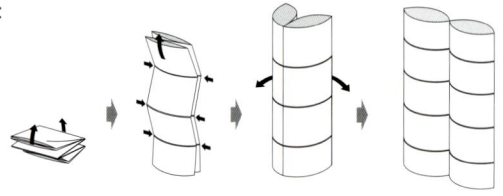

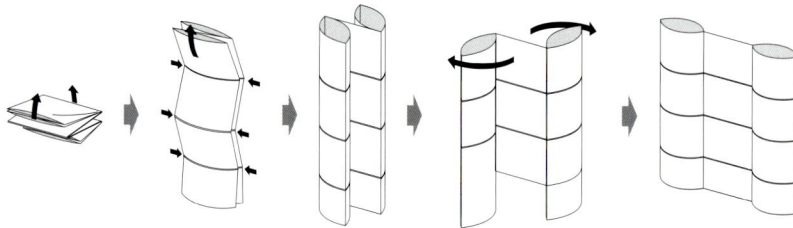

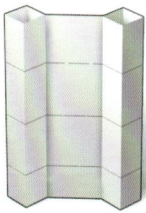

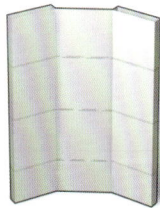

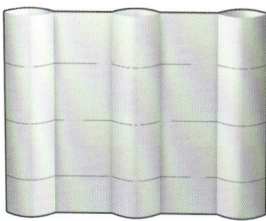

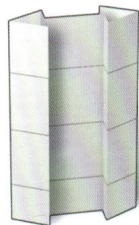

Duo

Possible shapes:

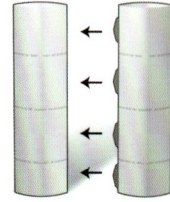

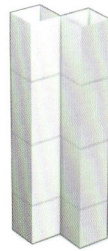

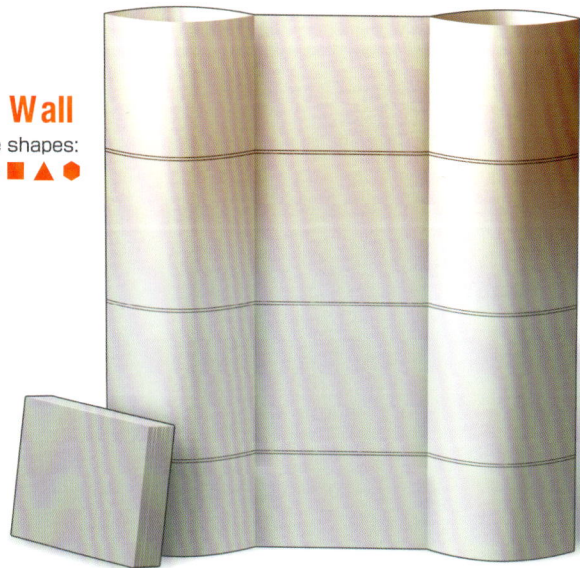

Assembly :
4 sec

Wall

Possible shapes:

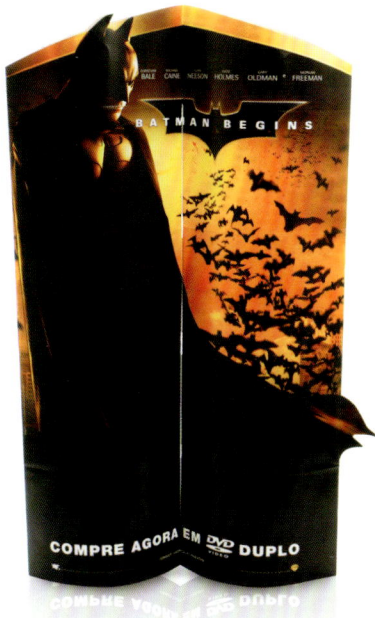

上からの形状

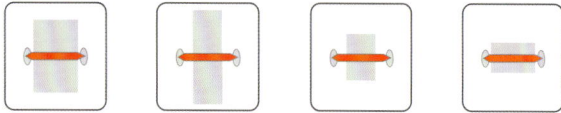

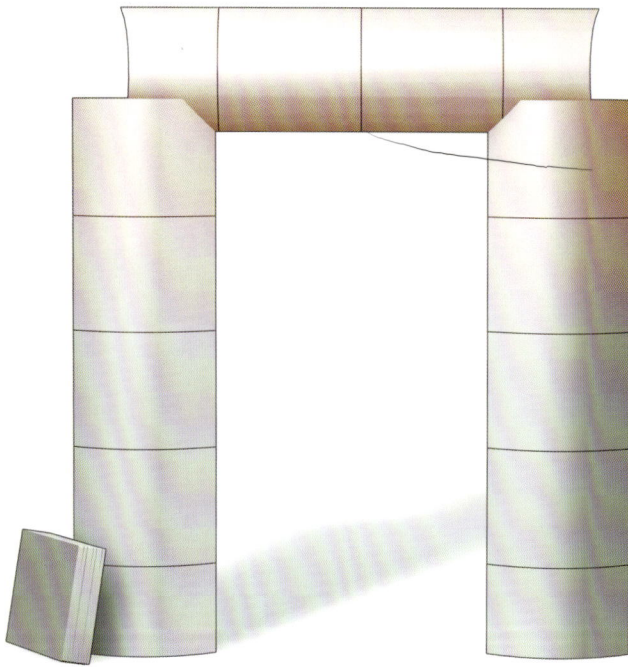

Gate

Possible shapes:

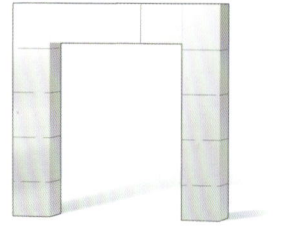

Square Gate

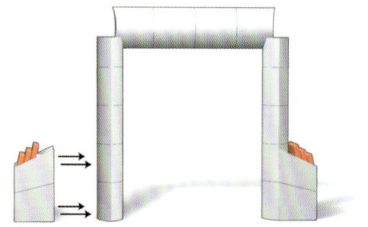

Gate + Bin

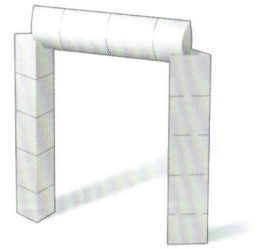

Triangle Gate

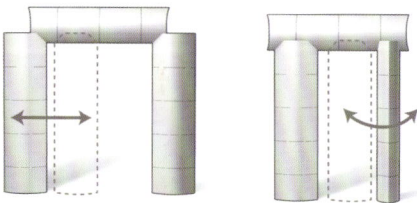

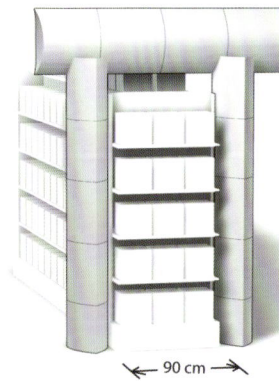

90 cm

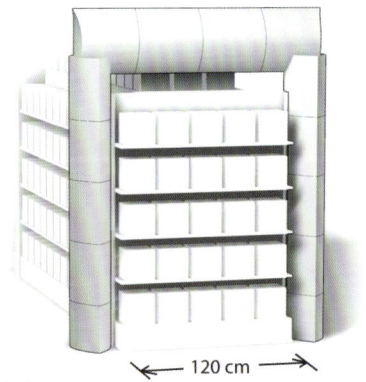

120 cm

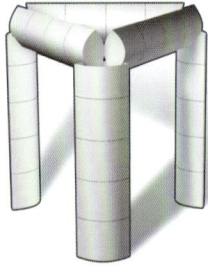

Tring

Possible shapes:
● ● ▬ ■ ▲ ⬠

Assembly :
40 sec

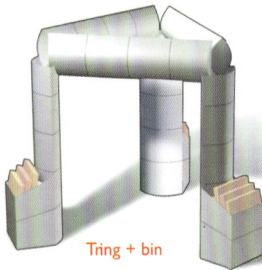

Tring + bin

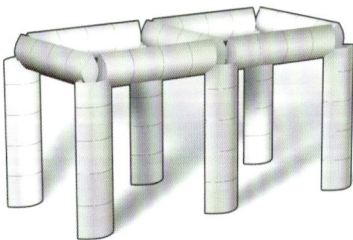

Double ring

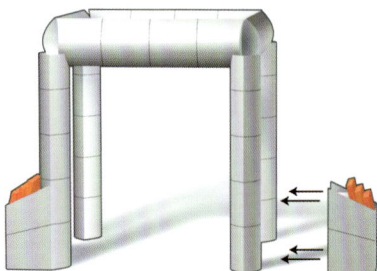

Bin

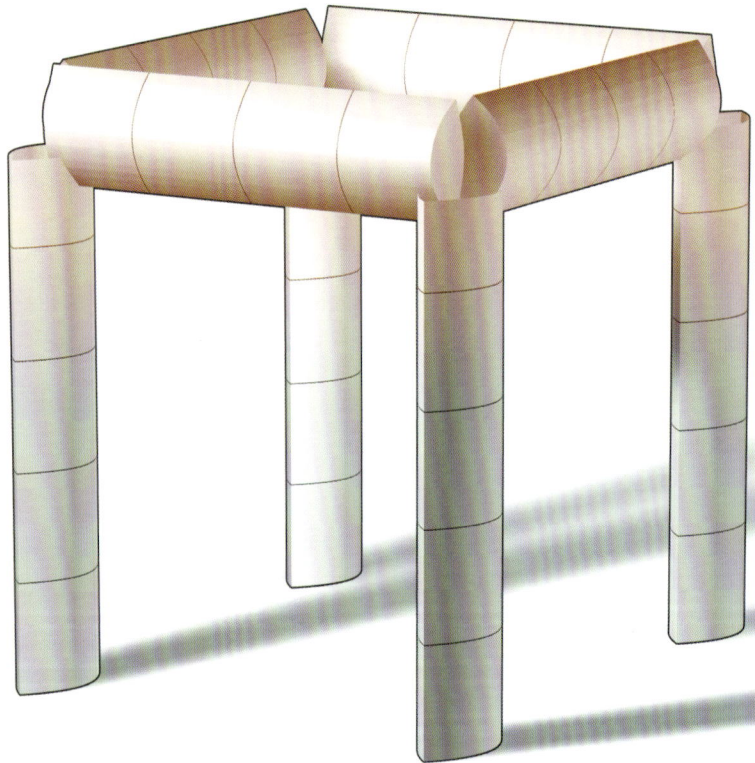

Ring

Possible shapes:
● ● ▬ ■ ▲ ⬠

上からの形状

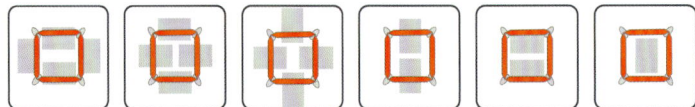

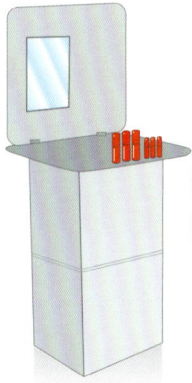

Open table

2 sides table

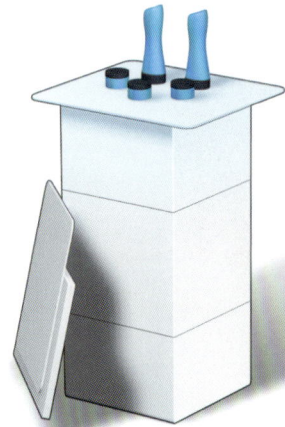

Square Table

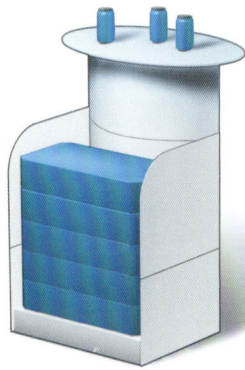

Case wrapper Table

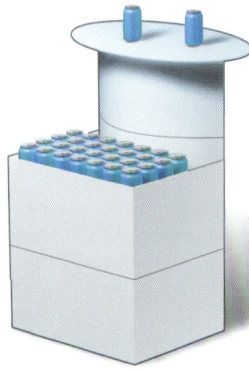

Bin Table

Assembly : 3 sec

天板

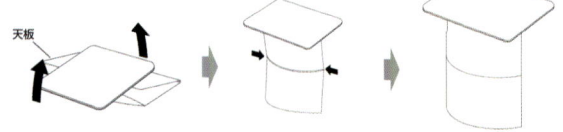

Table

Possible shapes:

●　●—■▲◆

Can table

Assembly : 2 sec

Assembly : 2 sec

天板

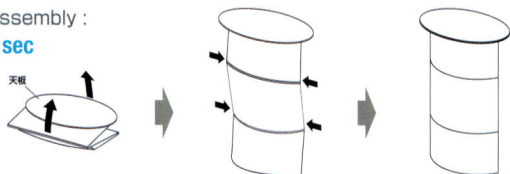

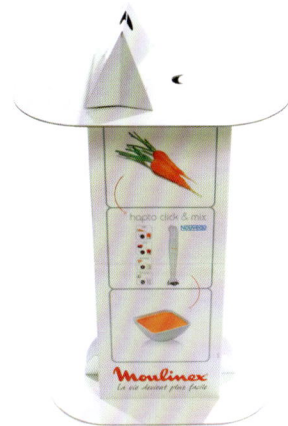

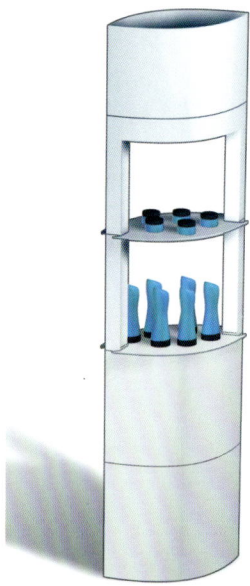

Tablama
2 steps

Possible

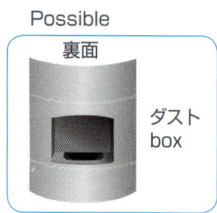

裏面

ダスト
box

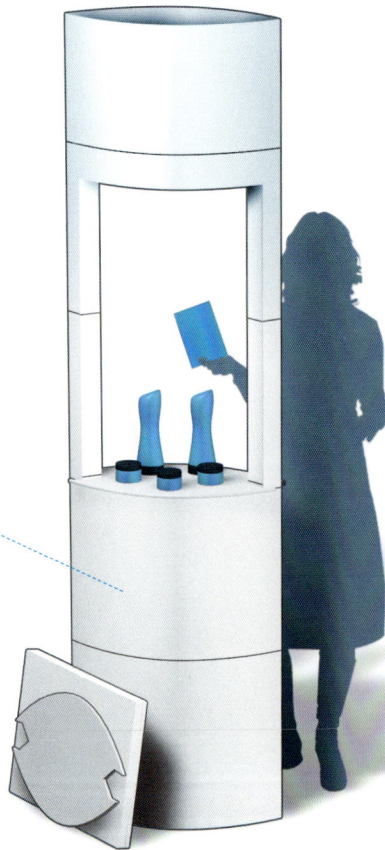

Tablama
Possible shapes:
● ● ━ ■ ▲ ⬠
Assembly :
5 sec

Bin Tablama
Possible shapes:
● ● ━ ■ ▲ ⬠
Assembly :
10 sec

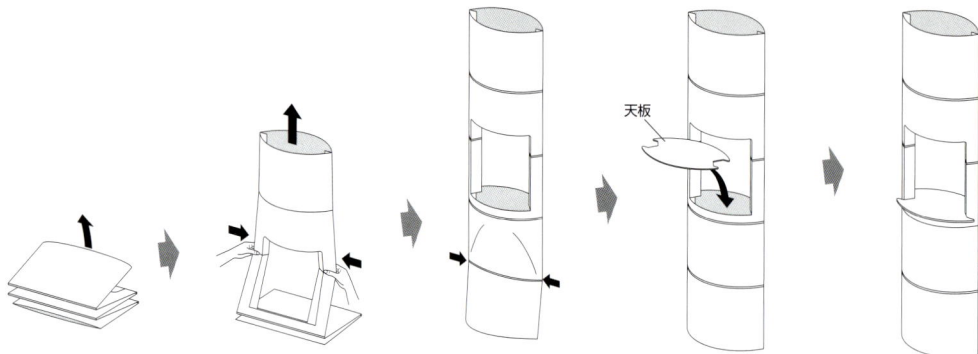

天板

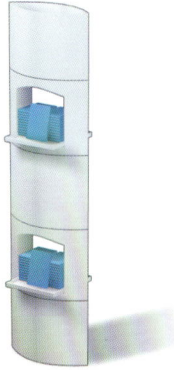

**Double
tablett**

**Double
sherpa**

**Shoes
display**

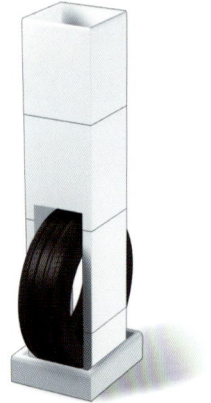

Tire display

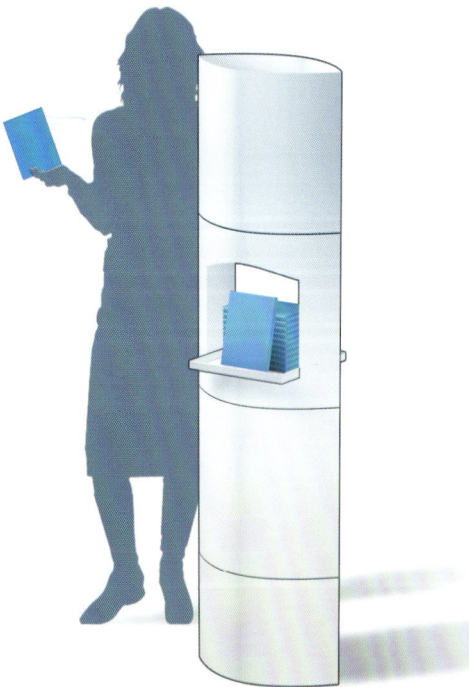

Tablett

Possible shapes:
● ● ━ ■ ▲ ⬡

Assembly :
10 sec

Sherpa

Possible shapes:
● ● ━ ■ ▲ ⬡

Assembly :
10 sec

**Square
Tablett**

Assembly :
30 sec

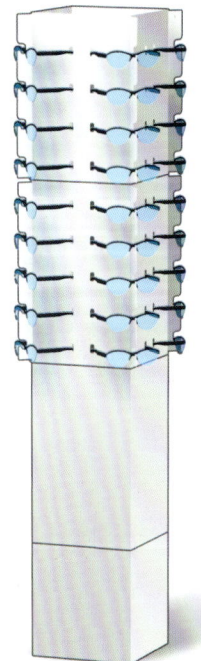

**Glasses
display**

Possible shapes:
● ● ━ ■ ▲ ⬡

Assembly :
4 sec

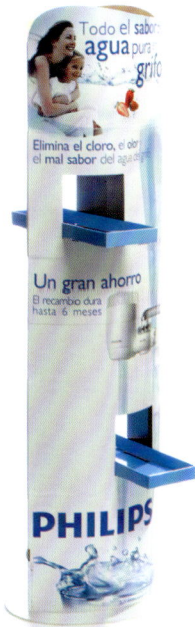
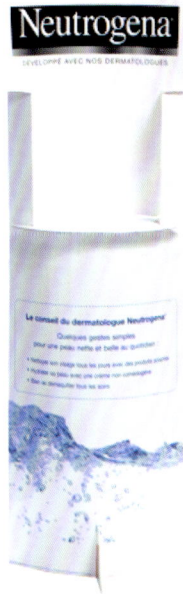

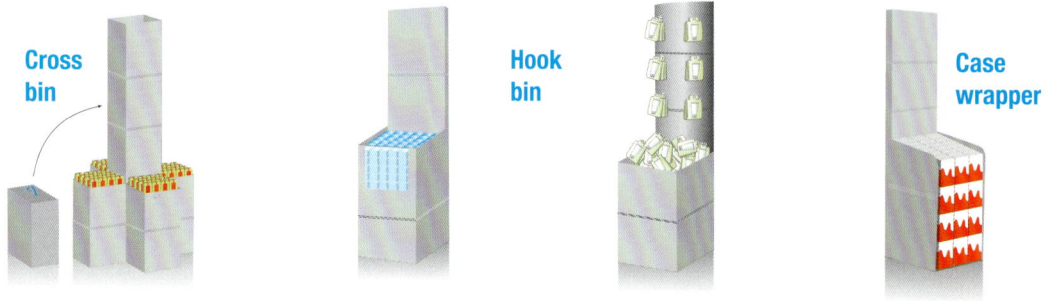

Cross bin

Hook bin

Case wrapper

Bin
Possible shapes:
● ● ━ ■ ▲ ⬠
Assembly :
1 mn

Top diecut bin
Possible shapes:
● ● ━ ■ ▲ ⬠
Assembly :
1 mn

360°bin
Possible shapes:
● ● ━ ■ ▲ ⬠
Assembly :
1 mn

Circle bin
Possible shapes:
● ●
Assembly :
1 mn

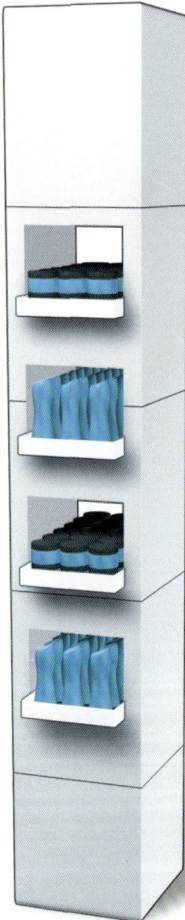

Lamastock
25 Kg
Possible shapes:
● ● ━ ■ ▲ ⬟
Assembly :
1 mn

Mozo
5□ Kg
Possible shapes:
● ● ━ ■ ▲ ⬟
Assembly :
1 mn

TX
Possible shapes:
● ● ━ ■ ▲ ⬟
Assembly :
1 mn

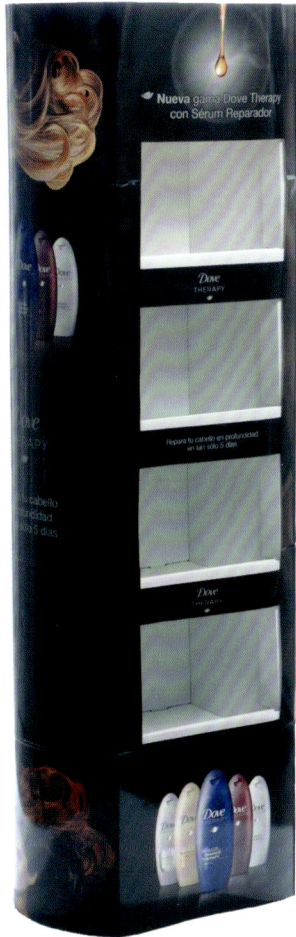

LA SÉLECTION
toutlevin
.com
Les Ormes de Cambras
Baron de Lestac
toutlevin

Senseo
Senseo
Senseo
PRIX
CADEAU !

Rowenta
Rowenta
Rowenta
100
ROWENTA
ROWENTA

Schweppes
Schweppes
Schweppes

EPSON
EPSON

Actimel
Actimel
Actimel

TOILETRY
【日用品】

COSMETIC
【化粧品】

PHARMACEUTICAL PRODUCT
【医薬品】

マンダム
mandom

GATSBY QUICK MOVING MIST

COUNTER P.O.P.
FLOOR P.O.P.

カウンターディスプレイ、フロアディスプレイは、店頭での強いインパクトと商品機能の訴求を重視しています。ハンガーディスプレイは、各アイテムの色がキレイに映えること、また多面展開を実現するために、訴求力を維持しつつ、コンパクト化を重視しています。

Both as a counter and floor display, this design focuses on creating appeal through strong impact and product functionality. As a hanging display, it maintains appeal, accurately reflecting the colors of the items and realizing diverse functions, while remaining compact.

A：電通関西支社
P：市川基商事
MATERIAL：紙類
W 330 × H 460 × D 230

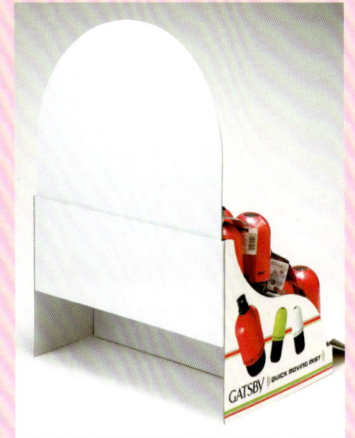

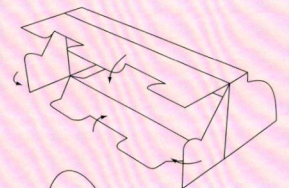

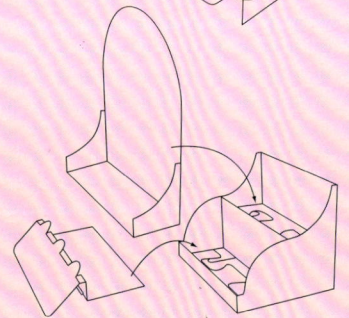

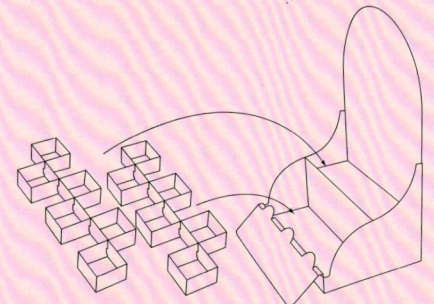

W 330 × H 1300 × D 230

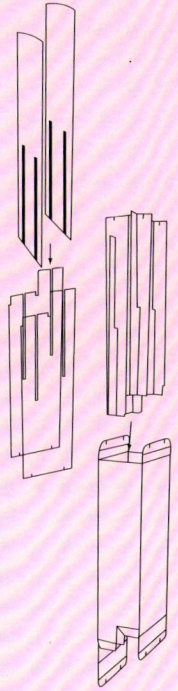

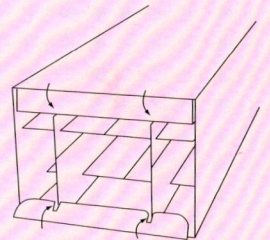

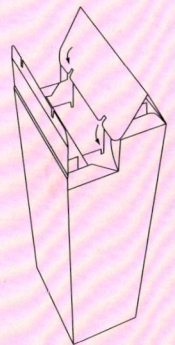

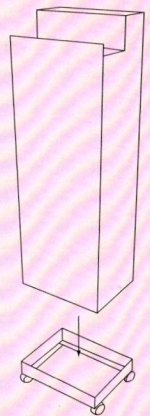

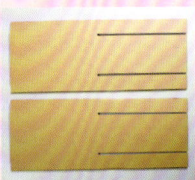

マンダム
mandom

GATSBY QUICK MOVING MIST

HANGING P.O.P.

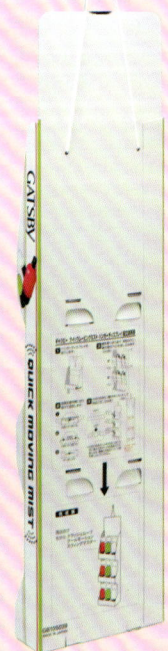

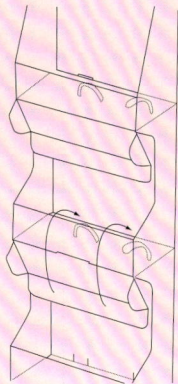

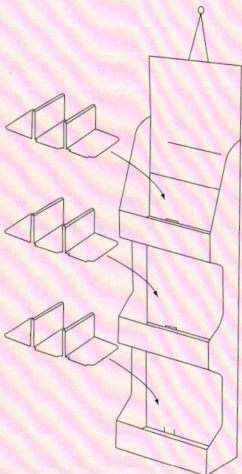

A：電通関西支社
MATERIAL：紙類
W 160 × H 675 × D 55

相模ゴム工業
Sagami Rubber Industries

sagami original 002

HANGING P.O.P.

本商品の最大の特長である 0.02mm のうすさをアピールするため、存在感がありなおかつ商品を取り出しやすい形状を採用しました。デザインはあえて奇をてらわず、シンプル、高級感を心がけました。箱と同じ白 × シルバーに、テーマカラーの赤を大胆に使い「究極！うさ 0.02 ミリ！」のキャッチコピーを際立たせました。

The shape of this display not only conveys presence, but also facilitates picking up the product as a way of selling its main feature of 0.02mm thickness. Efforts were made to keep the design simple and create a feeling of luxury. The display boldly uses the theme color red against white and silver to reflect the packaging, and as such, the catch phrase "The ultimate! Just 0.02mm thick!" was accentuated.

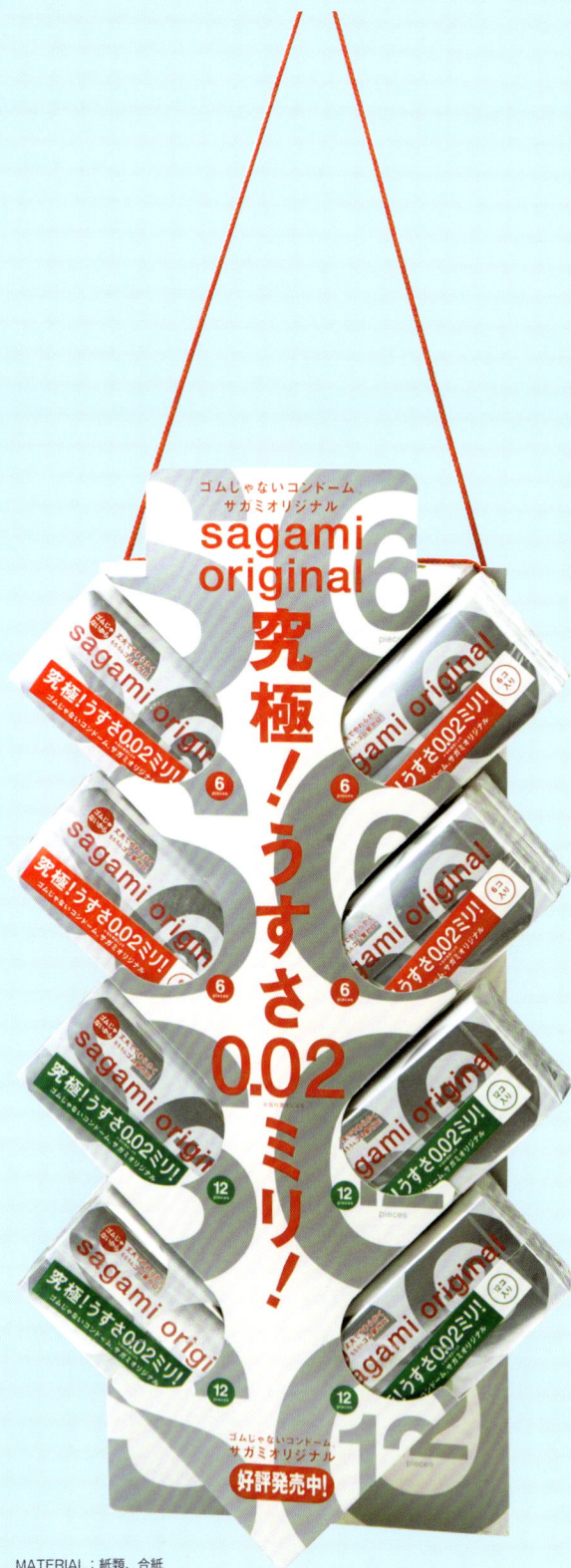

MATERIAL：紙類、合紙
W 200 × H 525 × D 65

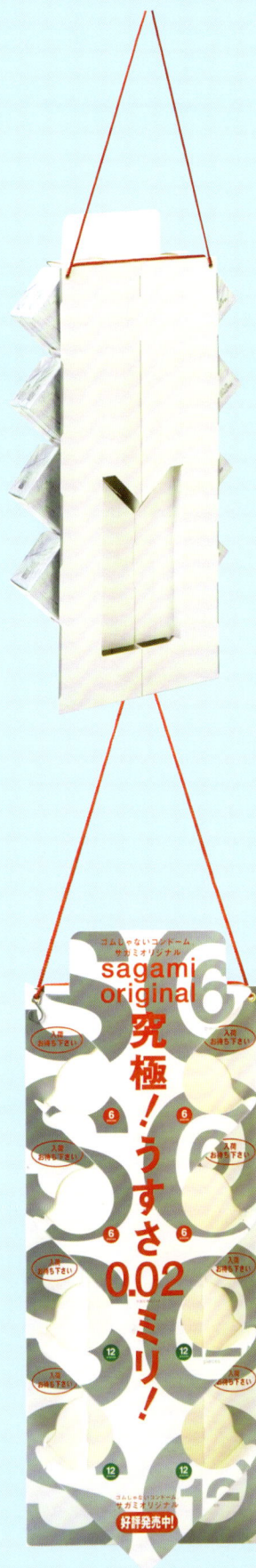

相模ゴム工業
Sagami Rubber Industries

sagami original 002 premium

COUNTER P.O.P.

さらにうすくやわらかく進化した「サ
ガミオリジナル 002 プレミアム」
の POP 兼ディスプレイです。衛生
的で使いやすいとお客様から評判が
高いブリスターパックを POP に活
用できないかというアイデアから生
まれました。組み立てが簡単でスペー
スが限られた店舗では POP とディ
スプレイを単体で使用することもで
きます。デザインはプレミアム品な
らではの高級感を心がけました。

A combination POP display for
"sagami original 002 premium,"
newly developed to be thinner
and softer. The display
originates from the idea that
the blister pack, highly
acclaimed as hygienic and
easy to use, could be used for
the design. Display setup is
simple and compact, and the
design gives a feeling of luxury
only offered by premier
products.

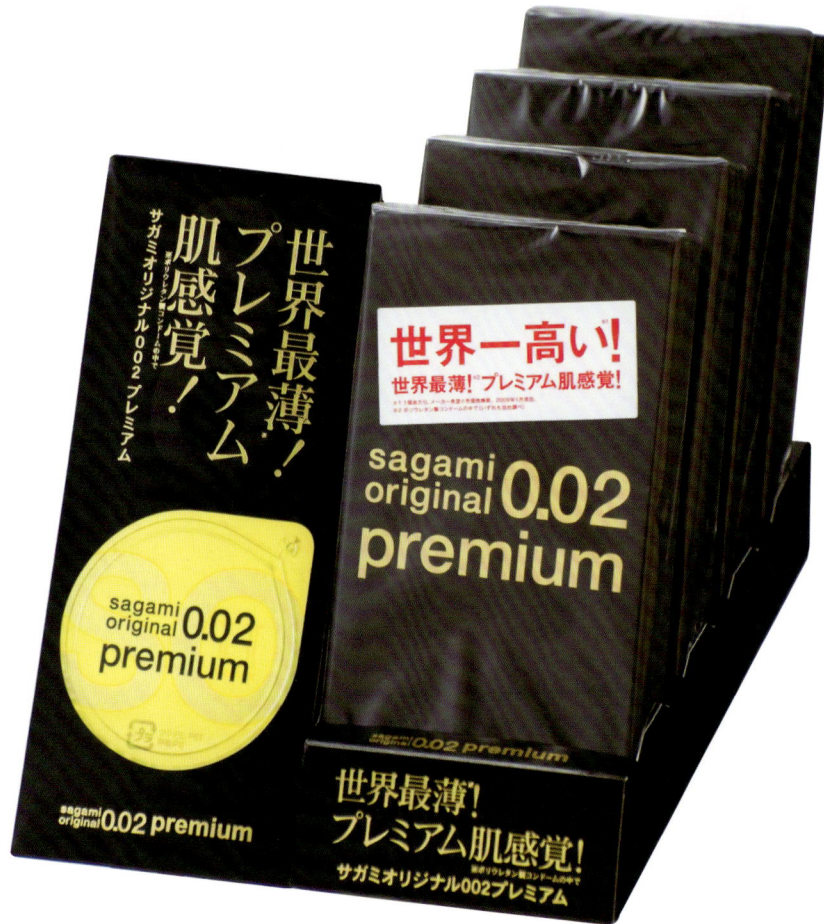

MATERIAL：紙類、合紙
W 125 × H 122 × D 198

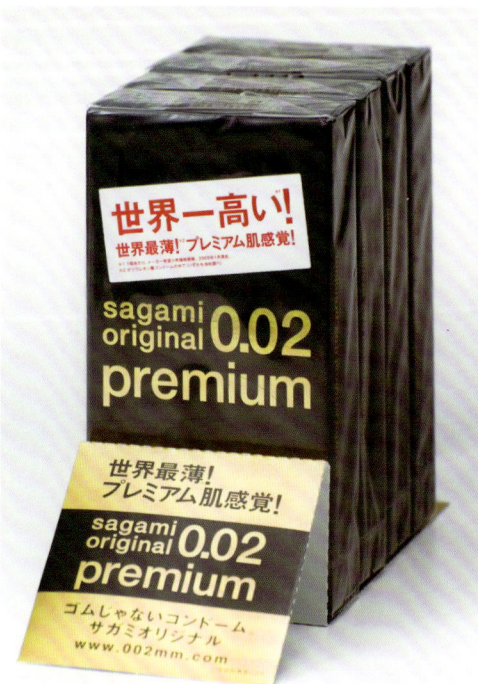

W 65 × H 40 × D 180

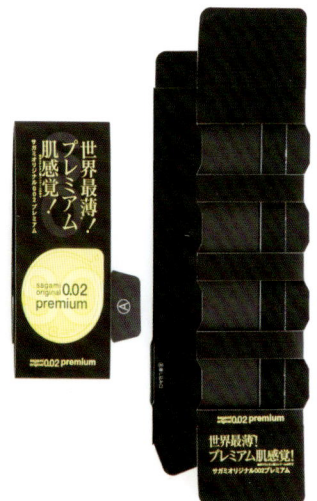

相模ゴム工業
Sagami Rubber Industries

sagami original 002

COUNTER P.O.P.
SWING P.O.P

サガミオリジナル 002 シリーズ（6コ入り、12コ入り、Lサイズ、クイック、プレミアム）をまとめて陳列でき、また店舗のスペースの都合で陳列するアイテム数を絞る場合にも対応できる多目的 POP です。デザインは、シリーズで陳列された時インパクトを出したかったのでメタリックな素材を使用しました。

A versatile POP display for the entire "sagami original 002" series (pack of 6, pack of 12, L size, Quick and Premium) that can also be used to display part of the series depending on available space. Metallic materials were used for the design to create impact when the products are displayed as a series.

W 65 × H 65

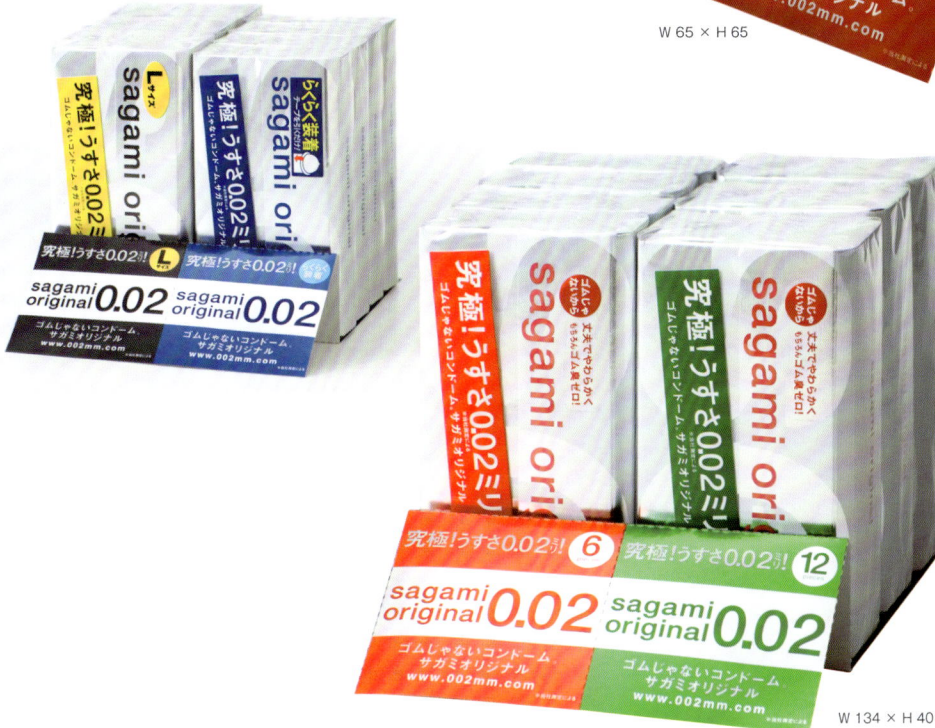

W 134 × H 40 × D 180

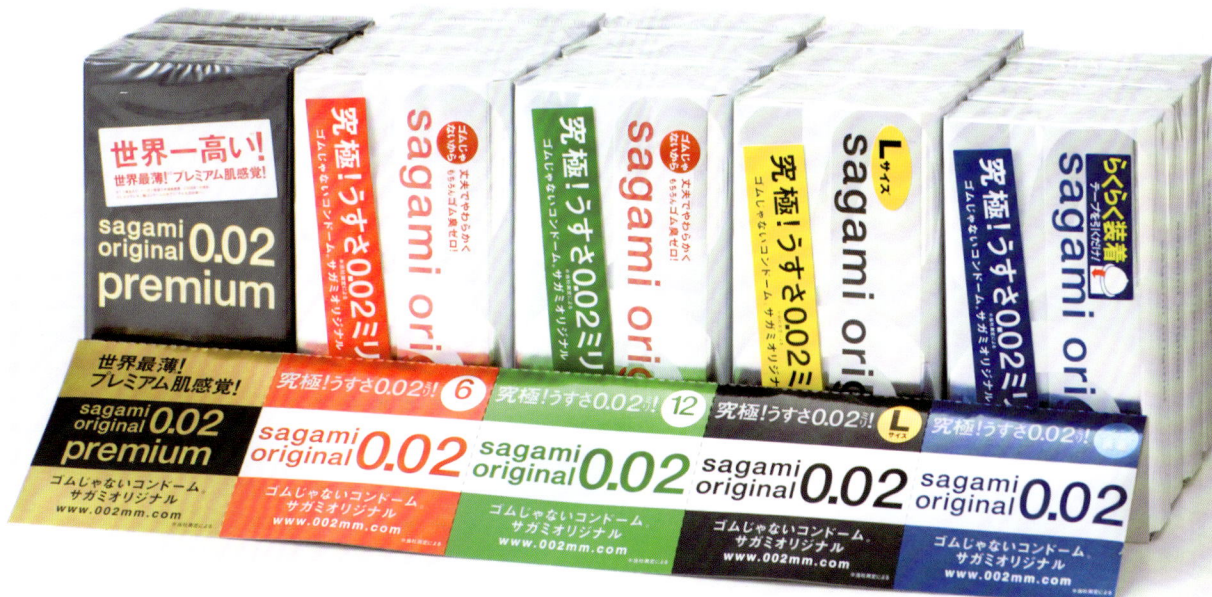

MATERIAL：紙類、合紙
W 330 × H 40 × D 180

プロクター・アンド・ギャンブル・ジャパン
P&G

Gillette Fusion PROGLIDE

COUNTER P.O.P.
FLOOR P.O.P.
HANGING P.O.P.
OTHERS P.O.P.

Gillette Fusion PROGLIDE を演出する際に大切にしたコンセプトは、「メカニカルな先進感」と「ストイックな本質の追究」です。カラーリングは、メタリック調のブルー&オレンジを PROGLIDE COLOR として徹底し、直線的なディテールの中になめらかな曲線をワンポイントあしらう事で、男性的な「鋭さ」と「やさしさ」を表現しています。

Important concepts for this Gillette Fusion PROGLIDE display were "advanced engineering" and "pursuing a stoic feel." Metallic blue and orange were selected for the coloring in keeping with the PROGLIDE brand colors, while adding a gentle curve as a feature amongst the otherwise linear detailing expresses macho-like "poignancy" and "simplicity."

P : C.C. レマン
MATERIAL : 紙類
W 680 × H 1700 × D 180

MATERIAL：紙類
W 420 × H 420 × D 205

Poster

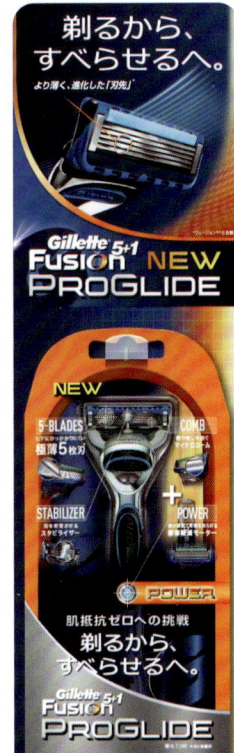

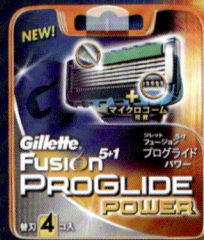

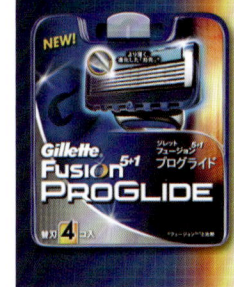

MATERIAL：紙類
W 110 × H 885 × D 25

プロクター・アンド・ギャンブル・ジャパン
P&G

Gillette Fusion

COUNTER P.O.P.
HANGING P.O.P.

P : C.C. レマン
MATERIAL：紙類
W 330 × H 422 × D 215

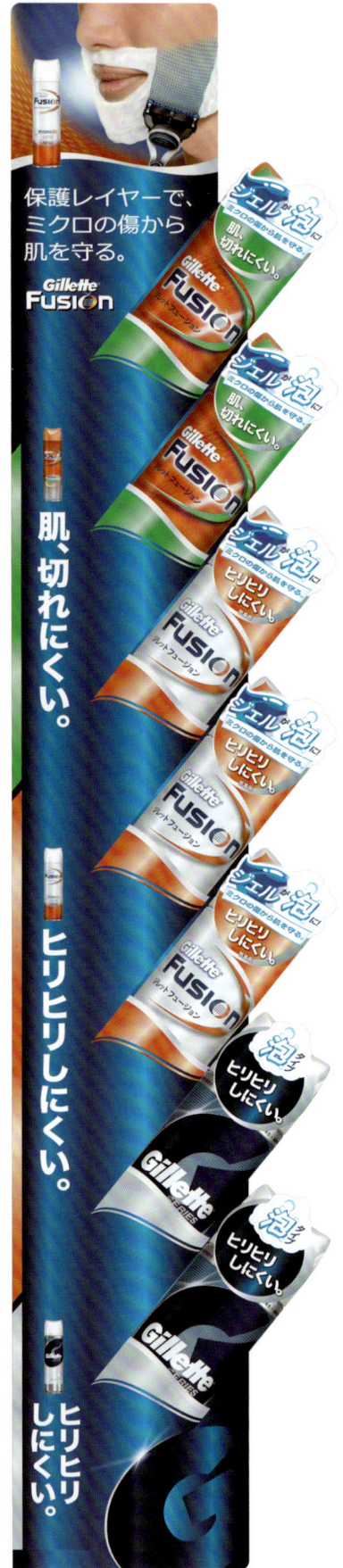

MATERIAL：紙類
W 125 × H 775 × D 58

P : 大日本印刷
MATERIAL : 紙類
W 300 × H 470 × D 300

P : 大日本印刷
MATERIAL : 紙類
W 300 × H 470 × D 300

プロクター・アンド・ギャンブル・ジャパン
P&G

Gillette Venus

COUNTER P.O.P.

2 種の製品のもつ各便益「女性初 5 枚刃」／「ソープ付き」を、黒・ダイヤ（＝上質感）／白・泡（＝さわやか）というカラーリングとグラフィックで対照的に見せ、パッケージでは訴求しきれなかった各製品および VENUS ブランドの世界観を表現しました。また、シェーバー本来の持つソリッドかつ硬質なイメージ、VENUS の高機能性をホットスタンプで表現し、女性らしいフェミニンさを曲線で表現しています。

Here, the benefits of 2 Gillette Venus products are displayed in contrast. The coloring and graphics for "the first 5-blade shaver for women" and "the soap shaver" were black with diamonds (for high quality) and white with bubbles (for freshness) respectively, and elements that could not be fitted on the packaging as well as the Venus brand ideology were included. Further, the display shows the solid and hard image of the shaver against the high functionality of the Venus brand, using curves to express femininity.

SPRジャパン
SPR JAPAN

samourai WOMAN PREMIUM

COUNTER P.O.P.
SWING P.O.P.

サムライウーマンプレミアムのテーマである「香り、バラ色。」の什器を製作しました。赤いバラを基調に仕上げ、まるでバラの香りが漂ってくるかのようなインパクトあるカウンター什器は1台でも2台連結でも使用できる仕様にしました。また、国内最大級のヘルス＆ビューティイベント「ドラッグストアショー」イベントブースでも什器と連動した赤いバラのインパクトのあるブースにしました。（2010年度）

Samourai Woman Premium's theme 'Aroma, Rose Red' is portrayed in its POP merchandising displays. Used individually or as pairs, the display dressed in rose red allures its viewers into a dramatic world of floral aroma. Exhibiting booth at the nation's largest annual health & beauty event 'Drugstore Show' was also embellished in rose red, leaving a theatrical impact to all welcomed visitors.

A：ビー・ブレーブ / フィード
P：コムクス
MATERIAL：紙類
W 190 × H 400 × D 220

W 100 × H 100

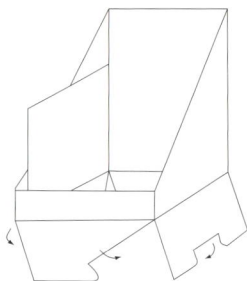

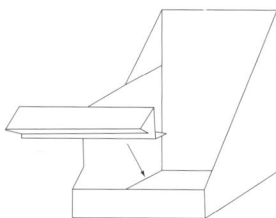

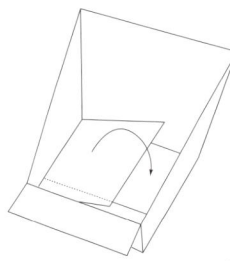

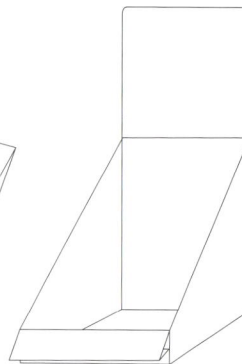

W 180 × H 255 × D 60

W 380 × H 400 × D 220

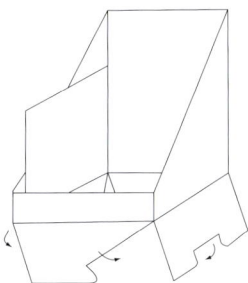

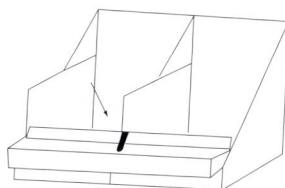

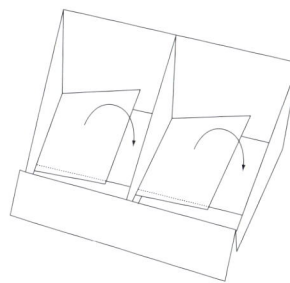

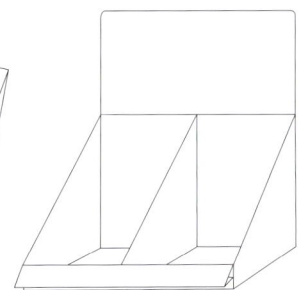

SPRジャパン
SPR JAPAN

samourai WOMAN PREMIUM

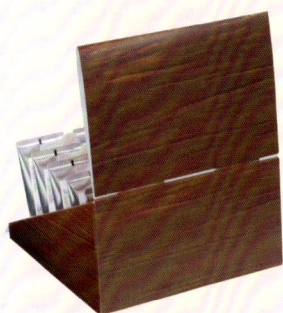

P：フィード
MATERIAL：紙類
W 250 × H 305 × D 280

SPRジャパン
SPR JAPAN

MVNE

COUNTER P.O.P.
SWING P.O.P.

MVNE（ミューネ）は美と幸せへの願いを込めて生まれました。世界中の人々を幸せでつつみこみ、生き生きと輝く喜びを与え続けます。ブランドコンセプトである天然の花々や果実のやさしい香りをイメージしたPOPを制作しました。

MVNE was created from a simple wish for beauty and happiness for all. A wish for everyone in the world to be touched by the brilliance of life to be happy. POP displays were designed depicting the brand concept of natural aroma's of gentle flower and fruits.

W 105 × H 115

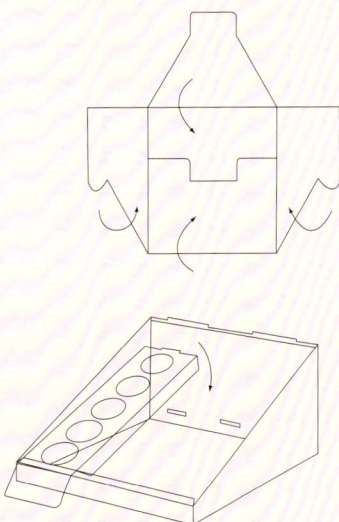

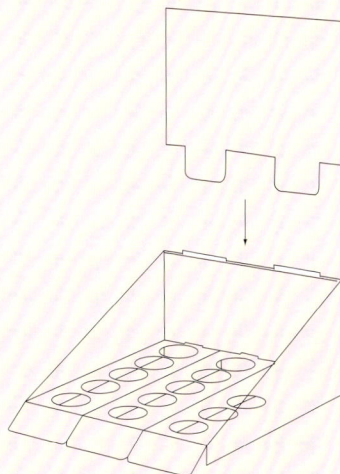

W 150 × H 210 × D 60

フィッツコーポレーション
FITS Corporation

セクシーガール ヘアコロン

COUNTER P.O.P.

ブランド・セクシーガールのミッションは、世界中の恋する女の子をセクシーにすること。さまざまなアイテムのなかで、一番人気のヘアコロンでは商品販促物にて商品の3大特徴を訴求しています。そして、バックパネルにてセクシーガールのブランドイメージを伝えています。

The mission of the "Sexy Girl" brand is to help girls in love all around the world to feel sexy. This display appeals to customers through the major characteristics of the brand's 3 hair colognes, the most popular of its product lineup, while the backing panel is used to convey the "Sexy Girl" brand image.

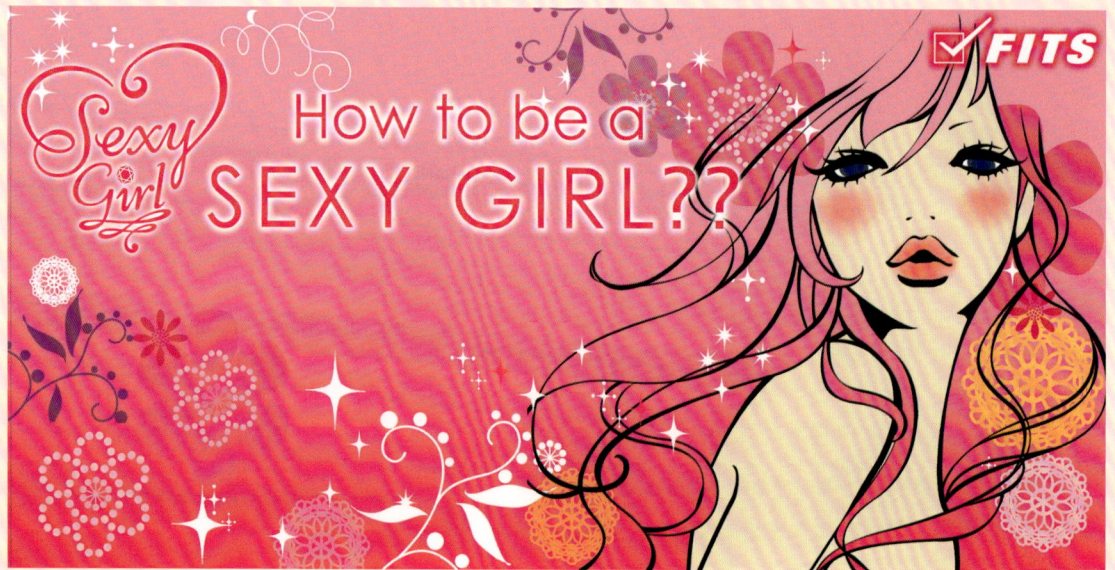

W 600 × H 300

W 180 × H 260

MATERIAL：紙類
W 300 × H 350 × D 250

W 880 × H 400

MATERIAL：紙類
W 210 × H 300 × D 270

W 180 × H 260

フィッツコーポレーション
FITS Corporation

セクシーボーイ フレグランスファイバー

COUNTER P.O.P.

セクシーボーイは、自分スタイルを香りで自由に表現するブランド。フレグランスファイバーはナカノとのコラボレーションで生まれた、香りが選べるヘアスタイリングワックスです。2段式什器はさまざまなスペースに対応できるように、B5POP は商品特徴をわかりやすく訴求するために作られています。そして、バックパネルにてセクシーボーイフレグランスファイバーの商品イメージを伝えています。

"Sexy Boy" is a brand emphasizing the freedom to create your own personal style with fragrance. The product "Fragrance Fiber," a hair styling wax that comes in a variety of scents, was developed in collaboration with Nakano. Designed to appeal through simple descriptions of the product characteristics, this B5-size POP display is 2-tiered, facilitating setup in most spaces, while the backing panel is used to convey the "Sexy Boy Fragrance Fiber" product image.

フィッツコーポレーション
FITS Corporation

クレイジー リベリュル アンド ポビーズ
COUNTER P.O.P.

2000年にIsabelle Masson-Mandonnaud によって設立されたフランスのブランドです。「可愛いだけはもう終わり お肌にやさしいスティック香水」というキャッチコピーに基づき、さまざまな販促物が作られています。また、ブランドイメージを伝えるために、各販促物にはブランドカラーである濃紫をバックに、プロダクトデザイナーのイザベルが「自由で好奇心が強く、個性的（クレイジー）」という魅力を感じたトンボがモチーフのブランドロゴが配置されています。

This French brand designed by Isabelle Masson-Mandonnaud in 2000 features a variety of products based on the catch phrase "No longer just cute: A stick perfume gentle on your skin." While the products are displayed against the brand color dark purple to convey the brand image, the product designer said that she used the dragonfly motif because it expresses "individuality (craziness) derived from freedom and inquisitiveness."

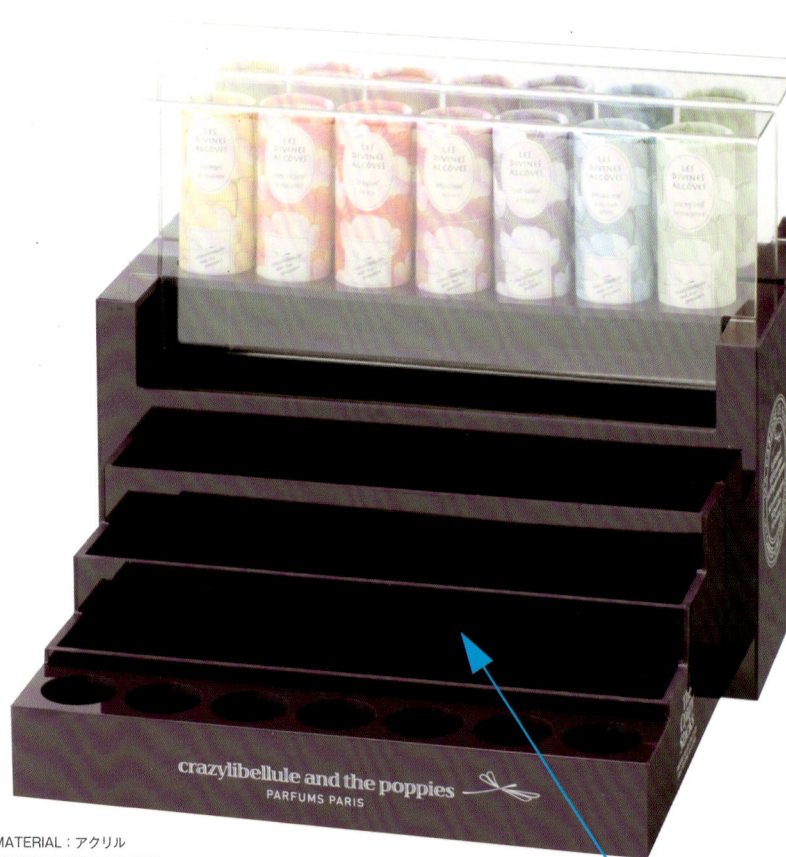

MATERIAL：アクリル
W 205 × H 200 × D 205

MATERIAL：紙類
W 300 × H 350 × D 310

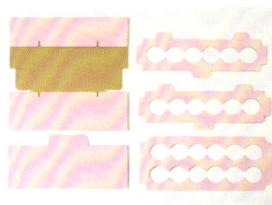

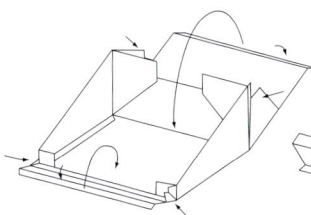

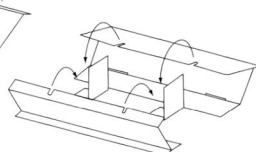

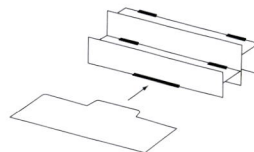

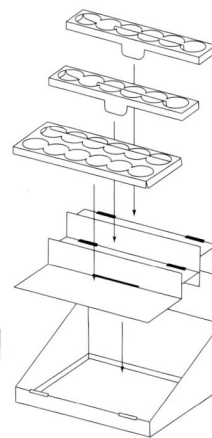

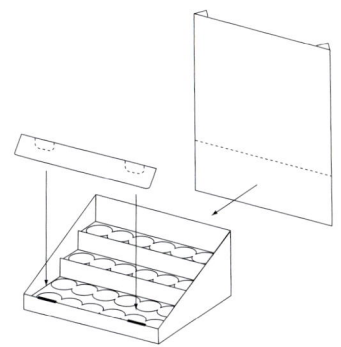

フィッツコーポレーション
FITS Corporation

セクシーガール ハンド&ボディバター

COUNTER P.O.P.

女の子に大人気のセクシーガールの、秋冬のボディケア商品 ボディバター。シアバターを配合し、保湿力は抜群。とろけるボディバターということを、コピーと画像でしっかりと訴求しました。コンセプトは「美味しいお肌のできあがり」。

A body care product from the fall/winter lineup of "Sexy Girl," popular among young girls, this body butter is a shea butter compound with excellent moisturizing properties. The display delivers strong impact through the use of a phrase and image that communicate the melting properties of the body butter. The concept was "Giving you delicious skin."

フィッツコーポレーション
FITS Corporation

ヴィーナススパ メディカル

身体の悩みに働きかける、医療部外品の商品たち。「効く」シリーズであることを伝えるために、可愛らしいディティールでありながらも、色味は落ち着かせたものにしました。

This lineup of quasi drugs is effective in treating physical ailments. In order to convey the message that this series "works," the display features subdued tones with charming details.

MATERIAL：紙類
W 300 × H 350 × D 275

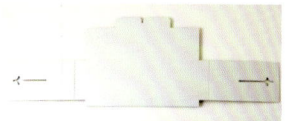

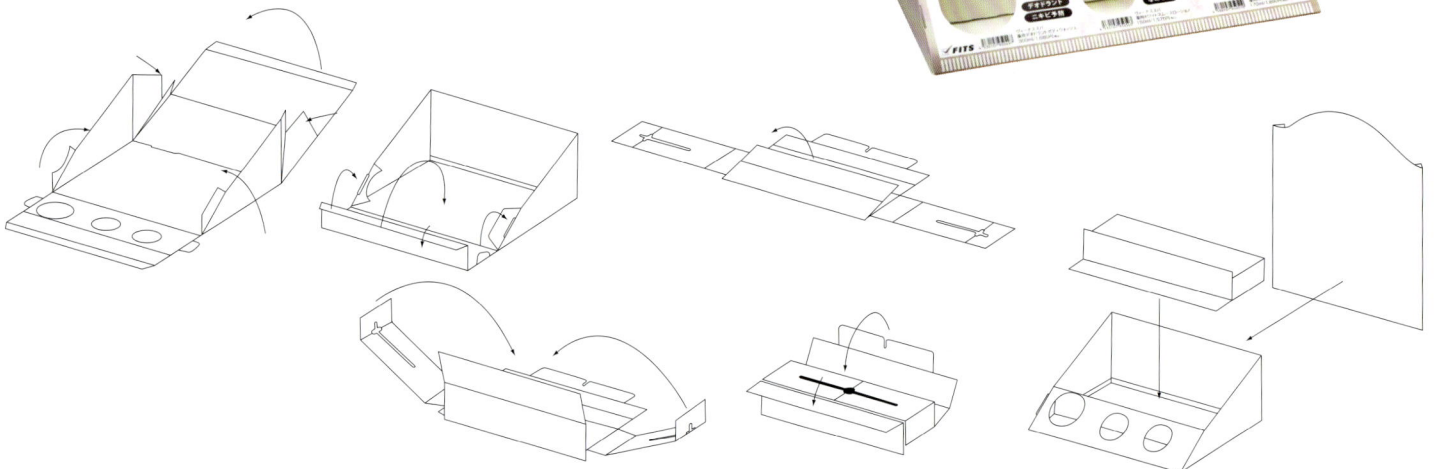

フィッツコーポレーション
FITS Corporation

トゥーザシーン ナチュラルアロマ

COUNTER P.O.P.

100%天然香料で出来た、ナチュラルなアロマスプレー。天然香料であること、また、心を穏やかにしたり潤わせる働きがあることを表すため、木目調の柄を施した落ち着いた什器になっています。

Natural aroma spray made from 100% natural fragrances. This serene display was designed with a woodgrain pattern to stress the use of the natural fragrances as well as the calming and moisturizing effect of the product.

MATERIAL：紙類
W 300 × H 350 × D 225

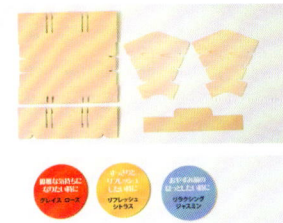

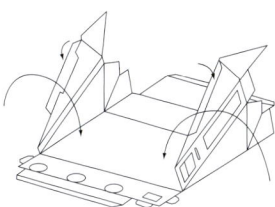

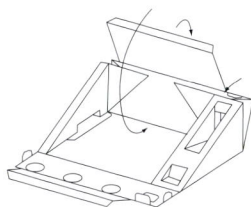

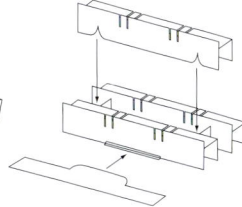

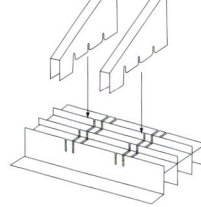

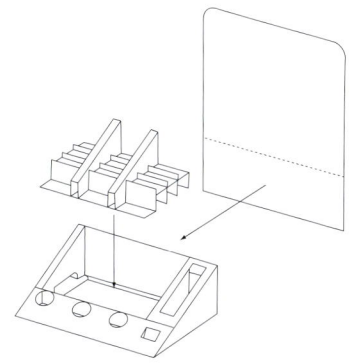

フィッツコーポレーション
FITS Corporation

ラブスイッチ ピンクブラウンアイライナー

COUNTER P.O.P.

大人スウィートな目もとをつくり上げる、ピンクブラウンのアイメイクシリーズ、ラブスイッチ。女の子のドレッサーを思わせるバックパネルで世界観を表し、2つのアテンションPOPで実際の使用感や印象を訴求しました。

"Love Switch" is part of the Pink Brown Eye Makeup Series for charming eyes. A touch of worldliness is added through the use of a backing panel in the likeness of a woman's dresser, while the two attention-grabbing pop-outs leave a lasting impression and show an example of actual use.

MATERIAL：紙類
W 300 × H 300 × D 205

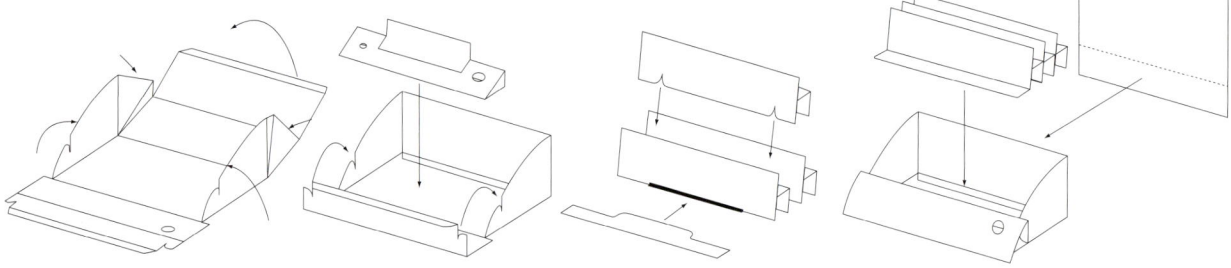

フィッツコーポレーション
FITS Corporation

ドラマティック コスメティックス

COUNTER P.O.P.

ドラマティック コスメティックス は、2010 年にデビューしたアイメ イク中心のメイクブランド。女の子 の毎日は、笑ったり泣いたり大忙し。 そんな毎日を、長いまつげや細く引 かれた綺麗なアイラインで、ドラマ ティックに彩ってくれます。楽しい 毎日を象徴するかのように、カラフ ルなディスペンサーはそれだけで心 が華やぎます。

Debuting in 2010, Dramatic Cosmetics is a makeup brand that specializes in eye makeup. Everyday, girls have a busy schedule filled with smiles and tears, and need a product that will give them long lashes adorned by a beautiful eyeline for dramatic coloring. Using a colorful dispenser adds a touch of lightheartedness as if to symbolize these fun-filled days.

MATERIAL：紙類
W 250 × H 50 × D 210

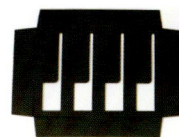

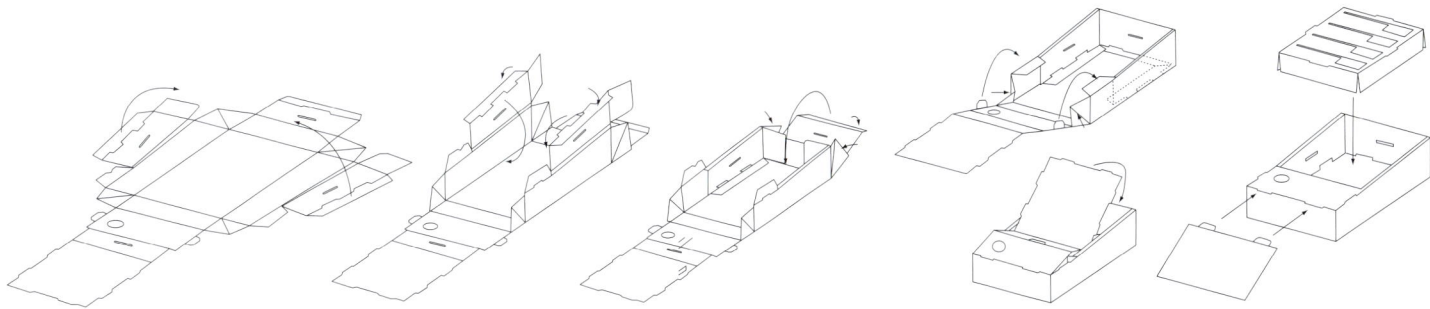

エステー
S. T.

消臭プラグ

自動でシュパッと消臭プラグ

COUNTER P.O.P.
OTHERS P.O.P.

2009 年秋に「デザイン革命」をテーマに、電子式消臭芳香剤「消臭プラグ」と「自動でシュパッと消臭プラグ」をフルモデルチェンジしました。商品パッケージは多くの色を使用せず、"パキッと"店頭映えするビビットカラーでブランドの統一感を出し、そのカラーを最大限に強調する「黒」をキーカラーとして全ての販促物を作成しました。店頭販促ボードは、シンプルでありながら優しさが伝わる商品フォルムを堂々と見せることで店頭でのお客様へのアテンションを引く狙いをこめました。

In fall 2009, the electronic type deodorant "Air Freshener Plug" and "Automatic Shupatto Air Freshener Plug" underwent a full model change based on the theme "design revolution." The product packaging uses limited coloring, and standardization for the brand was achieved through vivid colors that brighten up the store, and as such, all of the support materials for the display were "black" to accentuate the packaging. This simple design aims to grab attention by boldly displaying the product in a way that also expresses its gentle nature.

MATERIAL：スチレンボード
W 848 × H 497 × D 5

MATERIAL：アクリル
W 884 × H 243 × D 345

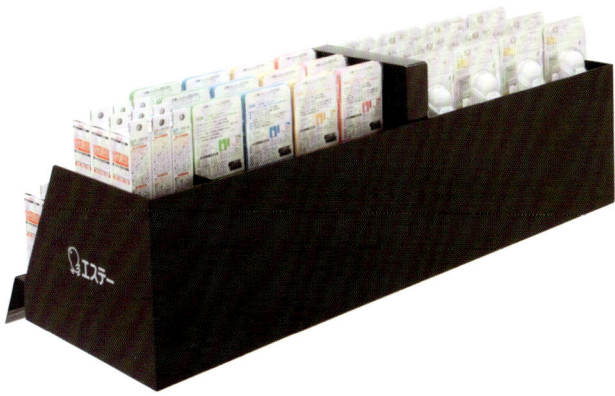

エステー
S. T.

消臭プラグ

自動でシュパッと消臭プラグ

COUNTER P.O.P.
OTHERS P.O.P.

W 65 × H 155 × D 117

MATERIAL：紙類
W 65 × H 155 × D 157

MATERIAL：紙類
W 228 × H 155 × D 229

MATERIAL：PET
W 100 × H 200 × D 57

エステー
S. T.

消臭プラグ

自動でシュパッと消臭プラグ

MOVING P.O.P.

MATERIAL：紙類
W 66 × H 210 × D 66

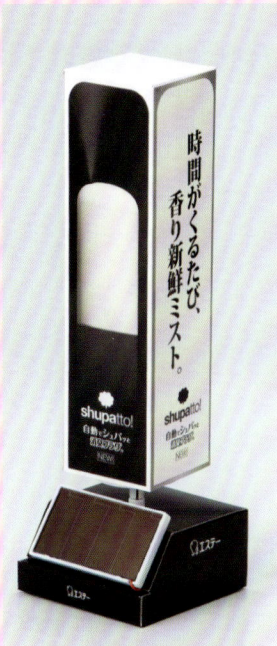

ユニリーバ・ジャパン
Unilever Japan

AXE

COUNTER P.O.P.
HANGING P.O.P.

ショッパーの注目を集めるため、遠くからでも目立つアックス フレグランス ボディスプレーをモチーフにした巨大 POP を作製しました。製品自体が POP になるため、ブランドの認識が即時にできる利点があります。テスターを設置するための POP は、香りの特徴を示すフレグランスマップを台座にしました。各香りのテスターをマップ上にレイアウトすることによって、フレグランスの特徴をしっかりコミュニケーションしました。ショッパーに複数の香り特徴を分かりやすく伝え、香り体験を促進するPOPです。

This POP display showcasing AXE fragrant body spray is extra-large to attract the attention of shoppers from afar. The shape of the product itself was used for the display, offering the added advantage of instant brand recognition. As testers were included, the base of the display was designed as a fragrance characteristics map, and each of the testers was set on the map so the information would be read. This display conveys the scent characteristics in an easy-to-understand way and encourages fragrance testing.

P：レンゴー
MATERIAL：紙類
W 200 × H 790 × D 115

P：レンゴー
MATERIAL：紙類
W 310 × H 455 × D 260

P：レンゴー
MATERIAL：紙類
W 340 × H 505 × D 230

P：レンゴー
MATERIAL：紙類
W 160 × H 500 × D 150

ユニリーバ・ジャパン
Unilever Japan

Rexena

COUNTER P.O.P.
HANGING P.O.P.

レセナドライシールドという新製品をはっきり認知してもらうためと、ブランドイメージにふさわしいプレミアム感のある色ということで、ブランドカラーとしてミッドナイトブルーを POP の基調色としました。またツールの種類は大型店から小型店までそれぞれの店舗スペースに合わせて選べるよう、スタンド式ディスプレイや、置き式にもハンガー式にも使えるスティック用ハンガーなど、バリエーションをもたせました。どんなスペースでの展開でも製品認知から理解までなされるようなツールを作成しました。

The brand color midnight blue was adopted as the base color for this POP display to promote easy recognition of the new product Rexena Dry Shield as well as provide a premier feeling appropriate for the brand image. In addition, variation was introduced through accessories that enable the display to be used as a countertop or hanging display as well as a standing display to suit the space available. But whatever the space size, this display was designed to act as a tool for facilitating product recognition and comprehension.

P：大日本印刷
MATERIAL：紙類
W 450 × H 475 × D 320

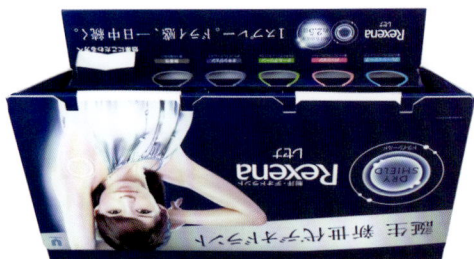

気づかれる前に、
毎日ワキ汗ケア

DRY SHIELD
Rexena レセナ

他人のニオイが気になる人⋯約80%

気づかれる前に、
毎日ワキ汗ケア

DRY SHIELD
Rexena レセナ

他人のニオイが気になる人⋯約80%

P：大日本印刷
MATERIAL：紙類、プラスチック
W 200 × H 805 × D 115

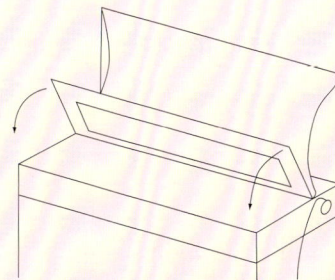

ユニリーバ・ジャパン
Unilever Japan

Rexena

COUNTER P.O.P.
HANGING P.O.P.

P：大日本印刷
MATERIAL：紙類
W 155 × H 525 × D 45

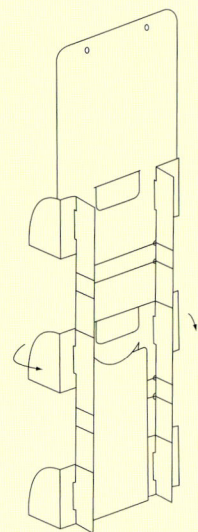

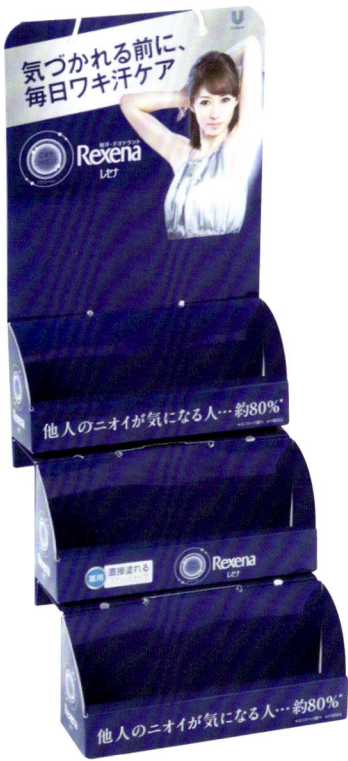

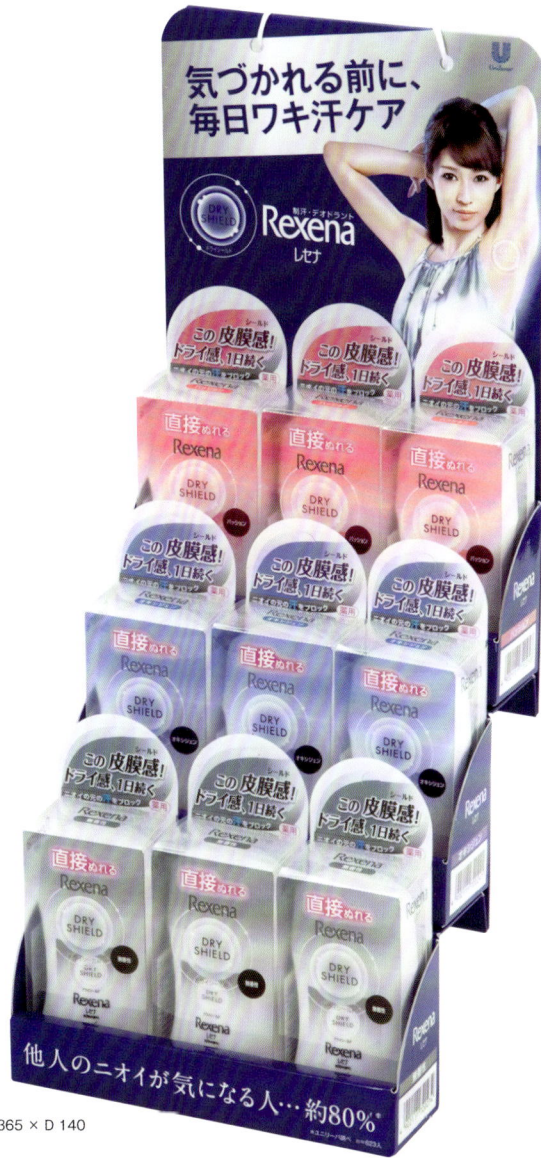

W 155 × H 365 × D 140

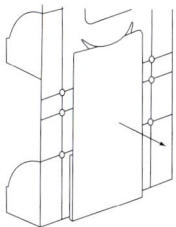

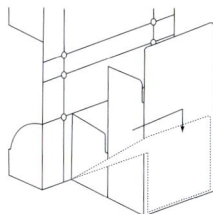

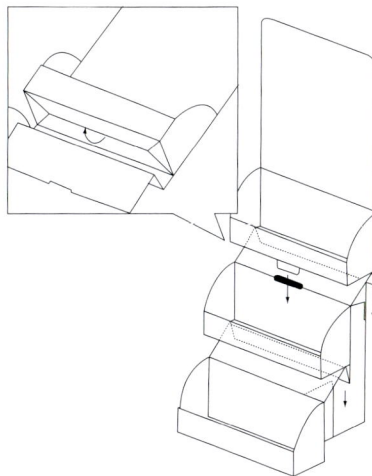

ユニリーバ・ジャパン
Unilever Japan

Rexena

COUNTER P.O.P.
SWING P.O.P.

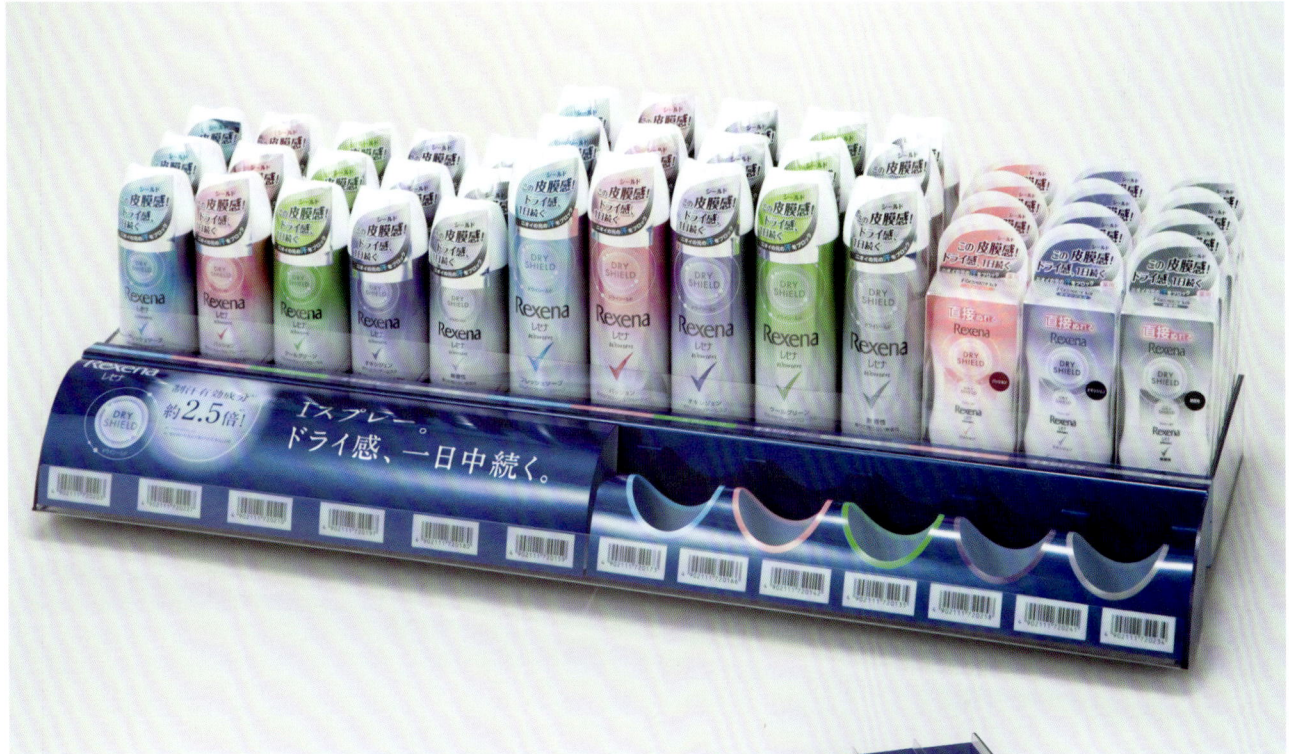

P：大日本印刷
MATERIAL：アクリル、プラスチック
W 630 × H 70 × D 230

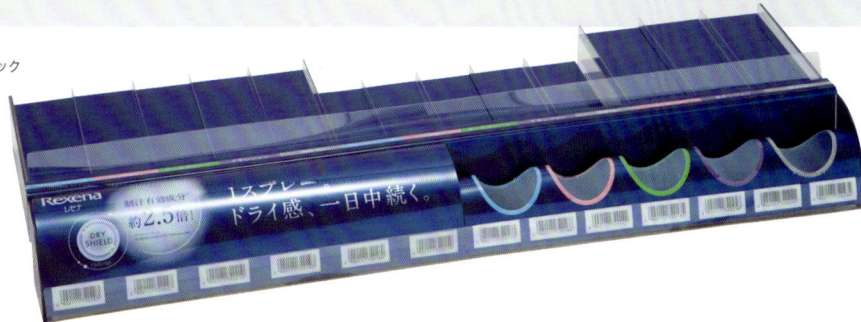

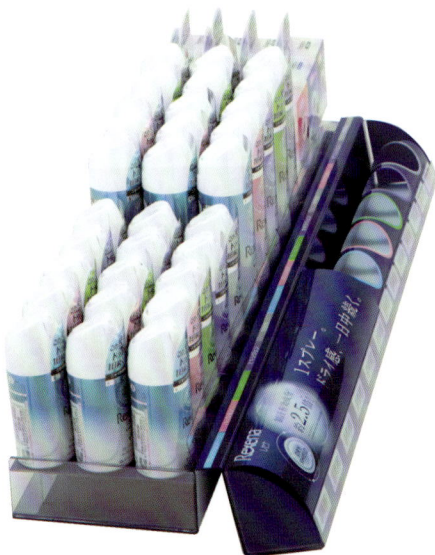

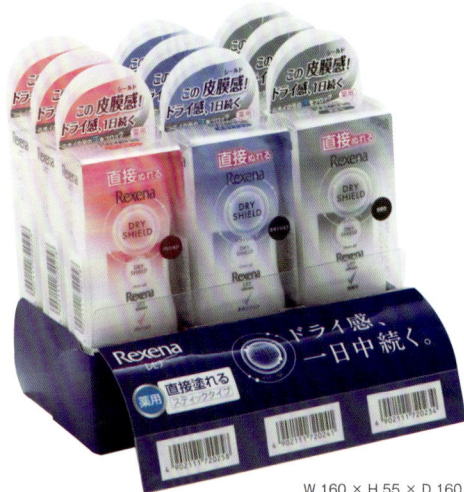

W 160 × H 55 × D 160

W 235 × H 55 × D 235

W 80 × H 80

W 80 × H 45

W 75 × H 65

W 60 × H 70

白元
HAKUGEN

フローラルミセスロイド

FLOOR P.O.P.

防虫剤を使ったことがない人、もしくは若い人に対して少しでも購入して頂きたく作成しました。コンセプトは「どこからでも見える販促物」。壁面に設置しても、購入者の目に触れるよう、180度開いたフロアディスプレイに仕上げました。また、2台組み会わせて使用すると、360度のフロアディスプレイとなります。商品コンセプトの華やかさも損なわないよう注意して作成しました。

This display was designed to encourage mothball purchases by first-time users and young people. The concept here is "a product that can be viewed from all directions." The design for this 180-degree 3D floor display aims to attract the attention of customers even when used as a wall display. Moreover, 2 displays can be combined to create a 360-degree floor display, and efforts were made to prevent interference with the colorful product concept.

※現在は使用していません。

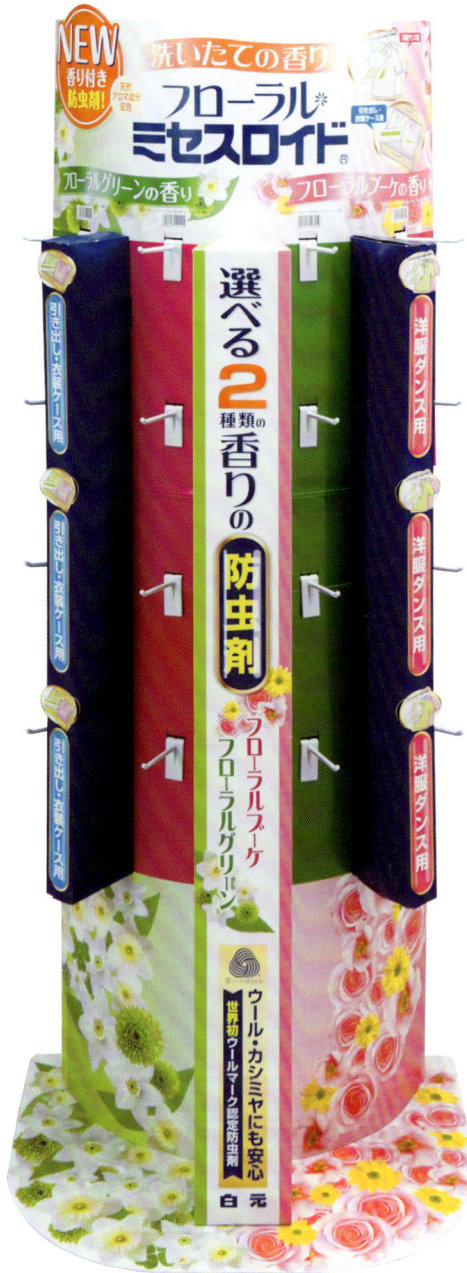

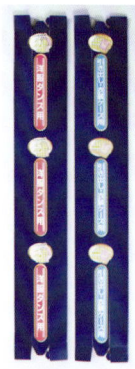

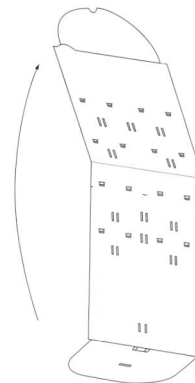

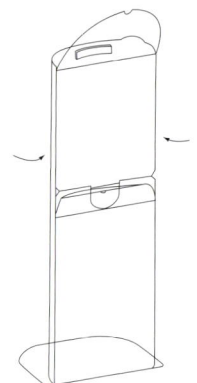

P：トーイン
MATERIAL：紙類
W 600 × H 1480 × D 460

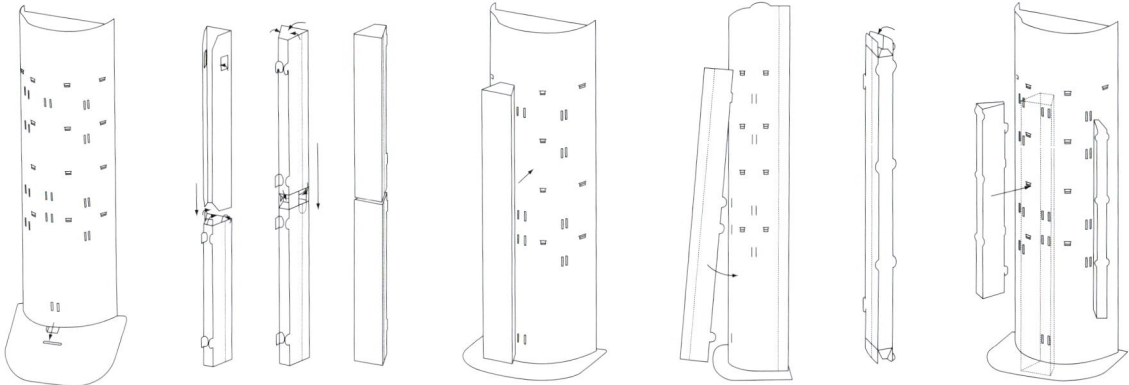

白元
HAKUGEN

フローラルミセスロイド

COUNTER P.O.P.

防虫剤を使ったことがない人、もしくは若い人に対して少しでも購入して頂きたく作成しました。コンセプトは「実際に香りを嗅いで購入」。自然に香りが漂いながら、いい香りの元を探ってもらい、そして実際に香りを嗅いでもらうため、香り見本をむき出しにしています。また、シェルフトーカーと一体型にすることにより、商品に直結した使用となっています。

This display was designed to encourage mothball purchases by first-time users and young people. The concept here is "sniff before purchasing." In order to get customers to seek out and sniff the lovely scent lingering in the air, the display features a sample of the fragrance. A shelf talker is also used to further connect the display and product.

※現在は使用していません。

A：協同広告
P：日本パルプテックス／北洋印刷
MATERIAL：プラスチック
W 120 × H 370 × D 330

白鶴酒造
HAKUTSURU SAKE BREWING

鶴の玉手箱

COUNTER P.O.P.
OTHERS P.O.P.

「鶴の玉手箱」は「毎日使うものにこそ こだわりを」そんな思いで白鶴酒造が作りました。古くから肌に良いといわれる日本酒や酒粕など、酒造りにまつわる原料や天然素材を配合した健やかな素肌のためのブランドです。入浴剤と手作り石けんの異なる商材の売り場を確保することを念頭にして、「酒蔵からお届けするちょっといいもの」と、お客様がパッと見てわかるように、屋根付きの酒蔵の陳列什器を作りました。さらに漆塗りの玉手箱をイメージした光沢のある陳列ボックスは、ひな壇としても利用でき、コーナー作りに大変好評でした。

The Hakutsuru Sake Brewing Company developed the "Tsuru no Tamabako" lineup based on the concept "Commitment to everyday items." The brand was created from a mix of raw and natural materials used in brewing sake such as sake and sake cake, said to be beneficial to skin since long ago, and aims to promote healthy skin. Consideration was given to a combination display of bath salts and handmade soap, and was designed in the likeness of a covered brewery to convey the message "Quality products delivered from the brewery." The glossy display box resembling a lacquered box can also be stacked vertically, making this a popular corner display.

P：モノリス
MATERIAL：紙類
W 100 × H 270 × D 130

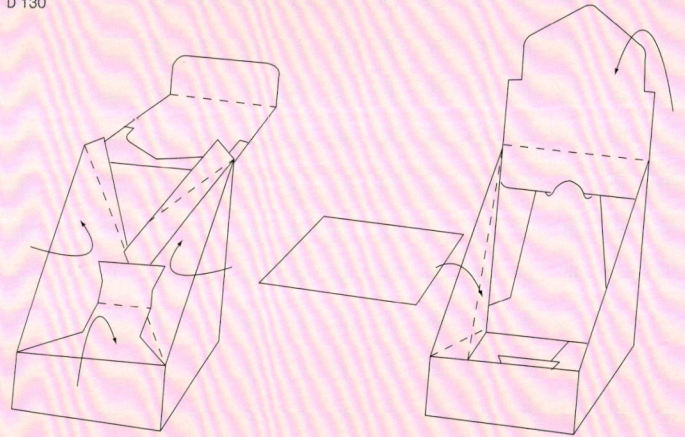

W 900 × H 400

P：モノリス
MATERIAL：紙類
W 510 × H 425 × D 310

ナリスアップ コスメティックス
NARISUP COSMETICS

Soft UV cut foam

COUNTER P.O.P.

製品の一番の特徴である"泡"タイプの日やけ止めを印象づけるため、什器自体を泡の形状で表現しました。また、泡の質感をパールの特殊紙を使って演出。カラフルな商品を引き立たせるよう、シンプルなデザインに仕上げました。

To emphasize this sunscreen's main"foam" type characteristic, the display outline was shaped like foam. Further, specialty pearl-finish paper was used to imitate the texture of foam. A simple design that makes this colorful product stand out.

P：イデイ
MATERIAL：紙
W 360 × H 405 × D 190

フマキラー
FUMAKILLA

虫よけバリア置き型

OTHERS P.O.P.

「虫よけバリア置き型」は玄関などに置くことで、家の中への虫の侵入を防ぐ商品です。屋内で使用する商品なので、香りにこだわっています。その香りを伝えるために、殺虫剤業界では珍しい香り見本をつくりました。置いたままにしておくより、揺れるとさらに効果が広がるという製品特長を、板バネを使用し、商品と同じように揺れるPOPで表現しました。

Placing this "insect repellent barrier" in areas such as your front entrance prevents insects from invading your home. As this product is for indoor use, the aroma is all-important, so an aroma sample rarely seen in the pesticide industry was developed. Rather than place the sample on a base, it was placed on the end of a spring so it moves around for greater effect, imitating the vibrations of the product..

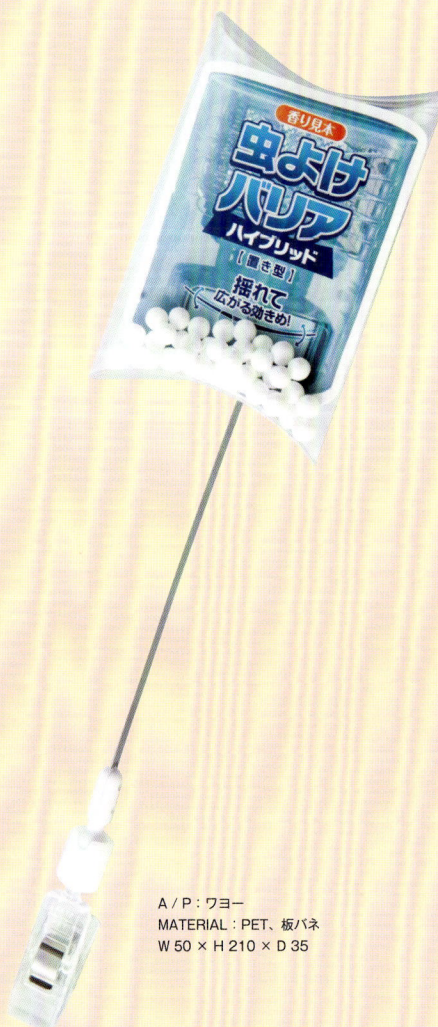

A／P：ワヨー
MATERIAL：PET、板バネ
W 50 × H 210 × D 35

ドクターシーラボ
Dr.Ci:Labo

A：凸版印刷
MATERIAL：紙類
W 500 × H 1290 × D 350

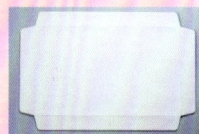

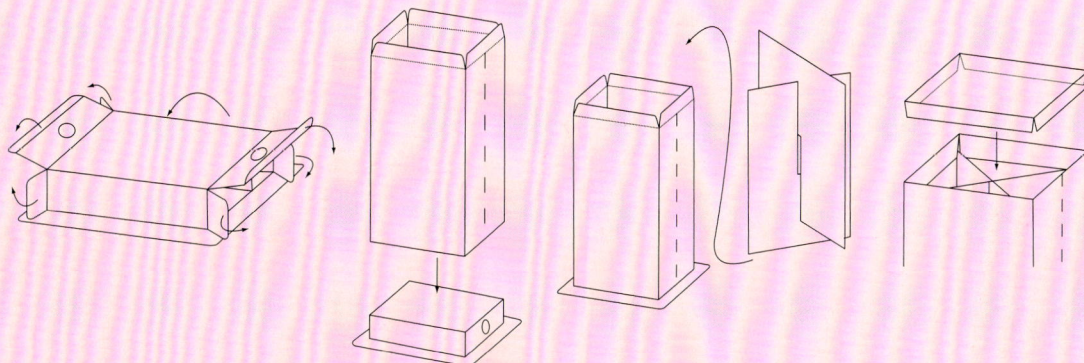

ドクターシーラボ
Dr.Ci:Labo

スーパーホワイト 377

COUNTER P.O.P.
OTHERS P.O.P.

「かつてない透明美肌へ。」をキーワードに、商品の世界観と登場感を出しました。ブライトニング商品なのであえて、単色にこだわり、白が際立つデザインにしました。

The product's ideology and presence was established via the catch phrase "For the whitest skin you have ever experienced," and although this display was for a brightening product, white was offset by the use of simple coloring.

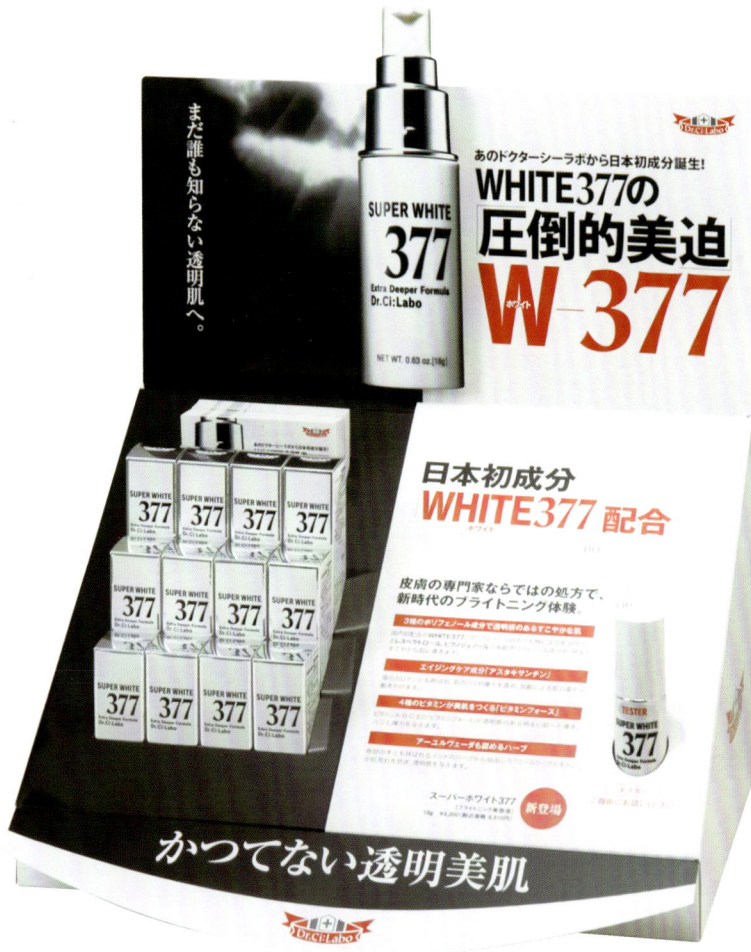

A：ミクプランニング
MATERIAL：紙類
W 400 × H 480 × D 310

A：デジタルガレージ
MATERIAL：スチレンボード
W 900 × H 600

A：ミクプランニング
MATERIAL：紙類

A：ミクプランニング
MATERIAL：スチレンボード、紙類
W 148 × H 210 × D 60

A：凸版印刷
MATERIAL：スチレンボード、紙類
W 148 × H 210 × D 60

A：ミクプランニング
MATERIAL：スチレンボード、紙類
W 148 × H 210 × D 60

COSMETIC

ドクターシーラボ
Dr.Ci:Labo

アクアコラーゲンゲル エンリッチリフトEX

COUNTER P.O.P.
OTHERS P.O.P.

シリーズのある商品のため、今までのゲルとの違いが什器中央のアテンションにて一目でわかるデザインにしました。また、陳列に関して、ピラミッド形式に並べつつも商品の取りやすさに留意し、内容量の違う商品を並べても全体のイメージを崩さないデザインを心がけました。

As this product is part of a series, the display focuses on the central area featuring an explanation of the differences between this and conventional gels. Further, consideration was given to easy product access by lining them up in pyramid style, and efforts were made to ensure that the overall image was not disrupted despite showcasing products differing in size.

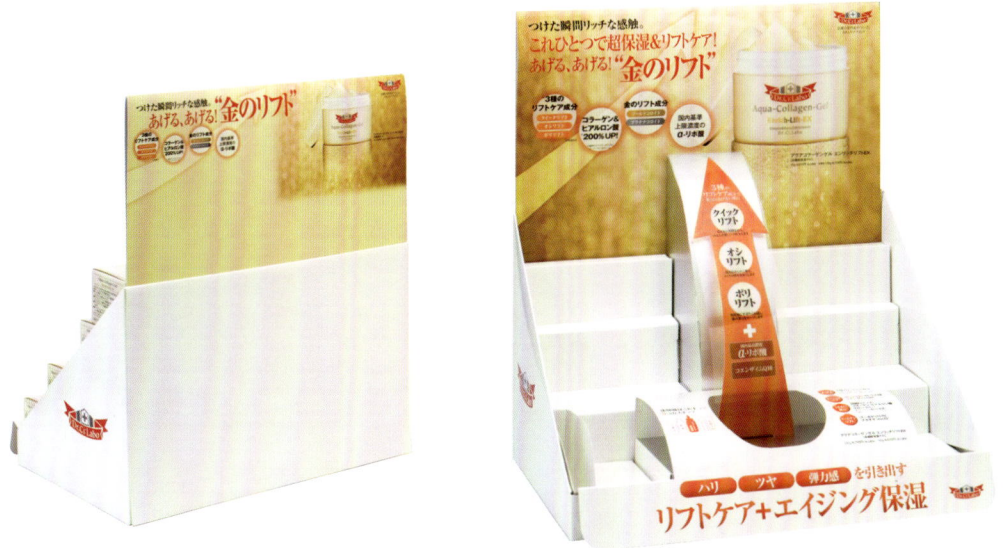

A：デジタルガレージ
MATERIAL：紙類、PET
W 400 × H 450 × D 280

A：デジタルガレージ
MATERIAL：スチレンボード
W 900 × H 600

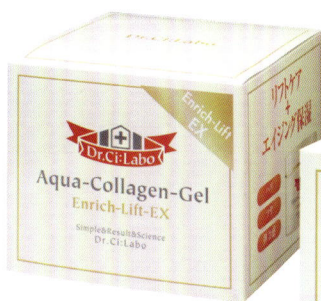

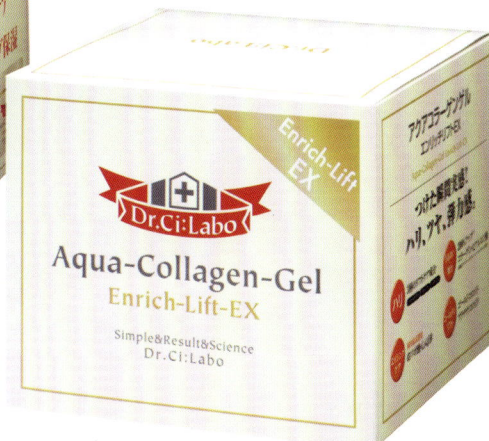

P：大光印刷
MATERIAL：紙類
W 200 × H 170 × D 200

A：凸版印刷
MATERIAL：スチレンボード、紙類
W 148 × H 210 × D 60

A：デジタルガレージ
MATERIAL：紙類
W 148 × H 210 × D 80

A：デジタルガレージ
MATERIAL：紙類
W 148 × H 210 × D 80

イミュ
Imju

déjàvu

COUNTER P.O.P.
FLOOR P.O.P.

マスカラの什器については、どこでどんな形の什器を見ても、すぐに製品を思い起こしていただけるように、製品色であるロングタイプの「赤」と、ボリュームタイプの「ピンク」を使用して、色の塊を出すことでわかりやすく表現しました。また、アイライナーの什器については、ラインがするする描けることを表現するために、ラインを螺旋状につなげて、トップビジュアルの芯と繋げ、なめらかさを演出しました。

This mascara display uses the "red" from the long type and the "pink" from the volume type packaging to create a clear link with the product regardless of the location or shape of the display. The purpose of the display is easier to understand by using color in such quantities. Further, smoothness is achieved for the eyeliner display with a continuous spiral line indicating how easily the eyeliner glides on and connecting the display with the top visual.

MATERIAL：合紙
W 400 × H 650 × D 290

MATERIAL：スチール、PET
W 900 × H 1550 × D 350

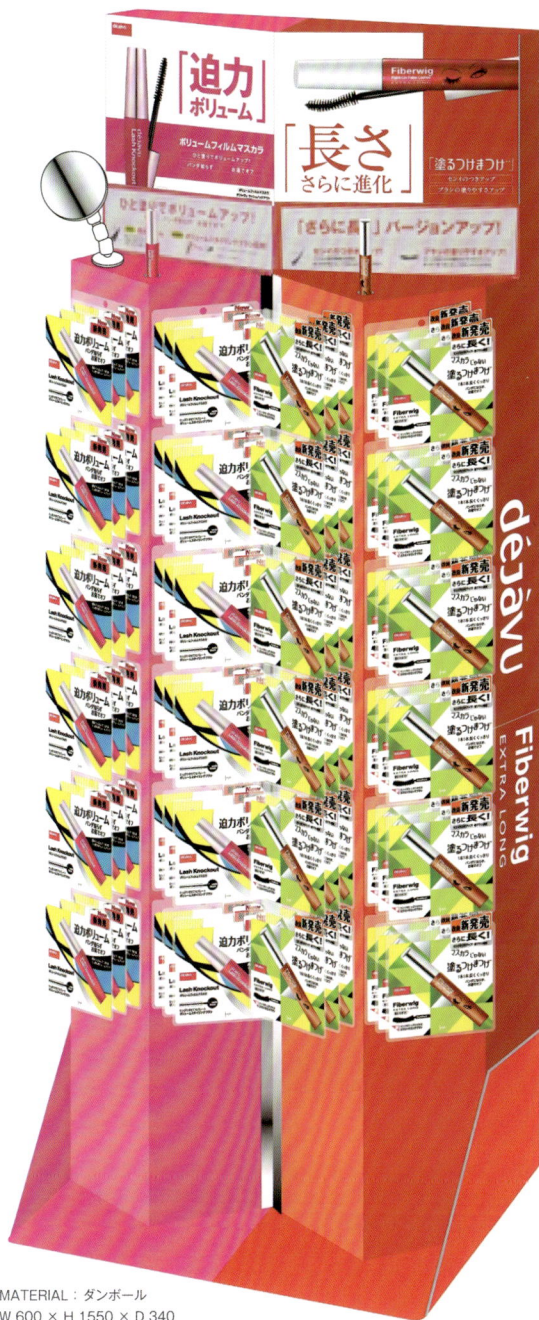

MATERIAL：ダンボール
W 600 × H 1550 × D 340

MATERIAL：紙類、ダンボール
W 450 × H 1550 × D 350

コージー本舗
KOJI HONPO

Dolly Wink

FLOOR P.O.P.

ドーリーウインクブランドプロデューサーの益若つばさを全面に押し出し、ひと目でどのような商品か分かることを心掛けました。ピンクにドットのドーリーウインクのパッケージデザインと揃えることで世界観を伝えられるようにしました。また、商品の陳列位置についても、見やすく取りやすい位置を意識しました。ちなみに、益若さんの身長も、正確に再現しています。

This display makes full use of the image of Tsubasa Masuwaka, the producer of Dolly Wink, and was designed so the product is obvious at a single glance. A feeling of unity was achieved by matching the display with the pink spotted Dolly Wink packaging. Thought was also given to the display location as well as high visibility and accessibility. The image size for Tsubasa Masuwaka was also accurately reproduced.

MATERIAL：紙
W 685 × H 1640 × D 400

MATERIAL：紙
W 350 × H 1400 × D 280

P：イデイ
MATERIAL：紙
W 465 × H 1600 × D 345

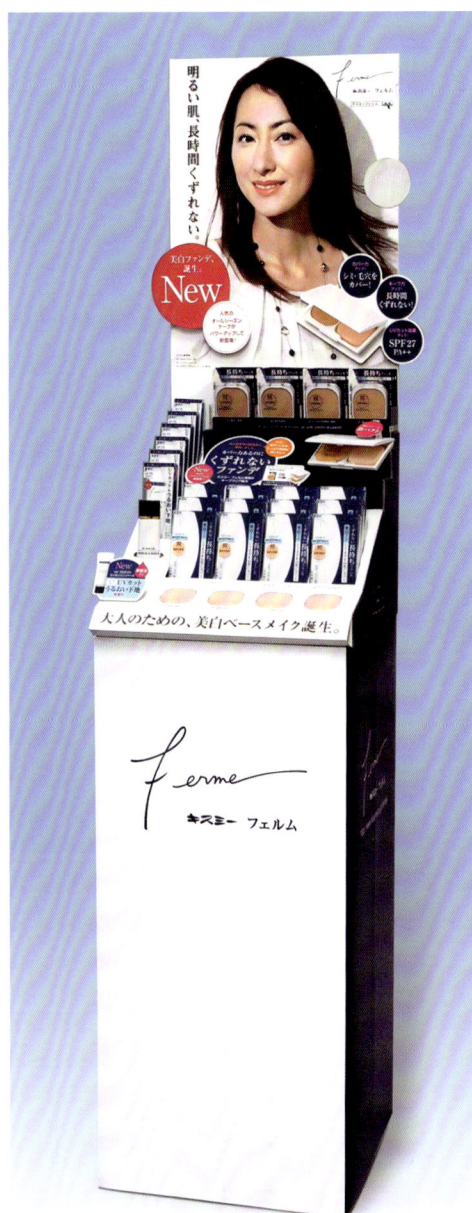

P：イデイ
MATERIAL：紙
W 450 × H 1600 × D 450

エリザベス
ELIZABETH

Savvy Brownie

FLOOR P.O.P.

ビジュアルにはシルエットのイラストを採用しながら、全体的にシンプルな表現でより商品を引き立てることを意識しました。ネイルのデザインサンプルを実際に落とし込むことで、買い手にネイルの仕上がりをイメージしやすい工夫を行いました。スタンドを使用せず、カウンターで設置出来る仕様になっています。

Featuring a silhouette for the main graphics, this display was designed to attract greater attention to the product through comprehensive simplicity.Actual samples of nail designs were included in the display, making it easier for shoppers to imagine the nail finish they can achieve. The display was not fitted with a stand as it was intended for countertop use.

伊勢半
ISEHAN

Kiss Me ferme

FLOOR P.O.P.

大人のための美肌メイクを表現するために、シンプルでありながら信頼感のあるデザインを目指しました。個々の商品特徴をしっかり伝えるためにコピーワークと共に、テスターもしっかりと使いやすく商品も取りやすい設計にこだわっています。設置スペースのことも意識しており、無駄の無いシンプルでコンパクトなサイズに設計。カウンターでも設置出来る仕様になっています。

Targeting adults, the design was kept simple, while aiming to create a feeling of trust. To adequately communicate the product characteristics, a catch phrase is used along with easy-to-use testers and a design that encourages customers to reach for the products. Installation space was also a concern, resulting in a simple and compact display without wasted space. Also suitable for countertop use.

ダリヤ
DARIYA

Palty Solid Fragrance

COUNTER P.O.P.
HANGING P.O.P.

パッケージのモチーフをそのまま取り入れてデザインしました。売り場に応じて、吊り下げても、置いても展開できるディスプレイです。質感や香りを体験していただけるようテスター置き場を設置しました。

The design for this display adopts the packaging motif. It can either be hung down or stood up depending on the sales location. Storage space for testers was added so that customers could test the fragrance and feel of the products.

A：I&S BBDO 名古屋支社
MATERIAL：紙類
W 150 × H 340 × D 215

W 150 × H 550 × D 135

ダリヤ
DARIYA

Palty Solid Fragrance

COUNTER P.O.P.

店頭で女の子から「カワイイ」と共感を得られるようデザインしました。商品コピーが "見えない香りのアクセサリー" ということで、アンティーク調の三面鏡の引き出しからアクセサリーが飛び出すイメージの立体型カウンターディスプレイです。商品が練り香水ということで、質感や香りを体験していただけるようテスター置き場を設置。容器のかわいらしさを見せるために、テスター置き場はクリアにしました。

This display was designed to evoke cries of "Oh, how cute!" Since the product catch phrase was "an accessory with a hidden scent," the image for the 3D counter display was accessories popping out of a drawer below an antique style three-fold mirror. The display was also equipped with storage space for testers so customers could test out the fragrance and feel of the products, which are solid perfumes. Further, the clear tester storage area was designed to show off the product's cute-look container.

A：I&S BBDO 名古屋支社
MATERIAL：紙類
W 490 × H 390 × D 120

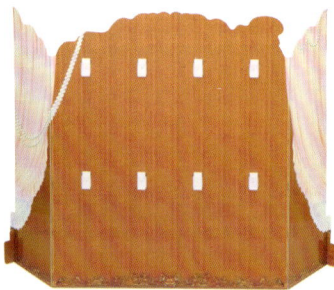

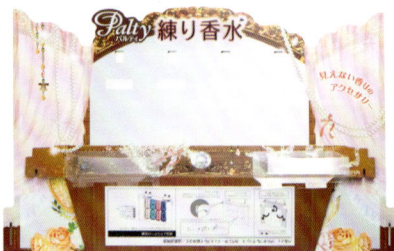

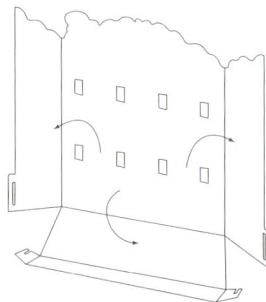

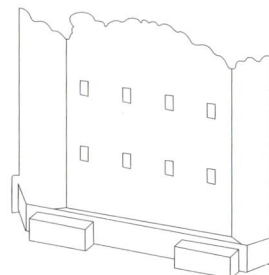

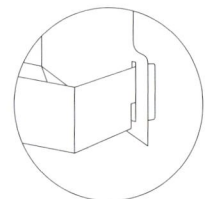

T-Garden
T-Garden

ジュエリッチ

COUNTER P.O.P.

新ブランドのアイラッシュ（つけまつげ）の発売に合わせ作成したプロモーションディスプレイです。『かわいい』が大好きな女の子がハッピーになれるブランドのコンセプトを大事にしました。ボードを大きくし、遠くからでも目立つようにしています。また、商品が無くなってもピンクの小花柄が見えるようにすることで、ガーリーな世界観を損なわないよう工夫しています。

This promotional display was designed in conjunction with the release of this new brand of false eyelashes. Great care was taken to impress that girls aiming for a "cute" look will be satisfied with the product. The backing board was enlarged so that it could be viewed from a distance. Further, by using a dainty floral pattern on the pink base, the feeling of girliness is not lost even if the product sells out.

P：スパイス
MATERIAL：紙
W 355 × H 430 × D 240

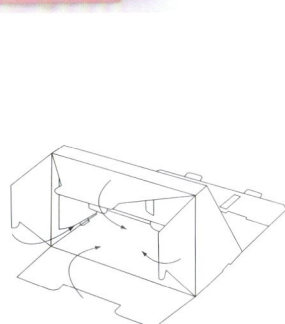

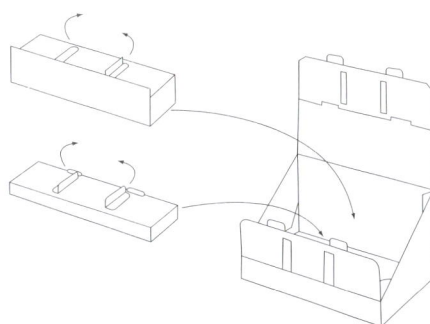

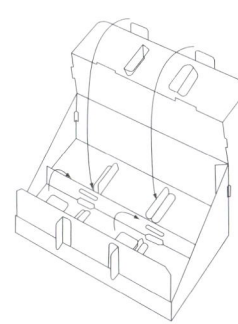

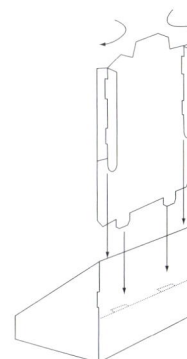

森下仁丹
Morishita Jintan

JINTAN116
HANGING P.O.P.

森下仁丹が創業116年の歴史で培った技術を集結させて生まれた「JINTAN116」の登場感を意識したPOPになっています。POPの上部には、商品のキャッチコピーでもある「生薬で息健康に」を強調して入れ込み、さらに、商標を顔にしたスタイリッシュなデザインに、商品特長を打ち出した5タイプのパッケージを展開しています。POPと商品のデザインを統一することで、売り場での存在感、商品の本物感を打ち出したPOPに仕上がっています。※5タイプのパッケージは、外装のみ期間限定。

This POP display was used to announce the debut of "JINTAN 116," the result of 116 years of accumulated technological wealth since the inauguration of Morishita Jintan. The upper part of the display prominently states the product catch phrase "Healthy breath through herbal medicine," and the 5 types of packaging showcase the product characteristics based on a stylish design featuring the brand's trademark face. Unifying the design of the display and product adds presence to the display and realness to the product. ※The 5 different packages are limited edition.

A：エムジェマ
P：美工
MATERIAL：合紙、プラスチック、塩化ビニル
W 85 × H 140 × D 40

生薬で
カラダの中から
"息"健康に!!

JINTAN
116
〈コクにが〉

円

只今品切れ中です

只今品切れ中です

1フェイスで
使う場合は、点線で
切り離しください。

生薬で
カラダの中から
"息"健康に!!

JINTAN
116
〈コクにが〉

円

NEW!
スタイリッシュな
携帯ケース入り

JINTAN
116
〈コクにが〉

7つの生薬。"息"健康に。

二日酔い 気分不快 口臭
ケース入り(100粒) 医薬部外品

NEW!
スタイリッシュな
携帯ケース入り

JINTAN
116
〈コクにが〉

7つの生薬。"息"健康に。

二日酔い 気分不快 口臭
ケース入り(100粒) 医薬部外品

A：エムジェマ
P：美工
MATERIAL：合紙、プラスチック、塩化ビニル
W 80 × H 320

森下仁丹
Morishita Jintan

JINTAN116

Package

Sampling

T-Shirt

大正製薬
Taisho Pharmaceutical

ジクロテクト

COUNTER P.O.P.
HANGING P.O.P.

２００９年６月の改正薬事法施行後、第１類医薬品（空箱）の陳列スペースが減少していたことから、省スペースで展開できるツールを作成しました。吊り下げて使用するだけでなく、カウンター上への設置も可能な仕様になっています。

As the display space for first-class OTC drugs (empty boxes) was decreased after the revised Pharmaceutical Affairs Act went into effect in June 2009, this display was designed as a tool for displaying in limited spaces. In addition to being used as a hanging display, it can also be used on a countertop.

A：電通
P：電通テック
MATERIAL：紙類
W 255 × H 485 × D 110

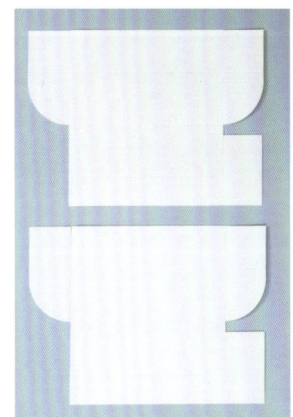

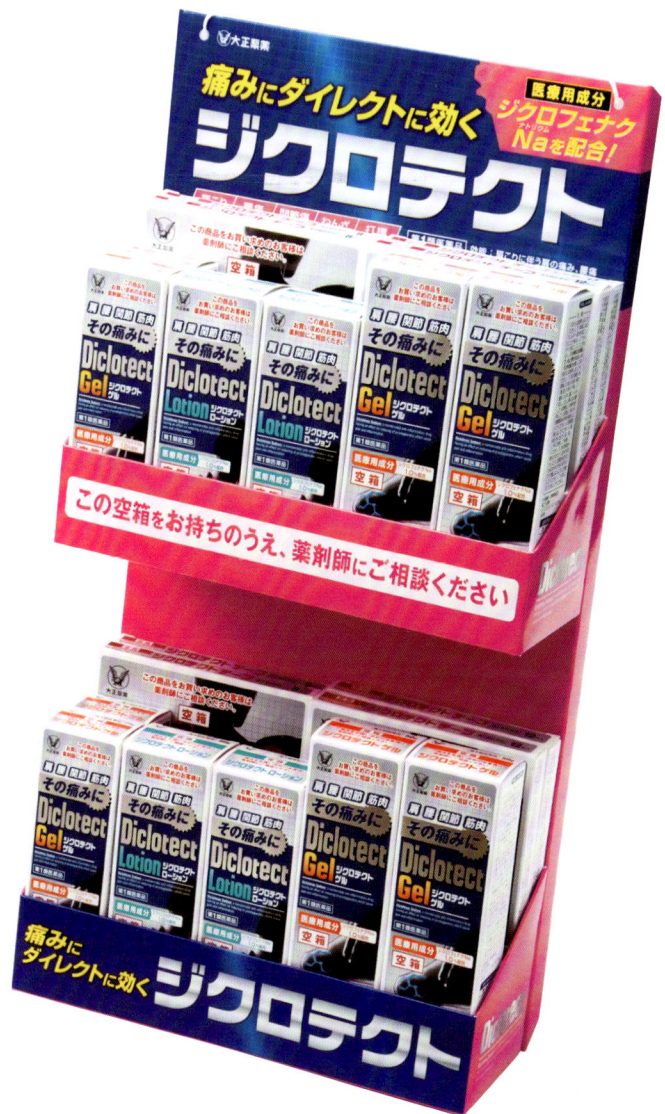

W 255 × H 485 × D 185

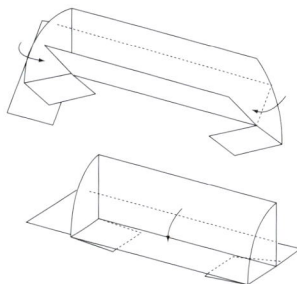

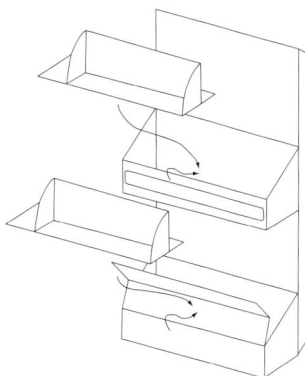

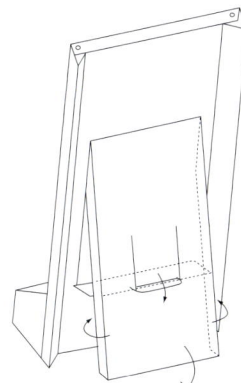

大正製薬
Taisho Pharmaceutical

ジクロテクト

COUNTER P.O.P.

外用鎮痛・消炎剤カテゴリーにおいては、久々のスイッチOTC製剤であり、生活者への注目度を高める目的で作成しました。製品パッケージを踏襲したデザインとし、ユーザーが求める先進性や高級感を表現しています。また、お得意先様の作業負担軽減にも留意し、短時間で組み立てられるように工夫しました。

This is the first switch OTC drug to appear in a long time in the category of external analgesics and antiphlogistics, and the display was designed to increase exposure. It closely follows the product packaging, and conveys the spirit of innovation and sense of luxury demanded by users. The display also aims to relieve the burden on store staff through quick assembly.

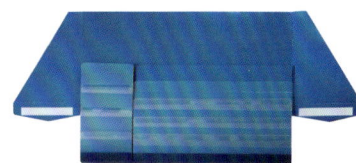

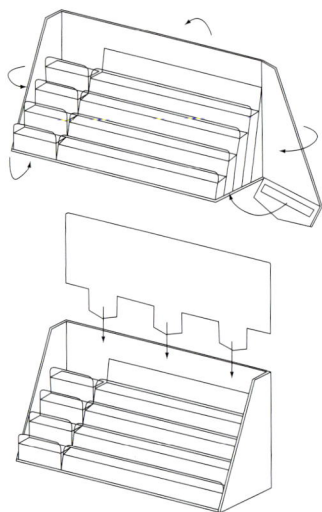

A：電通
P：電通テック
MATERIAL：紙類
W 620 × H 480 × D 210

A / P：興和紡績
MATERIAL：アクリル、スチレンボード
W 350 × H 600 × D 300

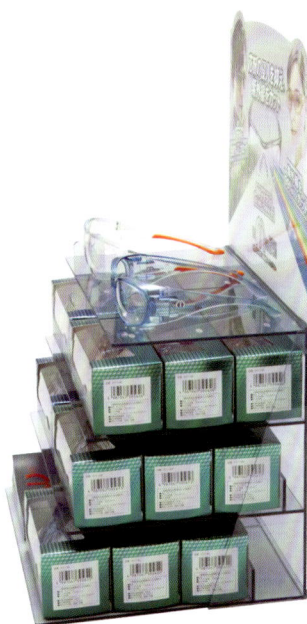

興和
KOWA

DIMENSION

COUNTER P.O.P.

商品新発売時の展開の際に使用した
ディスプレイで、テーマは新登場感
とブランドイメージに合わせ高級感
の演出。そのため、ディスプレイ本
体の素材はアクリルを使用しまし
た。また、見た目以外にも、エンド
陳列以外でも展開しやすいようにサ
イズの調整も行い、サンプルも取り
扱いやすいように製作しました。

This display was used in
conjunction with the release of
the product to deliver a feeling
of luxury that supports both the
new release and brand image.
As such, acrylic was adopted
as the material for the display
body. Attention went into not
only the appearance, but also
into making a size-adjustable
display that can be used as
more than just an end display,
and was designed so that the
samples were enticing to pick
up.

佐藤製薬
Sato Pharmaceutical

アラセナ S

COUNTER P.O.P.

アラセナSのSの字が、パッケージ上でもマークとして使われているので、このSを唇に例えてデザイン化し、コピーにも商品名の認知促進を図るため、アラッ！？という言葉を入れ込みました。また、レジ横にも置いて頂けるよう、コンパクトにし、商品のイメージカラーであるオレンジを多用することで、連動感とインパクトを高めました。

As the letter "S" of Arasena S is used on the packaging, here it was transformed into the shape of lips, and the phrase "Ara!" (Oh, my!) was added to emphasize the product name. The display was kept compact so that it could be placed next to the register, and overall coordination and impact were heightened through the abundant use of the product color orange.

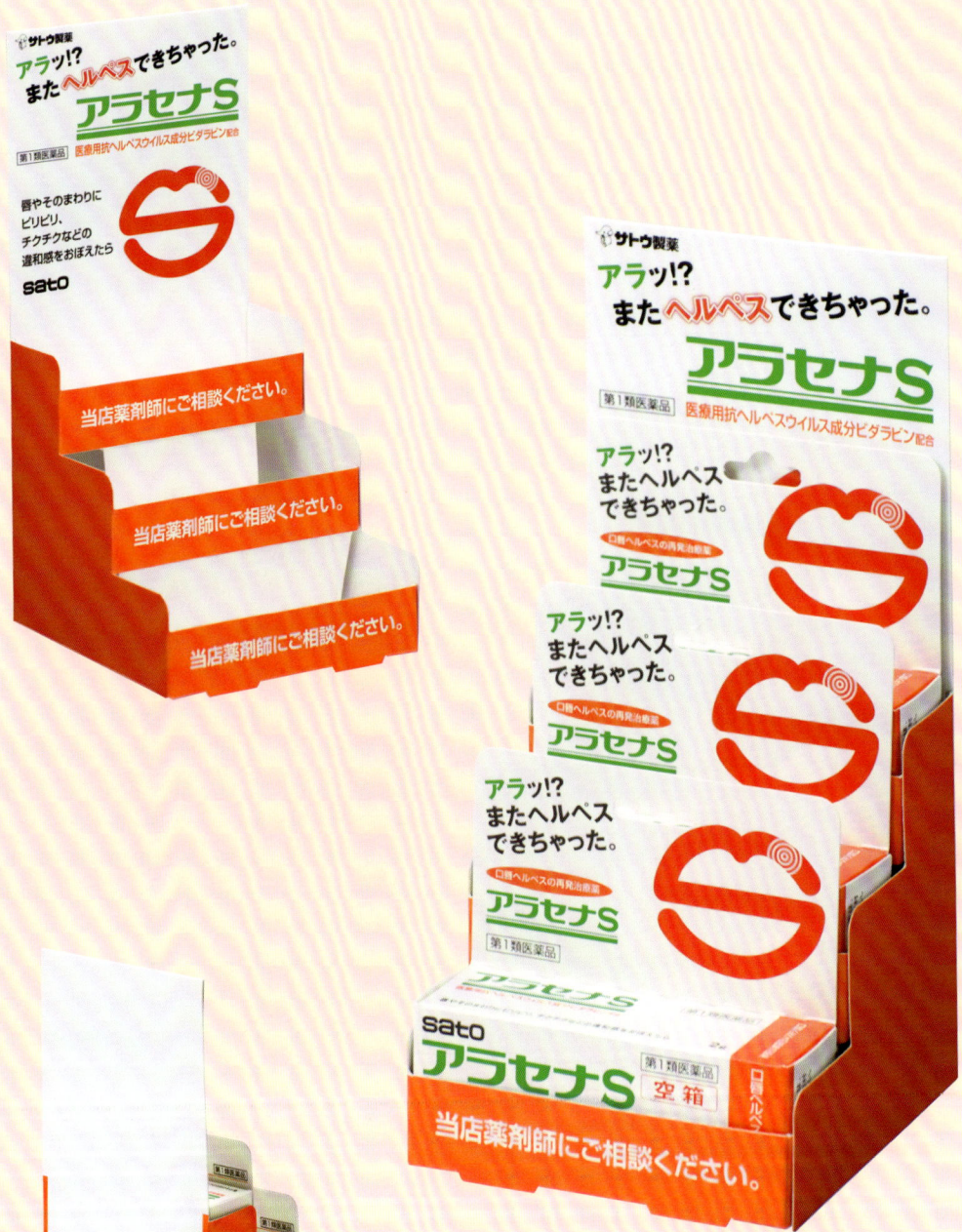

A：電通ヤング・アンド・ルビカム
P：インプレッション / ライザプロダクション
MATERIAL：合紙
W 92 × H 190 × D 96

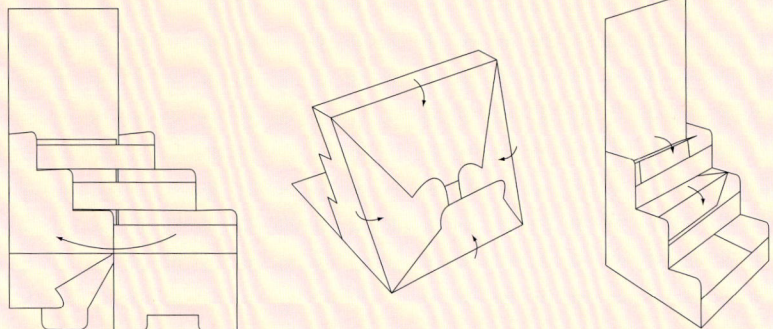

大鵬薬品工業
TAIHO PHARMACEUTICAL

ハルンケア
MOVING P.O.P.

ハルンケアの TVCM と連動し、夜トイレに起きてしまう「夜間頻尿」を訴求しました。店頭でのアイキャッチを高めるために、ムービング POP を使用し、効果的に「夜間頻尿」を表現しています。

In conjunction with the Harncare TV commercial, this display targets those troubled by "nocturia" causing nighttime toilet visits. Through a moving POP display, instore appeal is increased, and "nocturia" effectively described.

P：日本写真印刷
MATERIAL：紙類、PET
W 60 × H 150 × D 25

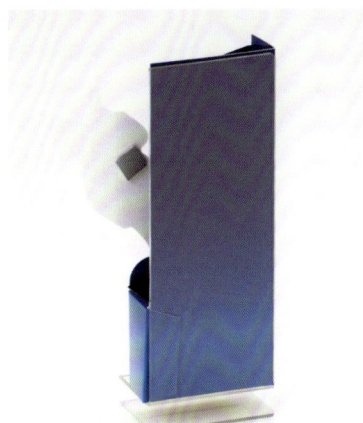

オムロン ヘルスケア
OMRON HEALTHCARE

歩数計 Walking style

HANGING P.O.P.

歩数計ではこれまでにないユニークなデザインの商品なので、その特長をひと目でアピールできるように商品の形状そのままの形の POP を制作しました。歩数計を用いて健康管理を行うことの楽しさを伝えることも意図しています。

As the pedometer features a unique design, this POP display was created in the same shape as the product to appeal to customers at a glance. The design also communicates the fun involved in using a pedometer to manage your health.

A：読売広告社
MATERIAL：紙類、合紙
W 360 × H 680

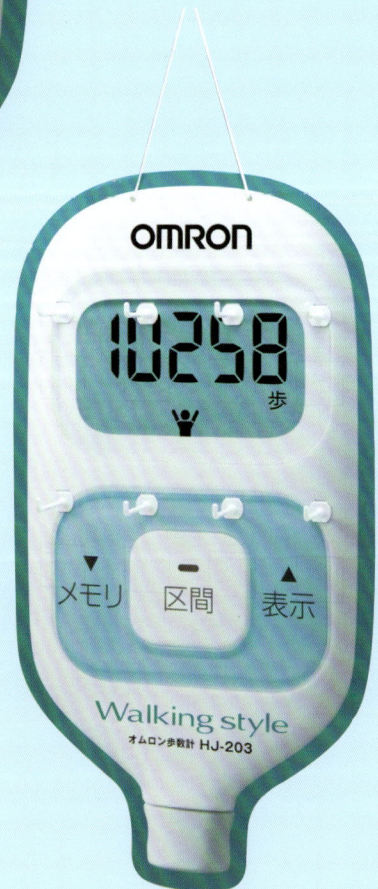

オムロン ヘルスケア
OMRON HEALTHCARE

上腕式手動ソーラー血圧計

COUNTER P.O.P.

ソーラーパネルを搭載し、太陽エネルギーで駆動するソーラー血圧計は、乾電池が不要となり廃棄物を削減できるほか、CO_2 排出量の削減が期待できる、環境にやさしい商品です。そこで、医療機器としての精度感だけではなく、地球へのやさしさやクリーンなイメージを POP でも表現しました。

The solar blood pressure monitor, mounted with a solar panel enabling it to run on solar energy, is an environmentally friendly product that does not need batteries, reducing waste, and also promising to reduce CO2 emissions. As such, this display not only conveys its accuracy as a medical instrument, but also its environmentally friendly and green features.

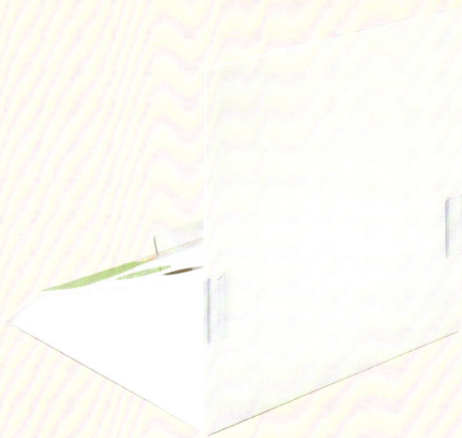

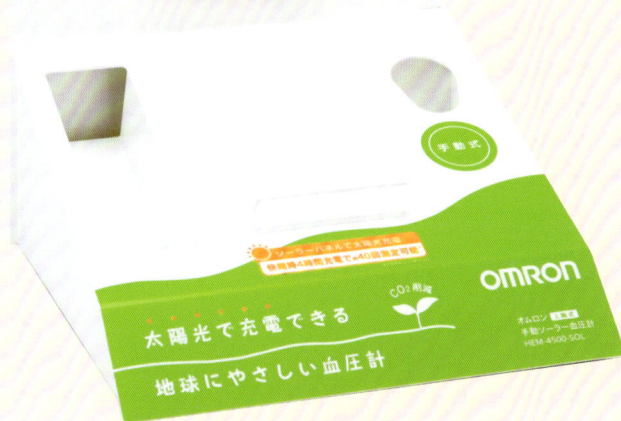

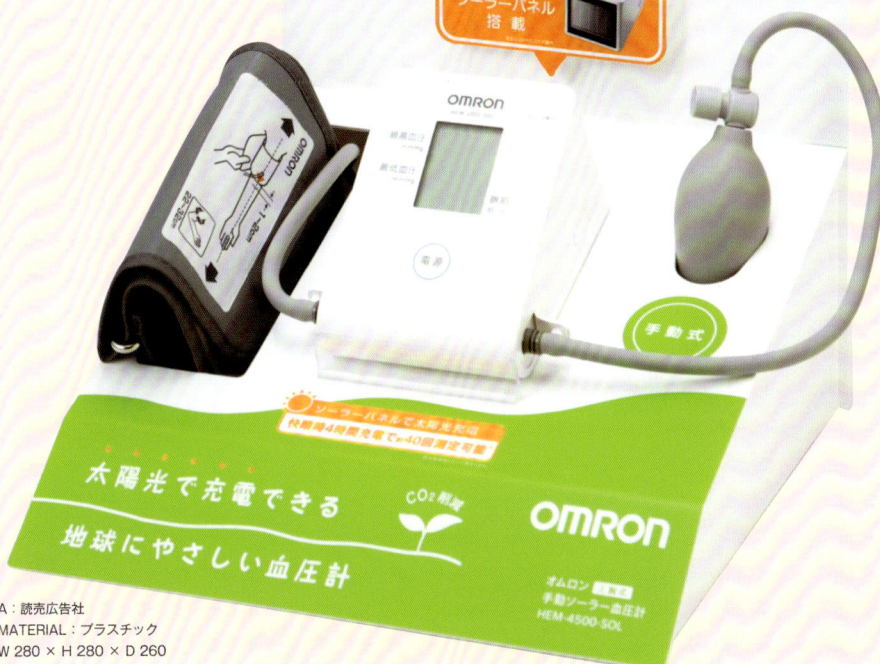

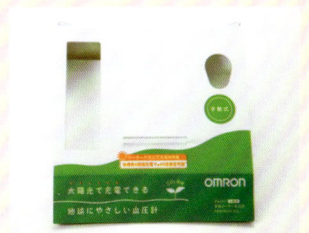

A：読売広告社
MATERIAL：プラスチック
W 280 × H 280 × D 260

103

タニタ
TANITA

カロリズム SMART

COUNTER P.O.P.
FLOOR P.O.P.

台と取り外しができるため、カウンター什器としてもフロア什器としても両方使用できるタイプのディスプレイです。

Since the base can be removed, this display can be used on either the counter or the floor.

W 410 × H 400 × D 250

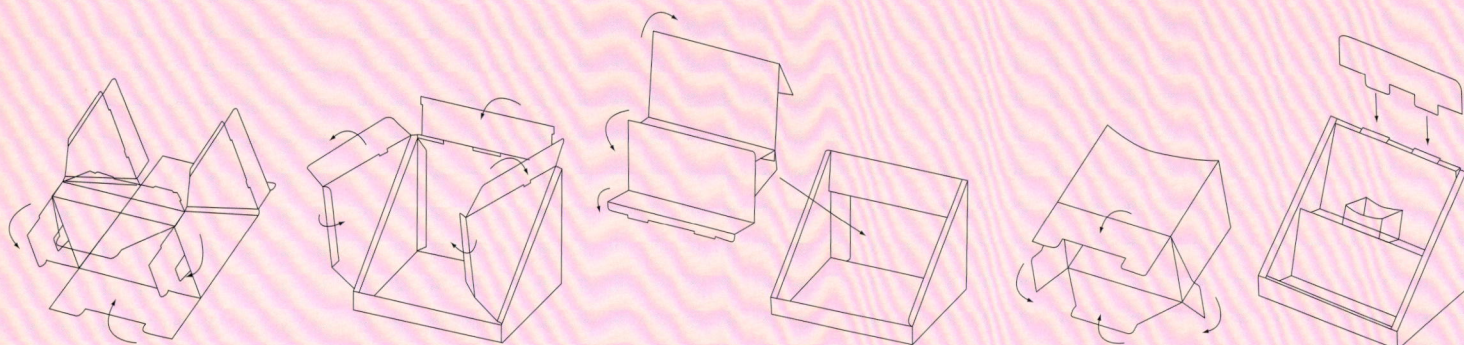

P：マスパック
MATERIAL：紙類
W 410 × H 1110 × D 250

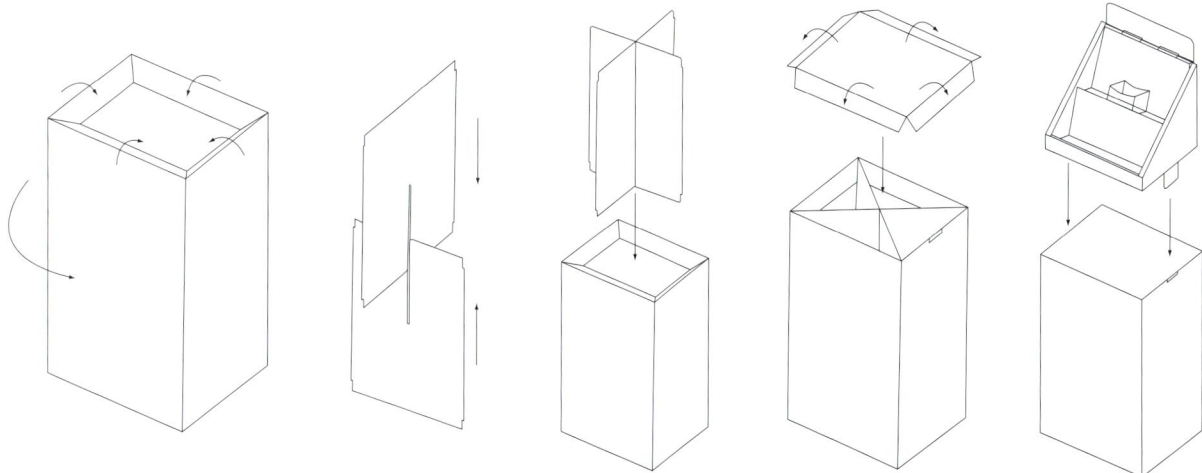

HOME APPLIANCE
【家電】

DIGITAL GADGET
【デジタル機器】

STATIONERY
【文房具】

東芝ホームアプライアンス
TOSHIBA HOME APPLIANCES

エアリオンワイド

COUNTER P.O.P.

東芝消臭デオドライザー〝エアリオン・ワイド〟の棚置き陳列に使用するカウンターディスプレイです。家電量販店舗内には消臭に関するカテゴリーが無いため、空気清浄機コーナーでの展開が中心となるので、空気清浄機と同じ目線になるよう、用途や最適な使用場所も大きく表示しています。また、素材はブルー基調のヘアライン合紙を使用して光沢感をだし、高級感溢れる助成物に仕上げ、店頭でも目立つように作成しました。

This counter display was used for the Toshiba deodorizer "Airion Wide." As there is no category for deodorizers within electronics stores, they are mainly displayed together with air purifiers, and as such, are viewed in the same way as air purifiers. Therefore, the display clearly shows types of application and locations ideal for use. It also uses blue-themed hairline paper to produce a glossy finish that fosters a feeling of extravagance, and was designed to stand out.

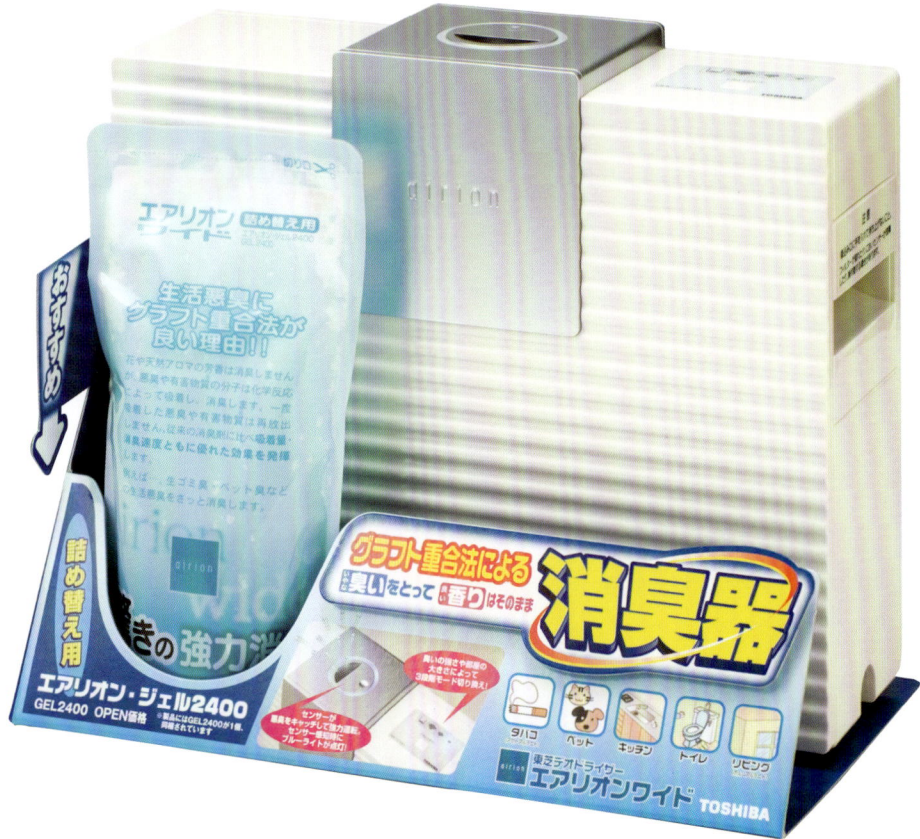

P：エキスプレス社
MATERIAL：合紙
W 310 × H 175× D 180

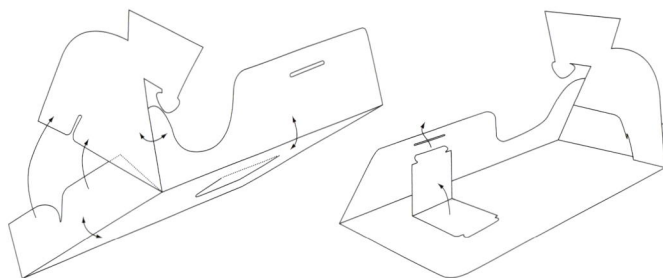

P：エキスプレス社
MATERIAL：合紙
W 470 × H 580 × D 240

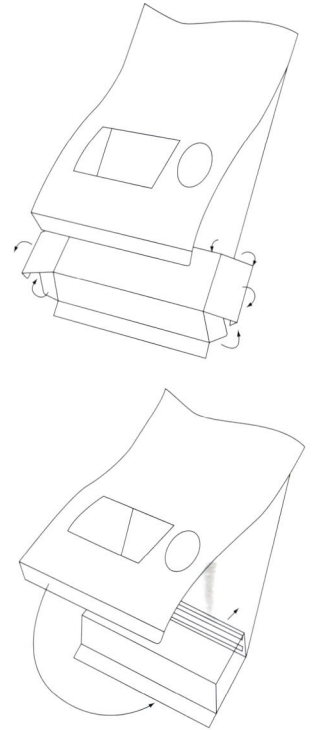

東芝ホームアプライアンス
TOSHIBA HOME APPLIANCES

グリル&フィッシュロースター

COUNTER P.O.P.

「お店でいただく本格焼き魚をご家庭で」をテーマに、料亭イメージでおいしさを表現しました。バックボードが可動式で奥行きの調整が可能なので、年末などの催事期には、山積み展示にも使用できる汎用性を備えています。

Based on the theme "home-grilled fish that tastes just like restaurant cooking," the image for this display was the delicious cuisine of Japanese-style restaurants. As the backing board is adjustable to change the depth, this versatile display can also be used as part of a larger display during party seasons.

P：エキスプレス社
MATERIAL：ダンボール合紙
W 485 × H 370 × D 360

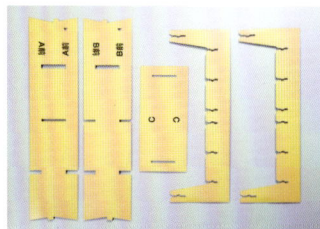

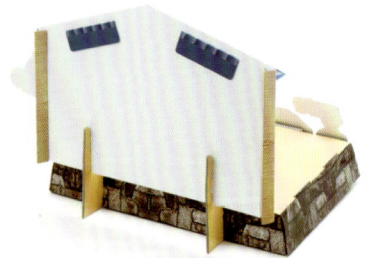

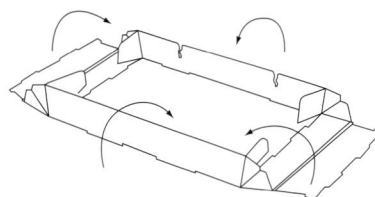

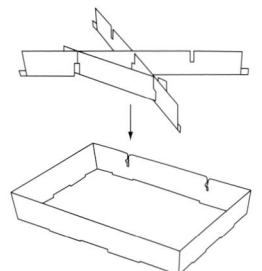

ワイドヒーターだから
頭から尻尾までパリッと焼き上げ！

東芝亭

TOSHIBA

本格焼き魚を
ご家庭で！

両面とも
パリッと
焼けてる！
すみずみまで熱が行き渡る！
両面焼き風遠赤外線ワイドヒーター

焼き上がりが
キレイ！
魚がくっつきにくい！
ブラックシリコーンコートマルチ焼網

丸洗いできて
とっても便利！
お手入カンタン！
分解丸洗い

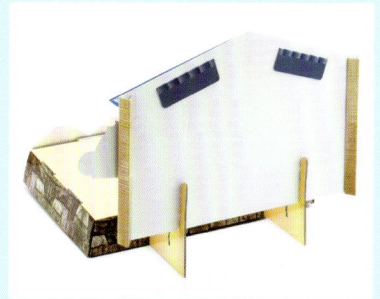

W 485 × H 370 × D 430

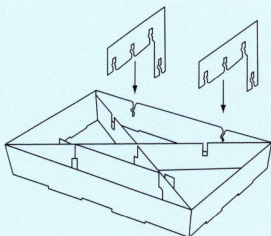

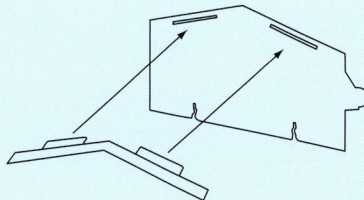

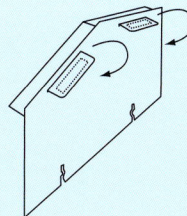

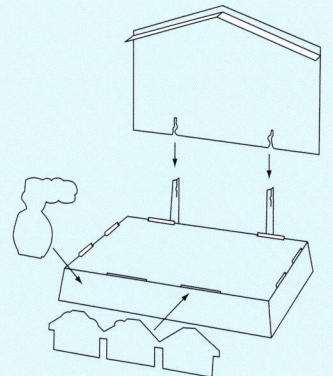

貝印
KAI

AdHoc
COUNTER P.O.P.

ワイン・シャンパンの関連商品を集め、手に取りやすい什器を作成しました。

This display was designed to hold wine and champagne related items that can be easily picked up.

MATERIAL：紙類、アクリル
W 400 × H 245 × D 125

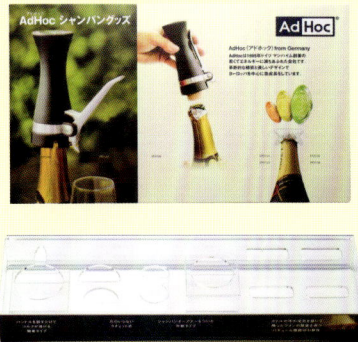

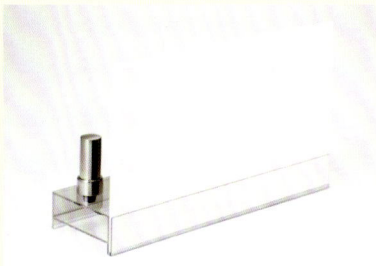

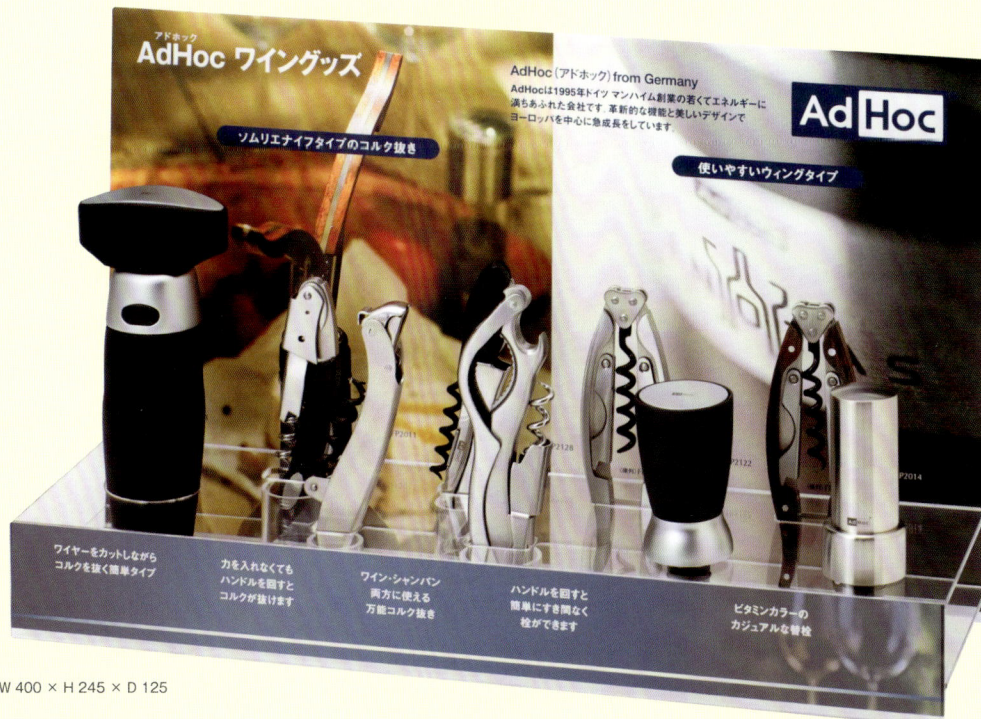

W 400 × H 245 × D 125

貝印
KAI

ちゅーぼーず3

COUNTER P.O.P.

シリーズの中で、部品のパーツが多く現品陳列のしにくい商品を作成しました。商品アピールと現品を出す際に管理しやすい役目を果たします。

This display was created for a product line that is hard to display due to the large number of parts in the series, and not only achieves product appeal, but makes it easy to manage the product on display.

MATERIAL：紙類
W 290 × H 250 × D 240

W 290 × H 250 × D 240

W 290 × H 250 × D 240

115

テスコム
TESCOM

Pure Black

COUNTER P.O.P.

白黒を基調にした製品カラーを踏まえ、「おいしさのキホン。」を全ての展示台のアイキャッチにしながら清潔感のあるシンプルなデザインに仕上げました。背面は各製品で使える食材を写真で見せることでどんな物が作られるのかを見る側に連想させ、ヘルシーなライフスタイルを提案。全面のアイコンでシンプルに分かりやすく機能訴求をしています。製品重量を考慮し、紙でも長期の展示で潰れないよう底の強度を強く仕上げました。

These stands all use the same black and white coloring as the product for an eye-catching effect, and the simple design carries a fresh, clean look. As pictures of sample ingredients are featured on the backing boards, viewers can easily imagine what they might make, promoting healthy living. The icons used throughout describe the features in a simple, easy-to-understand way. Further, the base of this paper display was reinforced to support the weight of the product over an extended period.

MATERIAL：紙類
W 280 × H 340 × D 275

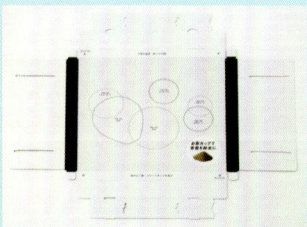

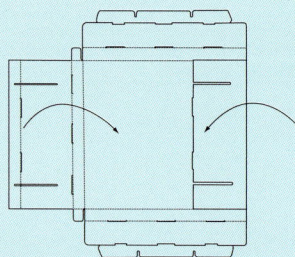

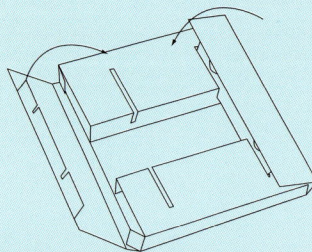

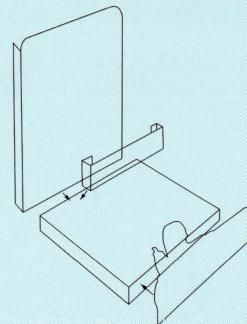

116

おいしいキホン。

① カラダの中からナチュラルに。
② ピュアデザインで気分もおいしく。
③ おしゃれ

はじめよう

丸洗いできる
セパレートバスケットで
後かたづけもラクラク。

Pure Black

のどごし
スッキリが
朝の
キホン。

ジューサー TJ110

TESCOM

おいしいキホン。

① カラダの中からナチュラルに。
② ピュアデザインで気分もおいしく。
③ おしゃれなのに機能的

はじめよう、ヘルシーライフをキホンから

のどごし
スッキリが
朝の
キホン。

TESCOM

おいしいキホン。

Pure Black

フローズン
シェイクが
元気の
キホン。

TESCOM

おいしいキホン。

大型チタンカッターで
クラッシュアイスもできる。

Pure Black

フローズン
シェイクが
元気の
キホン。

ジュースミキサー TMB16

TESCOM

テスコム
TESCOM

Metal Line
COUNTER P.O.P.

インテリアの一部として提案するスタイリッシュな製品デザインを踏まえ、生活の一部を切り取ったような展示台に仕上げました。背面は実際に製品を使用している場面を連想させる情景を映し、底をテーブルに見立てて生活スタイルを演出しています。デザイン家電では不安がられる機能面も、全面のアイコンで分かりやすく機能訴求をしています。製品重量を考慮し、紙でも長期の展示で潰れないよう底の強度を強く仕上げました。

While promoting this stylishly designed product as an interior item, the display stands aim to portray aspects of everyday living. Based on a lifestyle theme, the backing boards feature actual usage situations, and the bases were designed to resemble a table. As consumers often feel anxious about the features of designer home electronics, the icons used throughout describe the features in an easy-to-understand way. Further, the base of this paper display was reinforced to support the weight of the product over an extended period.

MATERIAL : 紙類
W 280 × H 340 × D 275

テスコム
TESCOM

ione

COUNTER P.O.P.

女性の定番人気色、ione シリーズの
キーカラーでもあるピンクを展示台
の全面に使用しました。背面のアル
グラスで高級感をプラスし、イオン
の形を表現する六角形を全体に散り
ばめています。前面の他に製品の背
面にも訴求を載せることで手に取っ
てすぐに製品情報が読めるよう工夫
しています。ラインナップで並べた
時の連なるピンクの迫力は存在感が
あり、どこからでも目立つブランド
ブロックに。耐久性を考慮した箱形
什器は、長期の展示でも対応出来る
つくりになっています。

Pink, a popular color choice
among women and the key
color for the "ione" series, was
used as the theme here. Adding
a glass-like and luxurious feel
to the backing boards,
hexagons symbolizing ions
were used throughout. In
addition to advertising on the
front, the stands were
constructed so that information
on the backing becomes visible
when the product is picked up.
When the various displays are
lined up, the "pink" grouping
stands out in all directions.
Further, the box-shaped
structure focuses on durability
for long-term display.

MATERIAL：紙類、金属
W 300 × H 290 × D 255

120

W 200 × H 270 × D 255

W 200 × H 290 × D 255

テスコム
TESCOM

nano ione

COUNTER P.O.P.

製品の上質感や美髪への憧れ・輝きを表現する色としてゴールドをキーカラーに採用し、展示台の全面に使用しました。背面のアルグラスで高級感をプラスし、イオンの形を表現する六角形を全面に散りばめています。手に取ってすぐに読めるよう背面に製品情報を入れ、フロントはキャッチコピーとイメージのみでシンプルに演出しています。ワンランク上の質感と輝きを主張する展示台を目指しました。耐久性を考慮した箱形什器は、長期の展示でも対応出来るつくりになっています。

Gold was adopted as the main color for these display stands since it indicates high quality as well as the allure of beautiful hair. Adding a glass-like and luxurious feel to the backing boards, hexagons symbolizing ions were used throughout. Product information was featured on the backing so that it would be read when the product was picked up, and the front was kept simple with a catch phrase and images. The aim was to create display stands that emphasize a greater feeling of quality and glossiness. Further, the box-shaped structure focuses on durability for long-term display.

MATERIAL：紙類、金属
W 300 × H 290 × D 255

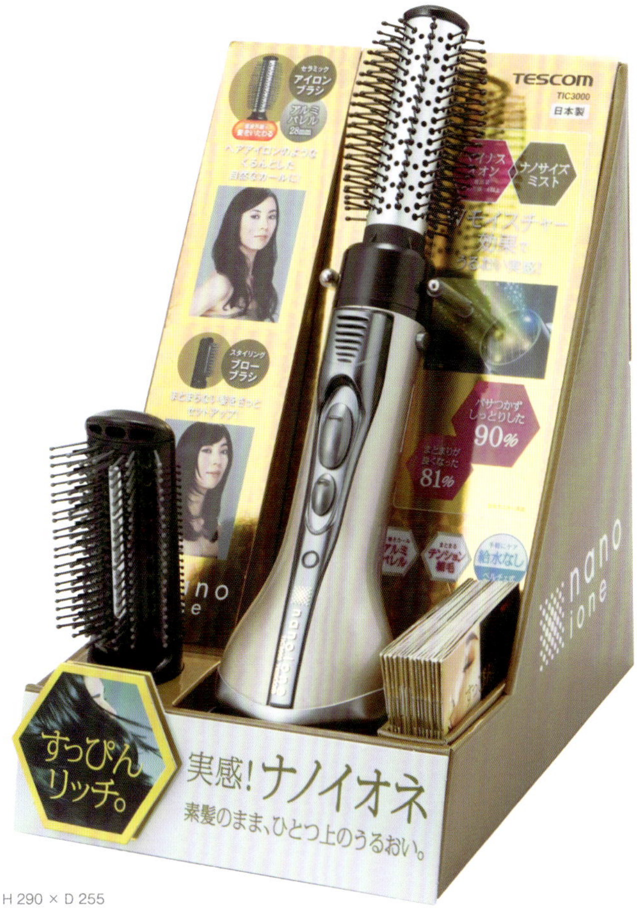

W 200 × H 290 × D 255

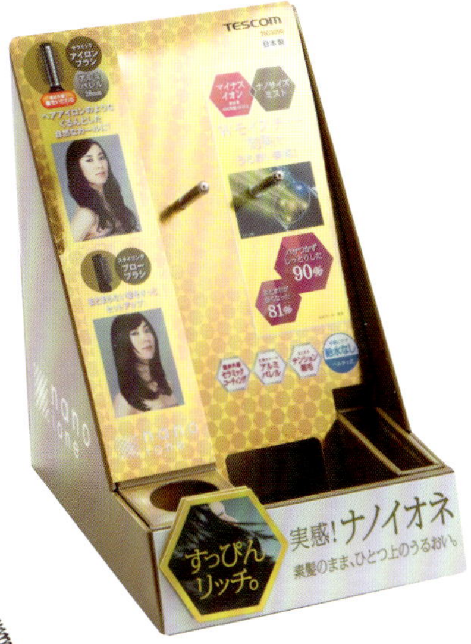

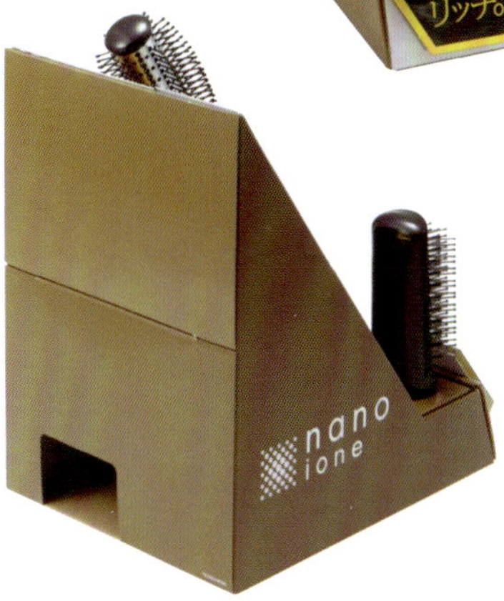

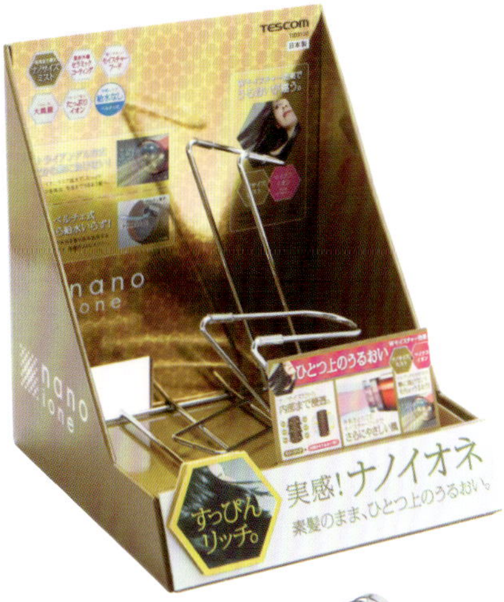

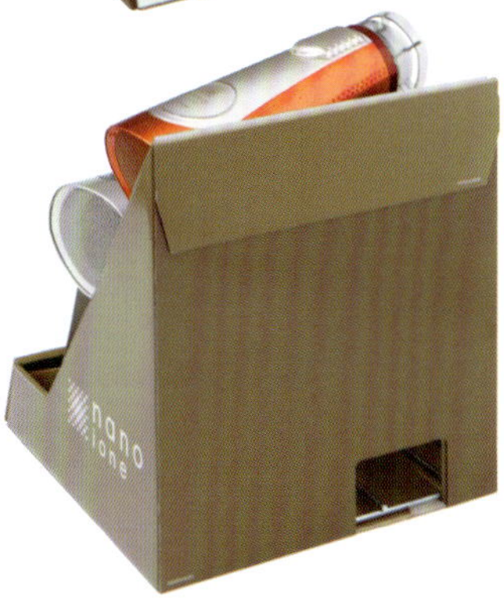

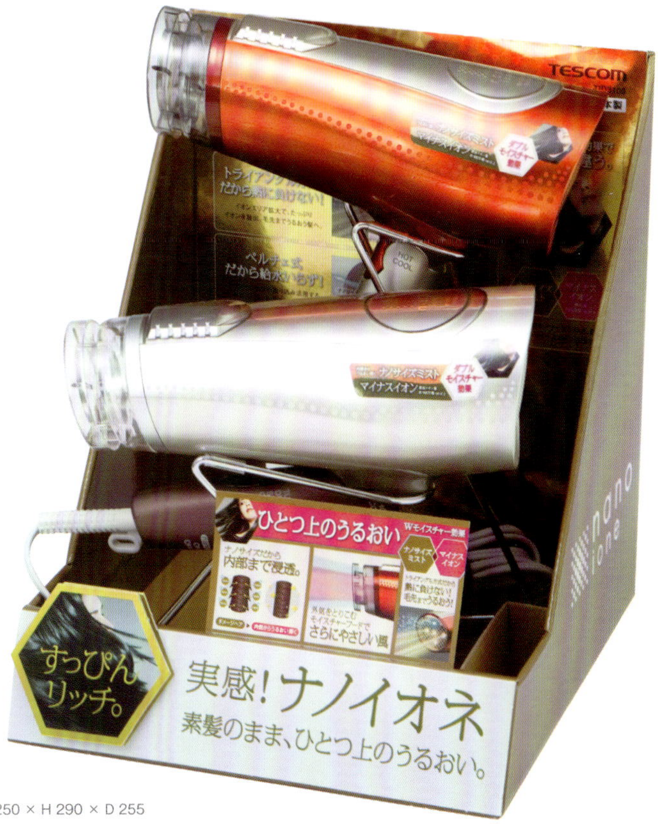

W 250 × H 290 × D 255

テスコム
TESCOM

OTHERS P.O.P.

各ブランドの世界観を統括するw900のボード。Pure Black・Metal Line は白黒のシンプルなカラーでまとめ、各ブランドの持つテーマを印象づけるものに仕上げています。ione、nano ione に関しては髪を魅せる製品ということを念頭に、「すっぴんリッチ。」というテーマと、憧れられる美しい女性のカットにこだわりました。ione はピンク、nano ione はゴールドのキーカラーをしっかり印象づけています。

These w900 boards aim to connect the ideology of the various brands. While the "Pure Black" and "Metal Line" boards were integrated through their simple black and white coloring, making the themes for these brands memorable, the "ione" and "nano ione" boards focus on images of hair based on the theme "natural richness," and use images of idol-like beautiful women. The boards feature pink and gold respectively as their main colors for a lasting impression.

W 900 × H 300

サーモス
THERMOS

ステンレスポット

COUNTER P.O.P.

片面印刷で組み立てやすい形状のカウンターディスプレイです。

An easy-to-assemble counter display with printing on one side.

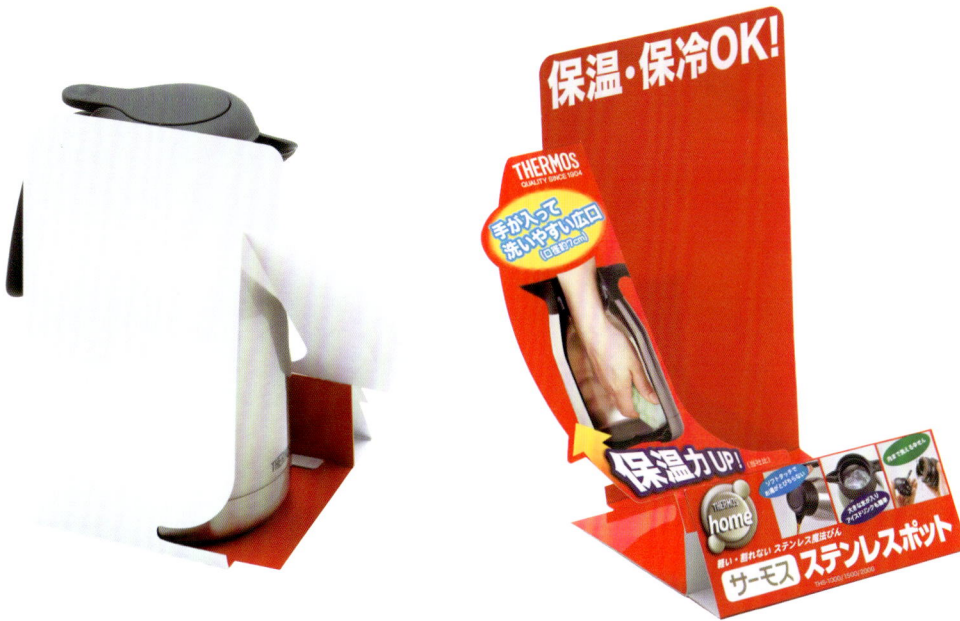

P：マスパック
MATERIAL：紙類
W 200 × H 250 × D 165

タイガー魔法瓶
TIGER

サハラ

COUNTER P.O.P.

「ファッション性」と「製品機能性と利便性」の融合をコンセプトとし、グラフィックとラインアップ陳列の組み合わせによりアピールするディスプレイです。店頭展開時のスペース確保と陳列を容易にするためBOX形状を採用、製品に直接セットする首掛けPOPで機能性を訴求しました。スタイリッシュで女性に受け入れられるデザインに仕上げています。

Based on the combination concept "fashion" and "product functionality and convenience," this display appeals to customers through its graphics and neatly arranged rows. A box shape was adopted so as not to take up excessive space as well as enabling easy display, and as the products can be placed directly within the frame, it attracts customers through functionality. The end result is a stylish display that aims to appeal to women.

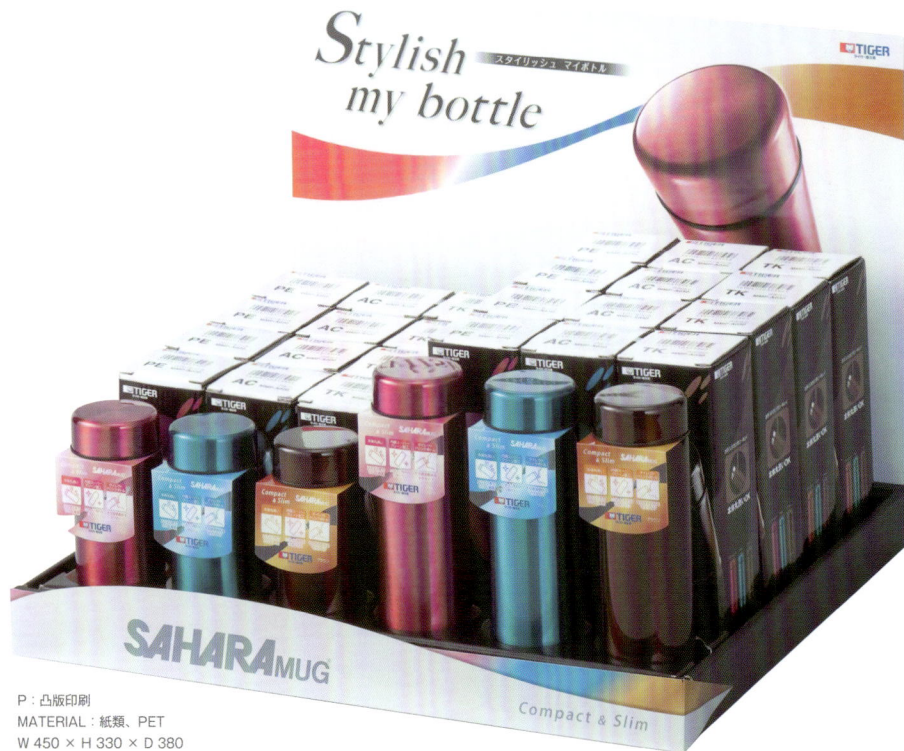

P：凸版印刷
MATERIAL：紙類、PET
W 450 × H 330 × D 380

ビジネスランチ

COUNTER P.O.P.

M-1世代の『弁当男子』をターゲットに、ビジネスバックに入るコンパクトサイズであることを第一訴求にした展示台です。ポイントは前面にビジネスバックのビジュアルをPOPとして使い、「バックにスッポリ入るコンパクトサイズ」を一目でわかるデザインにしたこと、ターゲットキャラクターを設定したPOPでユーザー目線からの商品特徴を訴求しました。また、全て紙製で簡易に組み立てることができ、棚置きから島展示まで幅広い陳列対応が可能です。

Targeting the M-1 generation of "lunch box men," this stand's major selling point is the way the compact size fits into a briefcase. A pop-out briefcase is used as the main visual at the front of the display, which was designed to quickly show that "the compact size fits neatly into your bag." Additionally, the product characteristics are displayed from the customer's viewpoint using a pop-out that features a target character. The entire display is made from paper and can be easily assembled, supporting a variety of applications, from shelf top to island displays.

P：タナックス 大阪支店
MATERIAL：紙類
W 300 × H 300 × D 200

アイシーエル
ICL

Afternoon Tea Lunch Box

COUNTER P.O.P.

ぱっとみてすぐわかる、をコンセプトに企画しました。立っていることでアイキャッチにもなり、見ただけでその商品の仕様や機能が分かる。そんな一石二鳥の POP になっています。

This display was based on the concept "instant comprehension." The vertical placement is eye-catching, and customers can take in the product specifications and features at a mere glance. A POP design that kills two birds with one stone.

P：ワヨー
MATERIAL：合紙
W 210 × H 360 × D 100

ダイキン工業
DAIKIN INDUSTRIES

うるるとさらら

クリスプ

HANGING P.O.P.
OTHERS P.O.P.

（上）冬の暖房需要期にお店に来店いただいた方に、エアコンの暖かみを端的に伝えることを考えながら、紙で作成することの意義や面白みを充分に踏まえた作品です。

（右）ダイキンエアコン（うるるとさらら）の加湿技術がつくり出すピュアな水分子"E-moist"。これを表現するのに、最適な手法を模索した結果、アルミの蒸着バルーン等を使用し柔らかな雰囲気を表現しました。

（左）業務用スポットエアコン『クリスプ』の堅いイメージの払拭と風量という目で見えないものを、視覚に表現する為に考えました。商品のアピールポイントをプロペラの回転により視覚的にキャラクターの持つイメージで柔らかく表現しています。

(Upper) This significant and interesting display made of paper directly communicates the warming effect of Daikin air conditioners to customers during the winter season when heating is in demand.

(Right) The humidification technology used in Daikin's Ururu and Sarara air conditioners produces pure water molecules known as "E-moist." After investigation into the best way of expressing this, items such as a UFO balloon were adopted for a soft image.

(Left) This display was designed to visually expel the stiff image for the commercial spot air conditioner "Crisp" and convey an invisible air flow. The image was softened by using a character to advertise the product's main feature via the rotation of a propeller.

P：タナックス
MATERIAL：紙、樹脂、PET
W 250 × H 510 × D 250

P：タナックス
MATERIAL：樹脂、金属
W 170 × H 210 × D 200

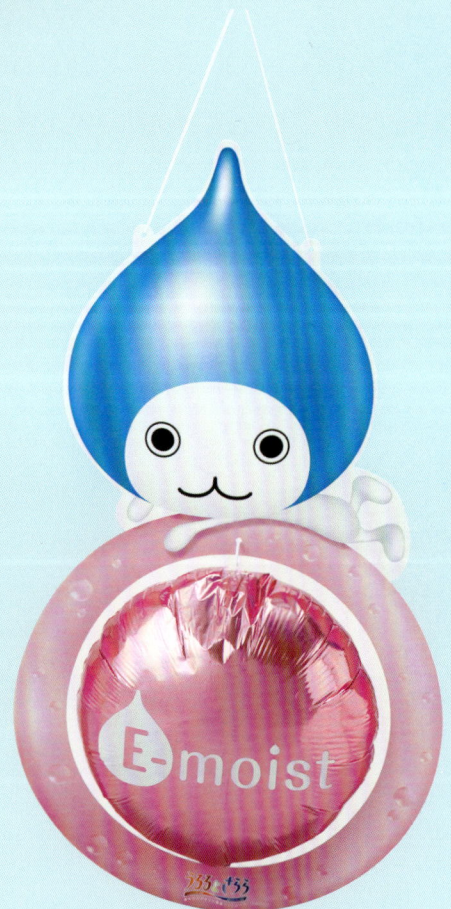

P：タナックス
MATERIAL：紙、樹脂
W 380 × H 600 × D 150

ダイキン工業
DAIKIN INDUSTRIES

うるるとさらら

MOVING P.O.P.

お店に置いて頂く上で、見て頂くことや、興味を持って頂くことを念頭において作成しました。立体的な構造やソーラームービングを使用することにより、星占い付きのカレンダーという注目ポイントをより引き立たせる作品になっています。

This fixture was designed not only to display the product, but also to appeal to customers and hook their interest. With a 3D construction and solar movement, it draws greater attention to the display's focal point – a calendar featuring astrological forecasts.

P：タナックス
MATERIAL：紙類
W 250 × H 300 × D 300

パナソニック
Panasonic

ポケット Doltz

COUNTER P.O.P.
HANGING P.O.P.

ランチ歯磨きをするOLをターゲット
に、手磨きから電動ハブラシへのス
イッチを狙いました。コンセプトは
「化粧ポーチに入れたくなる化粧品
のような演出」。ディスプレイは様々
な売り場での汎用性を考え、単品で
棚置きで展開できる他に、2つ並べ
て上部にコーナーボードをつけ、
コーナー感を演出する展開です。背
板にプラネジで取り付けて、上下に
吊り下げての展開も可能な仕様で作
成しました。

This display targets office
ladies who brush their teeth
after lunch, encouraging them
to switch to an electric
toothbrush based on the
concept "Designed to blend in
with the items in your makeup
bag." The stands are versatile
to suit any location, and in
addition to use as a
stand-alone or shelf top
display, the 2 can be joined
and a board mounted across
the top to create a more
prominent display. They can
also be mounted vertically onto
a backing board and hung from
the ceiling.

W 150 × H 270 × D 135

P：ファースト
MATERIAL：紙類
W 300 × H 340 × D 185

W 150 × H 640 × D 140

パナソニック
Panasonic

ポケット Doltz

OTHERS P.O.P.

ランチ歯磨きをするOLをターゲット
に、手磨きから電動ハブラシへのス
イッチを狙いました。コンセプトは
「化粧ポーチに入れたくなる化粧品
のような演出」。フック展開のスペー
スで、最小のスペースでいかに目を
引く訴求ができるかを考え、フック
に掛けるだけで簡単に設置でき、小
さいスペースでコーナー感が出せる
ような形状に作成しました。

This display targets office
ladies who brush their teeth
after lunch, encouraging them
to switch to an electric
toothbrush based on the
concept "Designed to blend in
with the items in your makeup
bag." This hook type display
aims to attract the greatest
attention using the smallest
amount of space. Setup
involves no more than hanging
the products, and the shape
was designed to deliver a
comprehensive feel within
limited space.

P：ファースト
MATERIAL：紙類
W 325 × H 275 × D 50

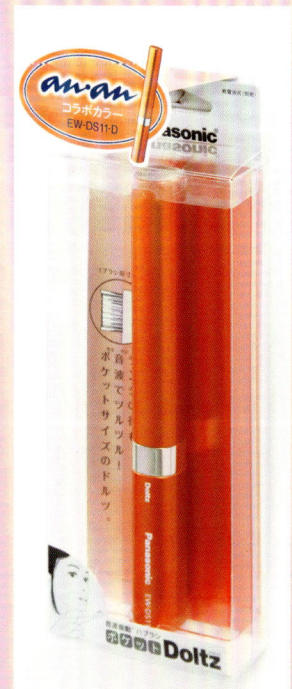

パナソニック
Panasonic

ポケット Doltz

FLOOR P.O.P.

ランチ歯磨きをするOLをターゲット
に、手磨きから電動ハブラシへのス
イッチを狙いました。コンセプトは
「化粧ポーチに入れたくなる化粧品
のような演出」。商品の美しさ、質
感をひと目で印象づけられるようメ
インの女性のビジュアルとキャップ
あり・なしの商品のカットアウトを
強調するためにPOPアップにしまし
た。また、店頭の様々な場所で展開
できるよう、できるだけスリムな形
状を考えました。

This display targets office
ladies who brush their teeth
after lunch, encouraging them
to switch to an electric
toothbrush based on the
concept "Designed to blend in
with the items in your makeup
bag." To highlight the beautiful
design and quality of the
product at a single glance,
pop-ups were used to draw
attention to the product
cut-outs along with the main
visual of a woman. Further, the
display was kept as slim as
possible so that it could be
used in a variety of locations.

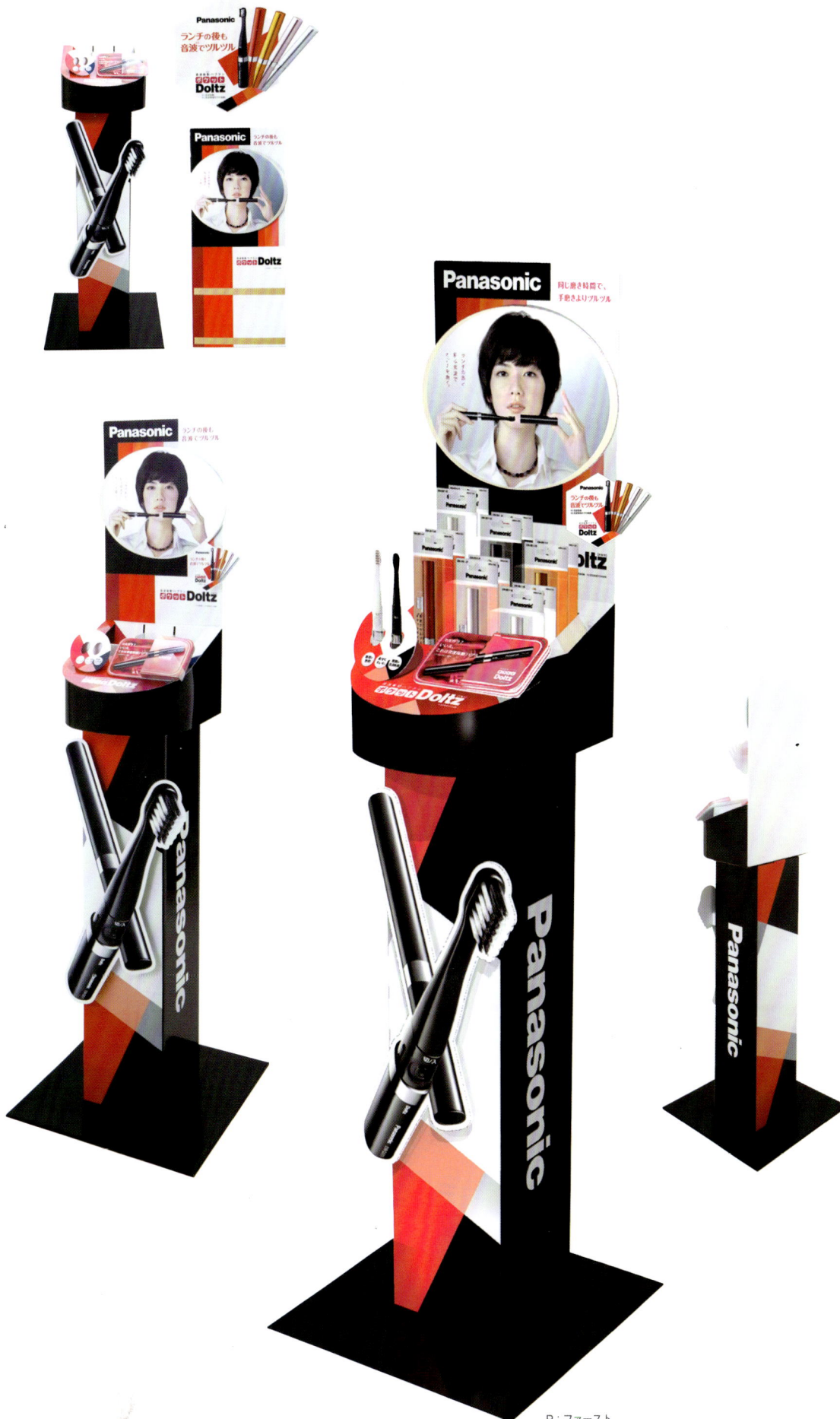

P：ファースト
MATERIAL：紙類
W 450 × H 1500 × D 450

133

パナソニック
Panasonic

ヘアーアイロン マルチ

COUNTER P.O.P.

商品の最大の特長である「アタッチメントを交換することで、1台で6通りのスタイリングができる」ことを、分かりやすく・楽しく伝えるため、6通りの髪型とアタッチメントを6色のカラーと対応させたカラフルなデザインにしました。同時に、展示した際に商品が映えるよう、ベースは黒で作成しています。また、一般的なヘアーアイロンと使い方が異なるので、使い心地をイメージしやすいよう、実際に手に取って使い方を実感してもらえるような仕様にしました。

"6 different styles with 1 unit simply by changing the attachment" – this is the main product feature, and a colorful display design was used to convey this in an easy-to-understand and fun way through 6 different hairstyles and 6 different attachment colors, while black was used as the base color so that the product stands out when displayed. Further, as the method of use differs from that of generic hair irons, the display was designed to allow customers to pick up the product and see how it feels.

P：スコープ・インターナショナル
MATERIAL：アクリル、プラスチック
W 220 × H 320 × D 255

W 435 × H 320 × D 255

パナソニック
Panasonic

ミキサー
COUNTER P.O.P.

野菜や果物のフレッシュなおいしさ
をそのままいただくことができる、
ミキサーの魅力を伝えたいと思い作
成しました。野菜や果実のビジュア
ルを外側、鮮やかなカラーを内側に
デザインすることで白い商品を目立
たせると同時に内側からのエネル
ギーを表現しています。展示台のラ
ウンドフォルムは有機的で、自然の
素材のイメージをより一層喚起させ
る狙いがあります。

These displays were designed
to highlight the attractiveness
of a mixer enabling consumers
to experience the delicious
taste of fresh fruits and
vegetables. They use images of
fruits and vegetables around
the edges and a refreshing
background color to make this
white product stand out as well
as express the energy that
comes from within. The curved
shape of the stand aims to
further enhance the image of
organic and natural materials.

P：ベストプロジェクト
MATERIAL：紙
W 335 × H 380 × D 320

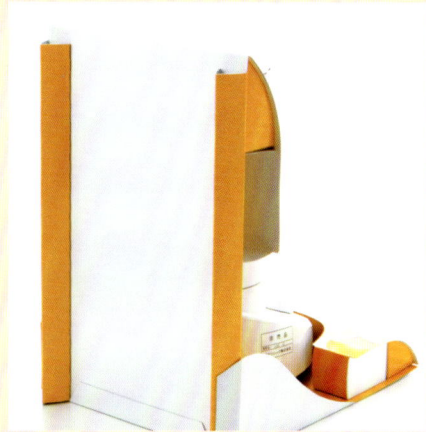

W 260 × H 380 × D 320

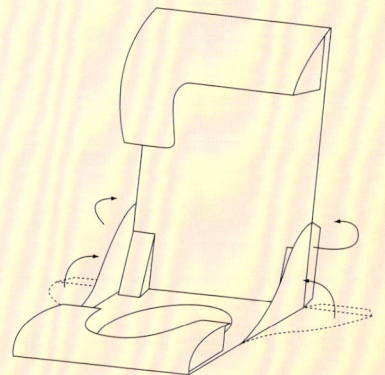

137

パナソニック
Panasonic

ミキサー

COUNTER P.O.P.

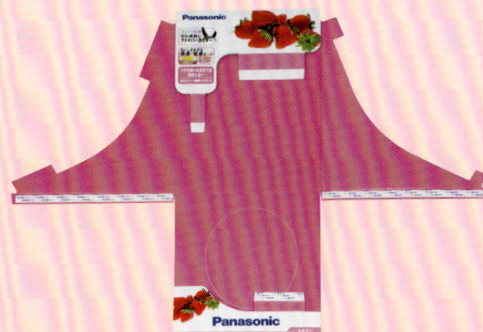

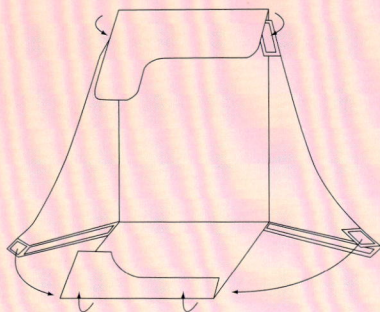

P：ベストプロジェクト
MATERIAL：紙
W 260 × H 380 × D 205

W 335 × H 380 × D 295

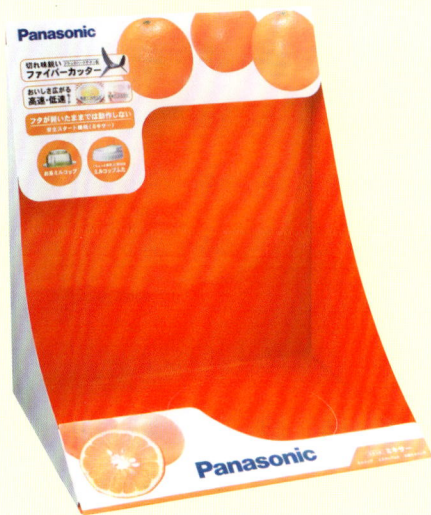

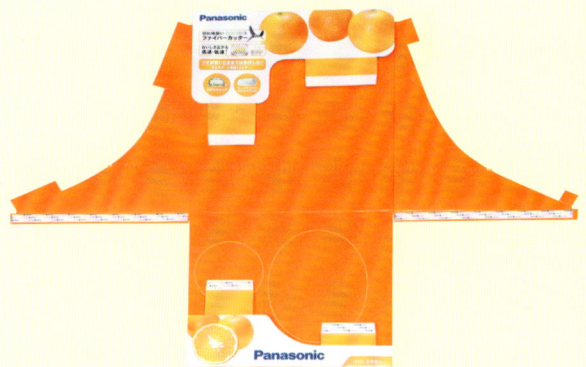

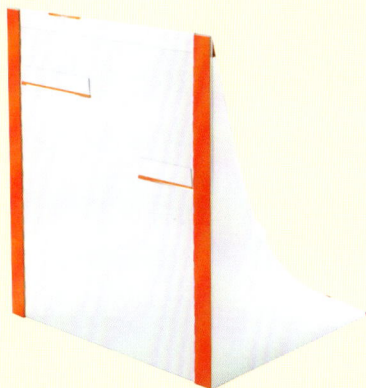

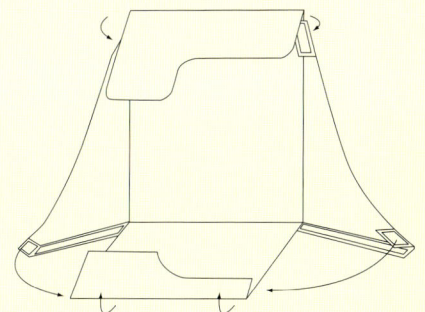

パナソニック
Panasonic

光速ビストロ
NEON P.O.P.

この電子レンジの特徴である遠赤外線で食材の外側を加熱、近赤外線で食材の内側を加熱するという機能を、実際にカットした状態の食品サンプル（さんま）で外側、内側を見せそれぞれの加熱をLEDで表現しました。熱のイメージはLEDの上から2種類の拡散フィルムを違った角度で仕込むことで、店頭でも目を引く新しい光の見え方を表現しています。

The way this microwave oven heats food is characteristic, using far-infrared rays and near-infrared rays to heat the exterior and interior respectively, and an LED was used to show a cross-section of an actual food sample being heated. The display achieves a new eye-catching method of lighting by laying 2 types of diffusion film at different angles over the LED to give the impression of "heat."

P：ベストプロジェクト
MATERIAL：樹脂、他
W 420 × H 440 × D 450

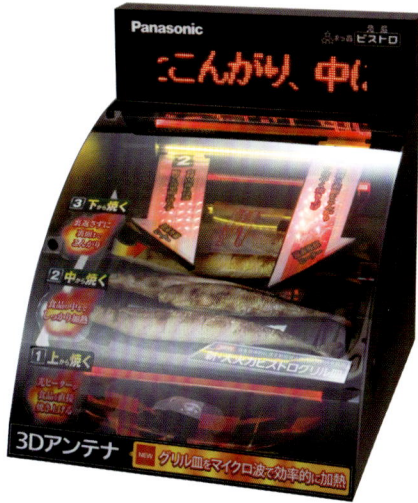

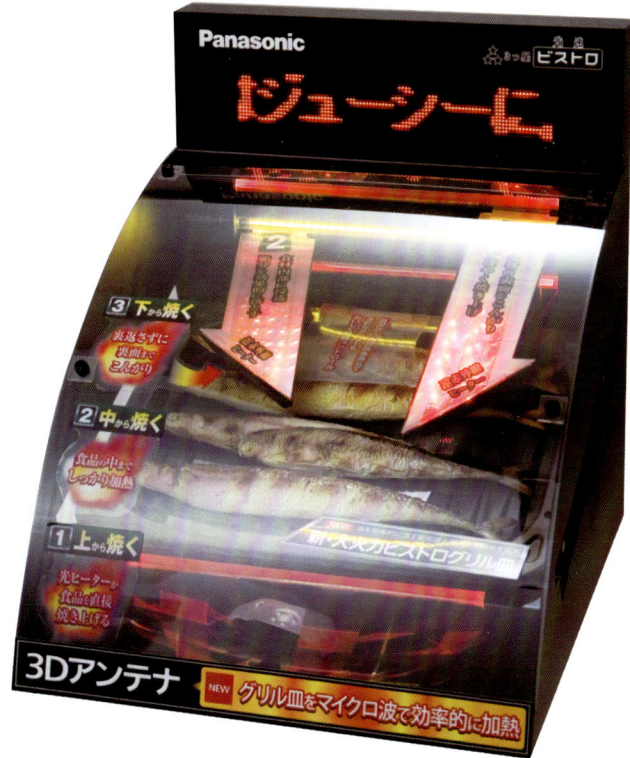

P：凸版印刷
MATERIAL：紙、樹脂

パナソニック
Panasonic

ななめドラム洗濯乾燥機
FLOOR P.O.P.

"eco ideas" を企業理念とするパナソニックは、販促物でもエコにこだわります。外装箱まで展示POPの一部。それはまさに「ゴミが出ないPOP」。制作コストを抑えるだけでなく、サイズも小さくなり、配送コスト削減も実現。パナソニックの先進性と商品の世界観を店頭で最大限にアピールしつつ、コストメリットも最大化したPOPです。

Panasonic's corporate philosophy is "eco ideas" and a green image is the focus for new-release products, right down to the external packaging and parts used in displays to reduce waste. This not only means reduced production costs, but also reduced display sizes, leading to lower transportation costs. This display was designed to emphasize Panasonic's spirit of innovation and product ideology, while taking advantage of these cost benefits.

P：大日本印刷
MATERIAL：紙、段ボール
W 1200 × H 1350 × D 500

P：美工
MATERIAL：紙、樹脂
W 900 × H 250 × D 200

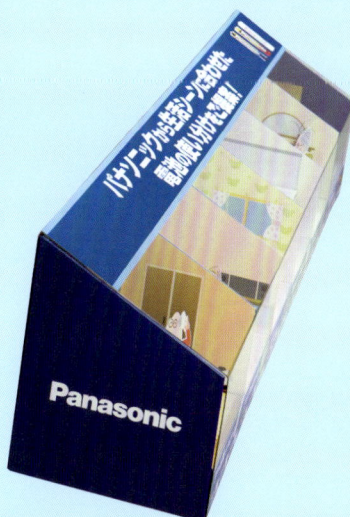

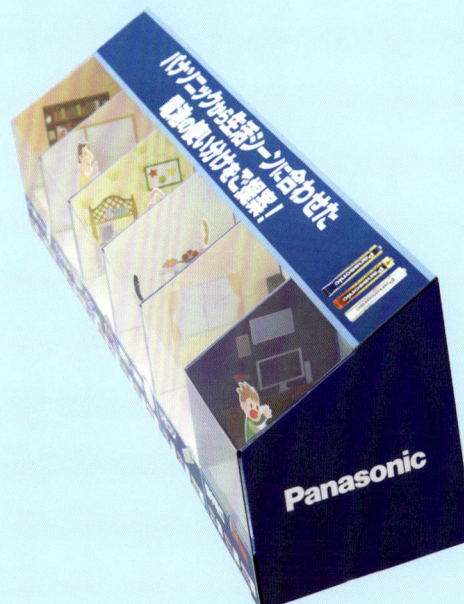

パナソニック
Panasonic

電池おすすめ分けアテンションハウス

COUNTER P.O.P.

お客様が自分に適した商品を選択しやすいよう各種の生活シーンをミニチュアで表現しました。電池に種類があること、使用機器によって品種に性能差があることを分かってもらうためのPOPです。コンセプトは「自分に必要な電池が何か一目で判断できる販促物」。機器の使用パターンを演出することにより、お客様が自分に適した商品を簡単に選択できるよう作成しました。

Various living scenes were displayed in miniature to make it easier for customers to select the appropriate product. This POP display aims to explain about the different types of batteries and the different types of performance they offer depending on the equipment they are used with based on the concept "a display that enables you to select the battery that's right for you." By showing samples of use, the display helps customers to easily select the most suitable product.

パナソニック
Panasonic

EVOLTA

MOVING P.O.P.

EVOLTA が世界 No.1 長もち乾電池であることを視覚的に演出し、作成しました。コンセプトは「アイキャッチ効果のある販促物」。ベース部分は表彰台をイメージしたデザインにし、その頂点にEVOLTAを立てることでNo.1を表現しています。さらに遠くからでも人を引きつけるムービング部分も、金メダルをモチーフにしNo.1を強調、視認性UPを狙いました。また、ギネス世界記録認定の訴求部分をPOPアップ仕様にし、世界基準で認められた記録であることをアピールしています。

This display was designed to visually show that EVOLTA is the world's longest-life dry-cell battery based on the concept "a display with an eye-catching effect." The product is displayed on a base area resembling a podium to show its No.1 status. To further emphasize this and increase visibility, moving parts were used to attract attention from afar, and a gold medal was adopted as the motif. Further, a pop-up is used to advertise the product's certification in the Guinness Book of World Records to emphasize that this is a world-recognized standard.

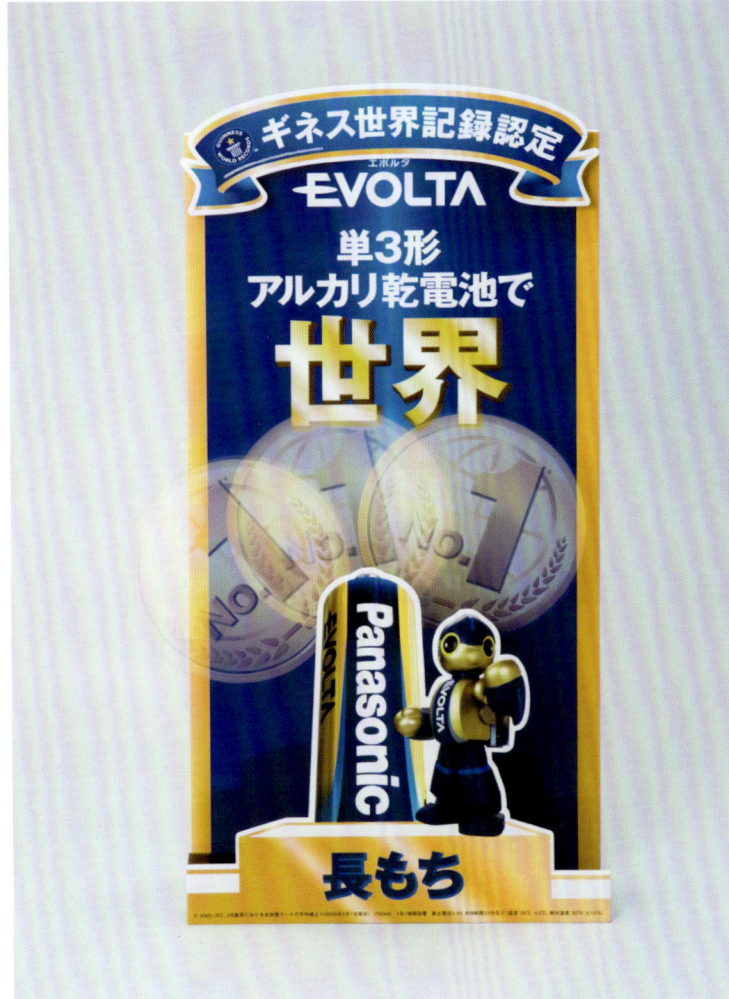

P：乃村工藝社
MATERIAL：紙類
W 280 × H 550 × D 75

パナソニック
Panasonic

EVOLTA

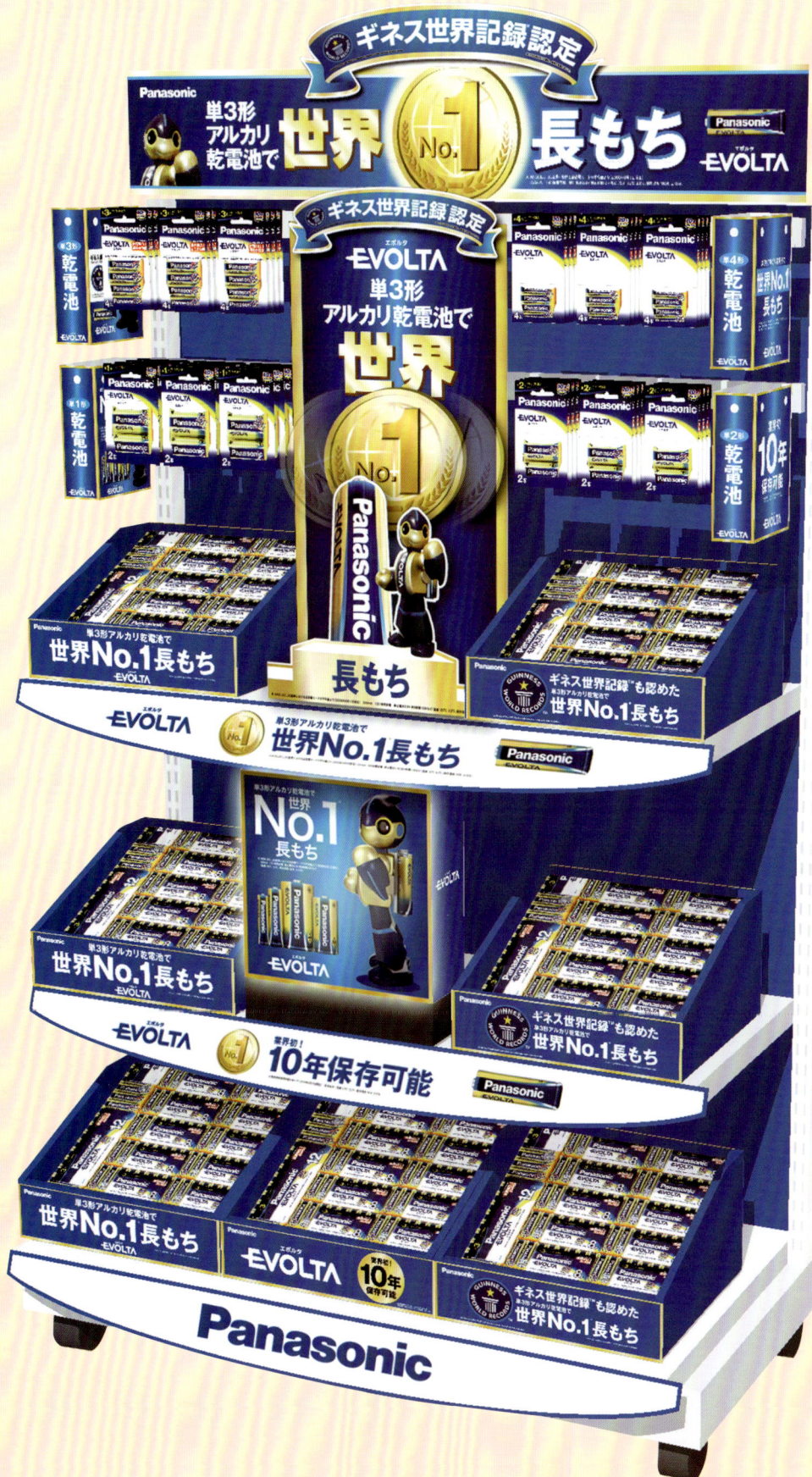

■展示例

パナソニック
Panasonic

LUMIX

MOVING P.O.P.

標準35mmレンズと3種類のワイド
レンズをそれぞれ比較訴求するの
に、回転式の三角柱ドラムを使い、
フレームが稼働することで、瞬時に
ワイド画面に切り変わる、という
ムービングPOPです。アイキャッ
チャーとしてのインパクトと省ス
ペースを実現しました。

Here, a rotating triangular drum
was used to provide a
comparison between the
standard 35mm lens and 3
types of wide lenses, and this
moving POP display switches
into a wide screen in the blink
of an eye based on a working
frame. A display that realizes
eye-catching impact as well as
conserves space.

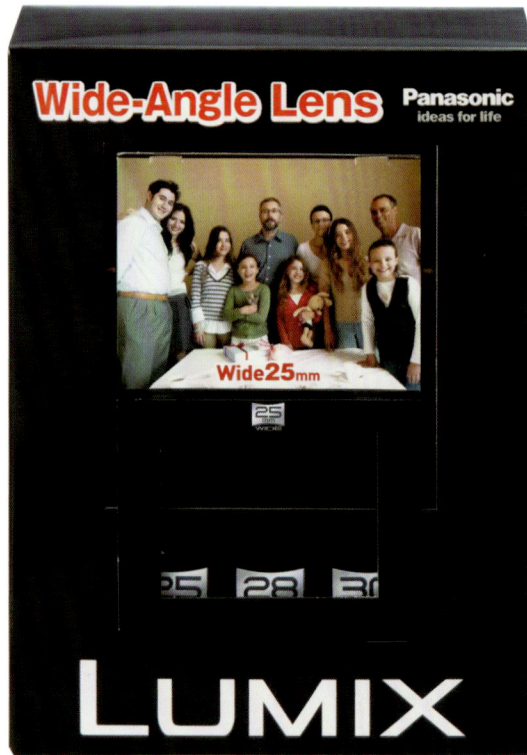

P：ワークトップ
MATERIAL：紙類、金属
W 145 × H 195 × D 75

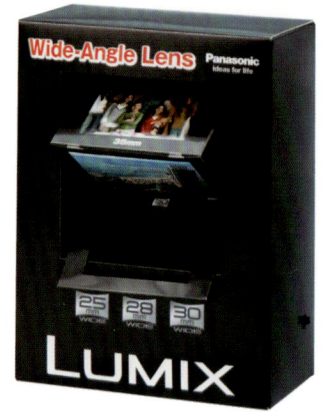

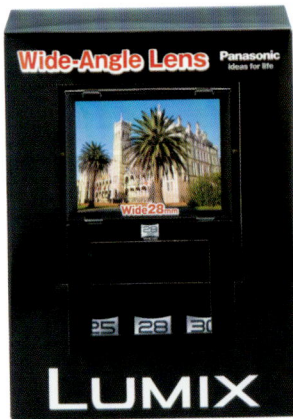

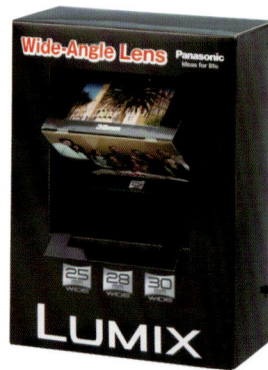

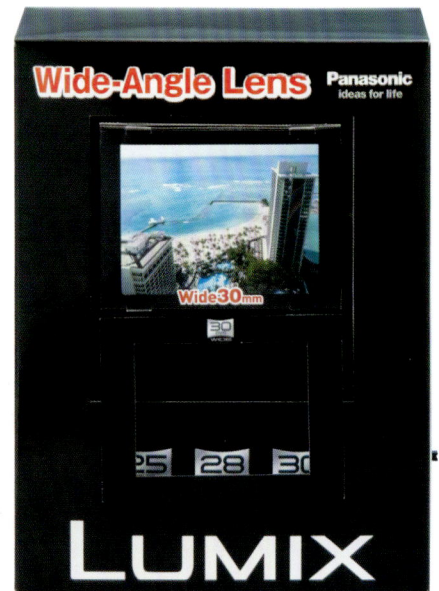

P：ワークトップ
MATERIAL：紙類、金属
W 145 × H 160 × D 50

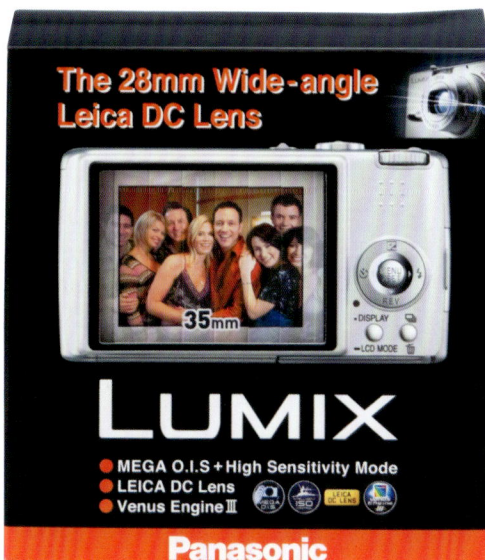

パナソニック
Panasonic

LUMIX

MOVING P.O.P.

ワイドレンズ28mmの画像を従来の35mmレンズの画像と比較するのに、2面チェンジ式のムービングを使って分かりやすく表現しました。

A double-sided moving display was used to show the difference between images taken with the 28mm wide lens and those taken with the conventional 35mm lens.

HOME APPLIANCE

パナソニック
Panasonic

デジタルビデオカメラ

COUNTER P.O.P.

高倍率ズームも手ぶれ補正機能付き
だからこそ実現可能という訴求と、
光学70倍ズームの迫力感をチェンジ
ングを使って表現しました。

This display shows what you
can achieve using a high-
power zoom and blurring
compensation function, and the
product is showcased using
images taken with a powerful
70x optical zoom.

P：ワークトップ
MATERIAL：紙類、プラスチック
W 95 × H 160 × D 45

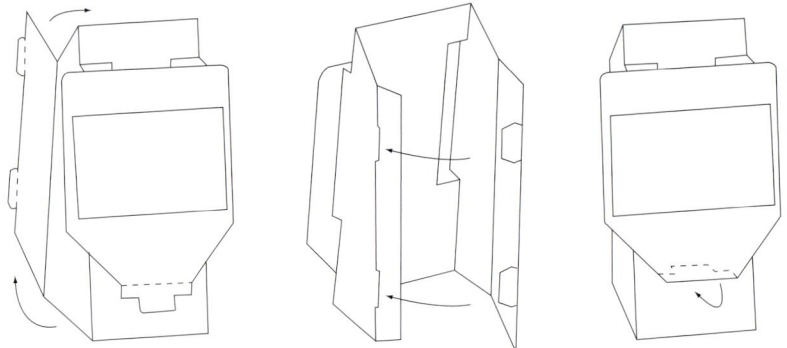

クラリオン
Clarion

SD AV-Navi

HDD AV-Navi

MOVING P.O.P.

P：大日本印刷
MATERIAL：紙類
W 170 × H 180 × D 50

クラリオン
Clarion

SD AV-Navi

HDD AV-Navi

COUNTER P.O.P.

2010年クラリオンより展開したPOPは、クラリオンのカラーであるクラリオンアズーロを中心としながらもそれぞれの製品イメージの黒とアップルグリーンを使ったナビ展示コーナー作りをしました。また立体物に関しては、それぞれのPOPに3色の色使いで人目に留まるようにすることと、製品の特長やポイントがわかるように入れています。平面物に関してもより製品のことが店頭での販売員からお客様への説明で機能ポイントが理解されるよう、ナビ選びに適切なツールをご用意しました。

Developed by Clarion in 2010, this display was used to advertise navigation equipment, and while the Clarion brand color blue was used as the main color throughout, the product colors black and apple green were also adopted. These three colors were used for the various 3D displays to make them stand out as well as highlight characteristics and selling points. Brochures were also prepared as a useful tool for customers in selecting a navigation system, and explanations of the main features were provided by sales staff.

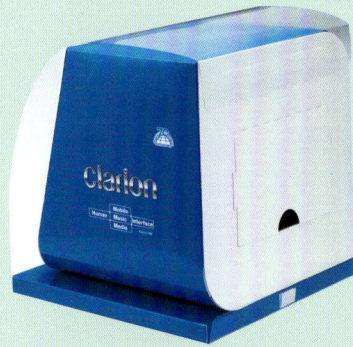

P：大日本印刷
MATERIAL：紙類、樹脂
W 280 × H 300 × D 290

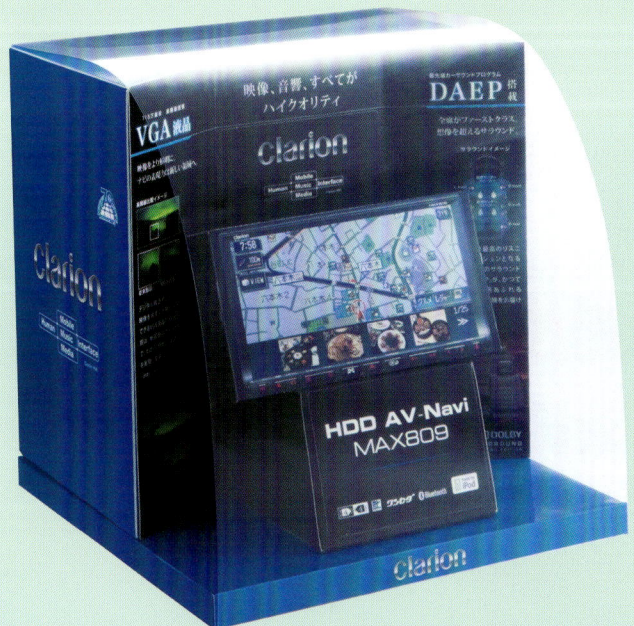

P：大日本印刷
MATERIAL：紙類、樹脂
W 280 × H 300 × D 290

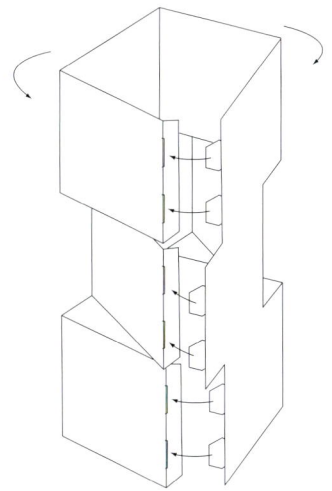

P：大日本印刷
MATERIAL：紙類
W 170 × H 260 × D 170

クラリオン
Clarion

SD AV-Navi

HDD AV-Navi

FLOOR P.O.P.

P：大日本印刷
MATERIAL：紙類
W 290 × H 290 × D 290

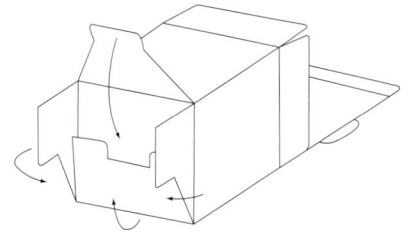

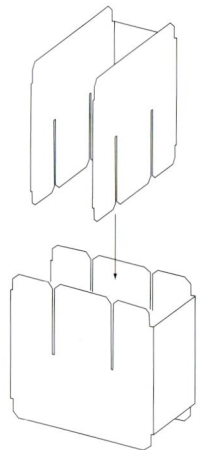

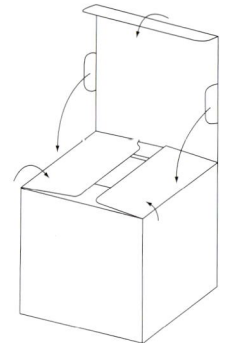

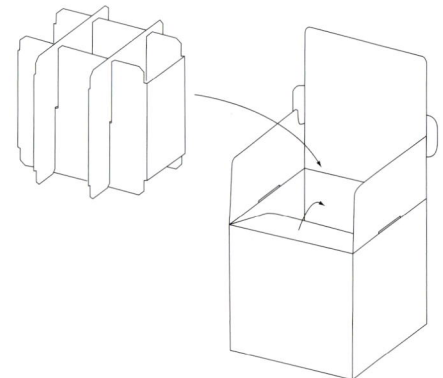

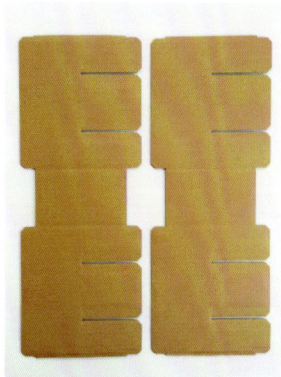

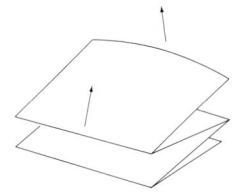

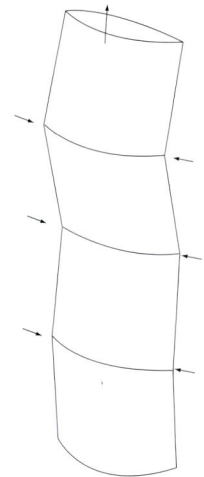

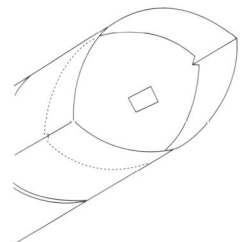

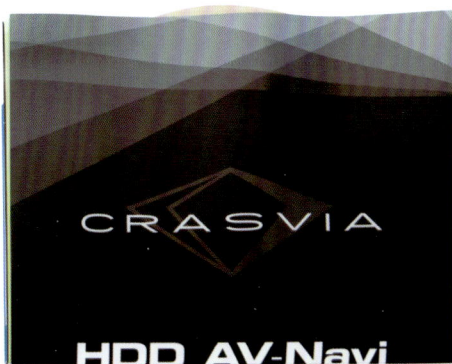

P : passot
MATERIAL : 紙類
W 500 × H 1500 × D 230

富士通テン
FUJITSU TEN

ECLIPSE

COUNTER P.O.P.

AVN7500 のウリとなる 4 つの特長機能を分かりやすく説明したショーケースのサイドに設置する機能訴求POP、立体感のある仕様で高いアイキャッチ効果が期待できるマップオンデマンド訴求ツール、店舗のイベントやフェア告知用に活用できるスタンドサイン、差し替えボードによる簡易フェア什器として継続展開でき、常に新しい話題を発信する売り場づくりを可能にするアイランド什器など、バリエーションに富んだ販促展開をしています。

This POP display is comprised of a showcase with side advertising that appeals to customers through easy-to-understand descriptions of the AVN7500's 4 main selling features. It functions as an extremely eye-catching 3D tool for this map-on-demand, and the standing sign can be used for instore events or advertising at fairs simply by using the replacement board. This display offers great variety as it can be used as an island type fixture, etc. for transmitting the latest information.

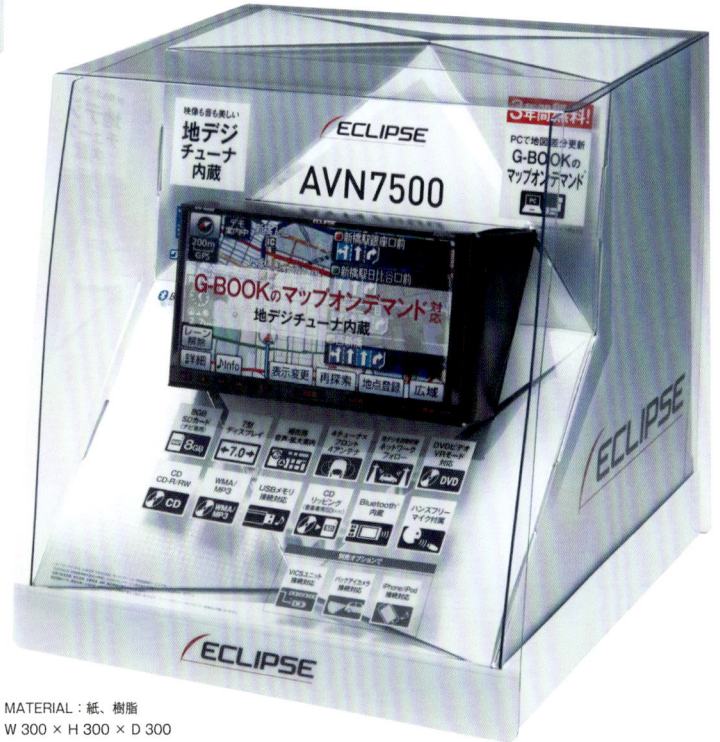

MATERIAL：紙、樹脂
W 300 × H 300 × D 300

MATERIAL：紙、樹脂
W 300 × H 370 × D 300

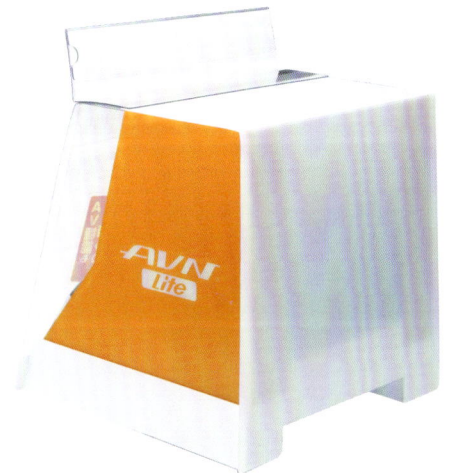

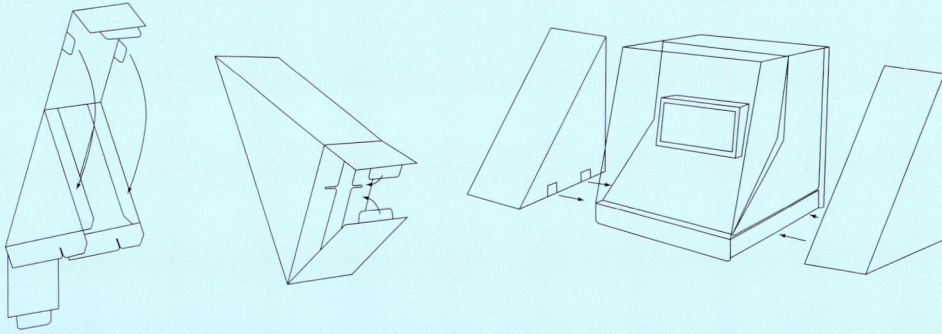

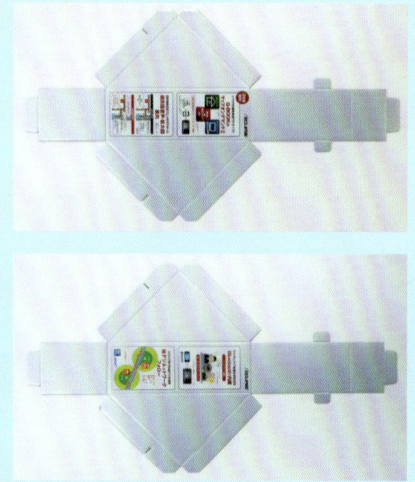

MATERIAL：紙、樹脂
W 600 × H 300 × D 300

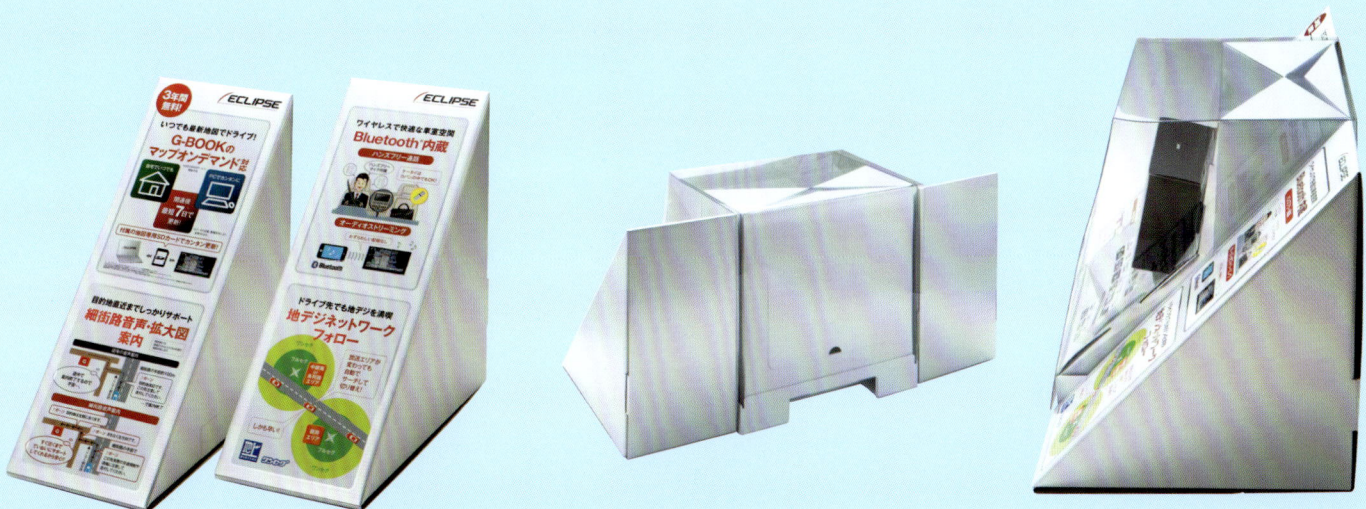

富士通テン
FUJITSU TEN

ECLIPSE

COUNTER P.O.P.
FLOOR P.O.P.

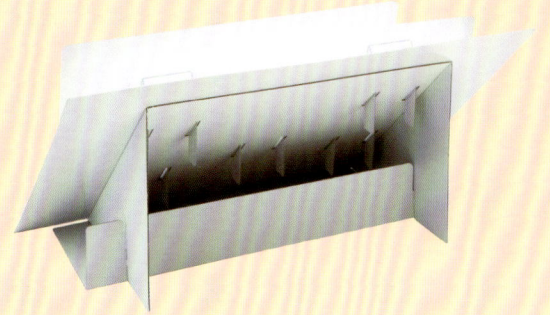

MATERIAL：紙
W 600 × H 320 × D 300

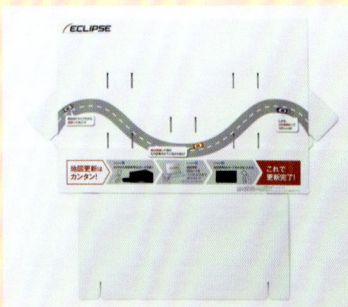

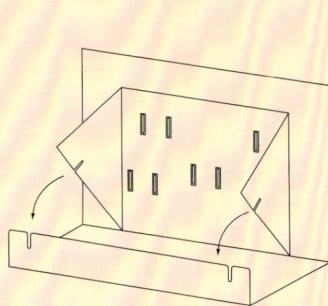

MATERIAL：紙
W 930 × H 1460 × D 450

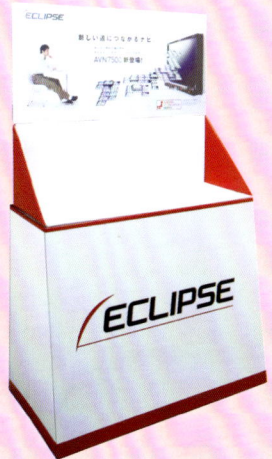

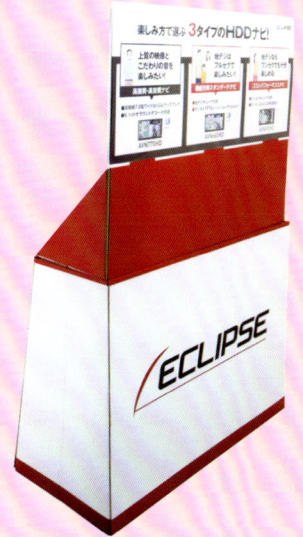

富士通テン
FUJITSU TEN

ECLIPSE

FLOOR P.O.P.
MOVING P.O.P.

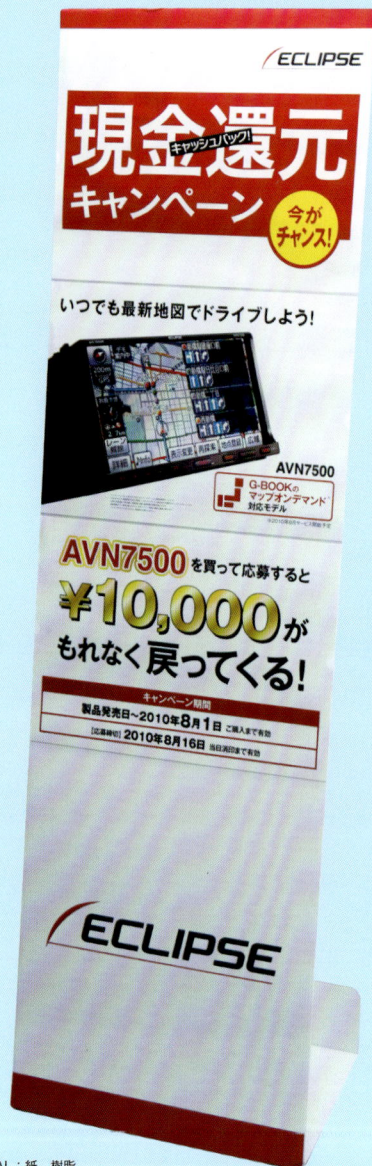

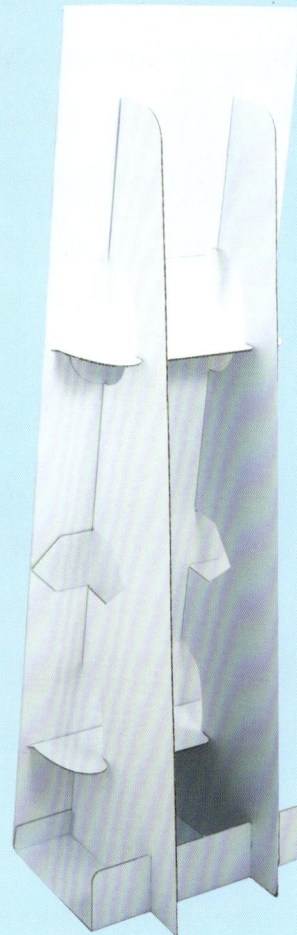

MATERIAL：紙、樹脂
W 420 × H 1430 × D 290

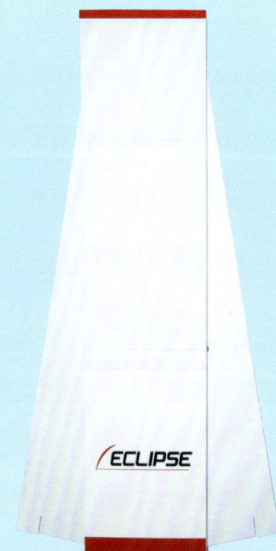

衝撃や**加速度**を感知して、
前後20秒間の**映像**と**音声**を記録。
ドライブレコーダー
記録データはパソコン・車載モニターで確認!

記録方法は3種類!
● イベントメモリー機能(20秒動画)
● ビデオメモリー機能(動画)
● ワンショットメモリー機能(静止画)

大容量
1GB
SDカード
(付属)

衝撃を
感知!

高画質カメラ

セパレート&コンパクト設計

ECLIPSE ドライブレコーダー **DREC3000**

MATERIAL：紙
W 300 × H 380 × D 280

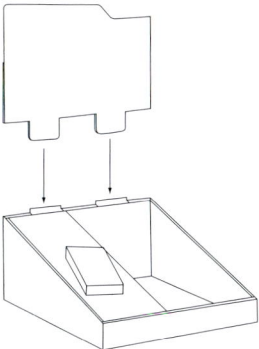

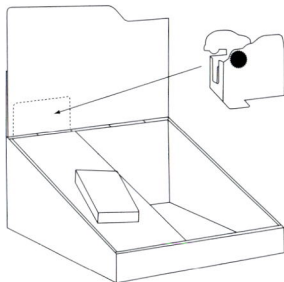

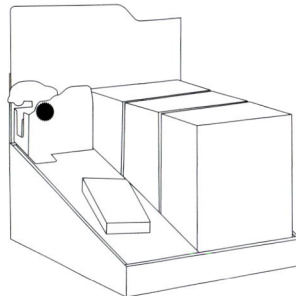

HOYA
HOYA

PENTAX K-x

COUNTER P.O.P.

ハイスペックをカラフルに楽しもう。デジタル一眼がもっとかんたん、もっとカラフルに。商品コンセプトが店頭で初めて「K-x」を知った方にも伝わる様な店頭 POP として製作し、展示スペースに合わせてシングルタイプ、ワイドタイプの 2 種類を用意しました。

Enjoy a high-specification product in a variety of colors! This new digital single-lens camera is simpler and more colorful than ever before. The POP display aims to inform customers new to the "K-x" about the product concept, and both a narrow and wide type of display were developed to suit the available space.

A：アサツー ディ・ケイ
MATERIAL：合紙、アクリル
W 225 × H 260 × D 225

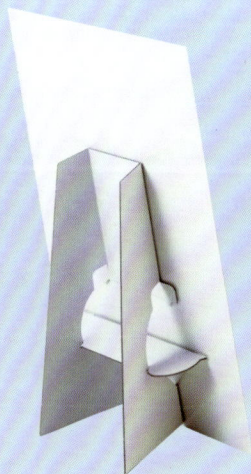

W 450 × H 260 × D 225

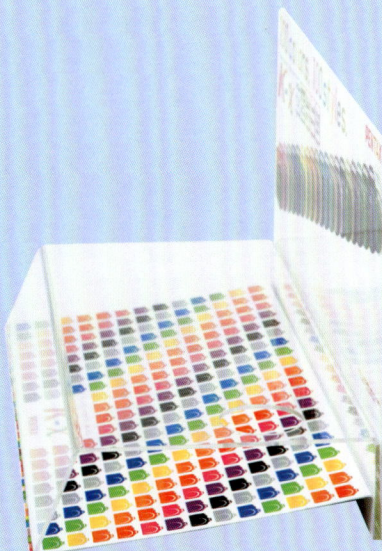

HOYA
HOYA

PENTAX K-x

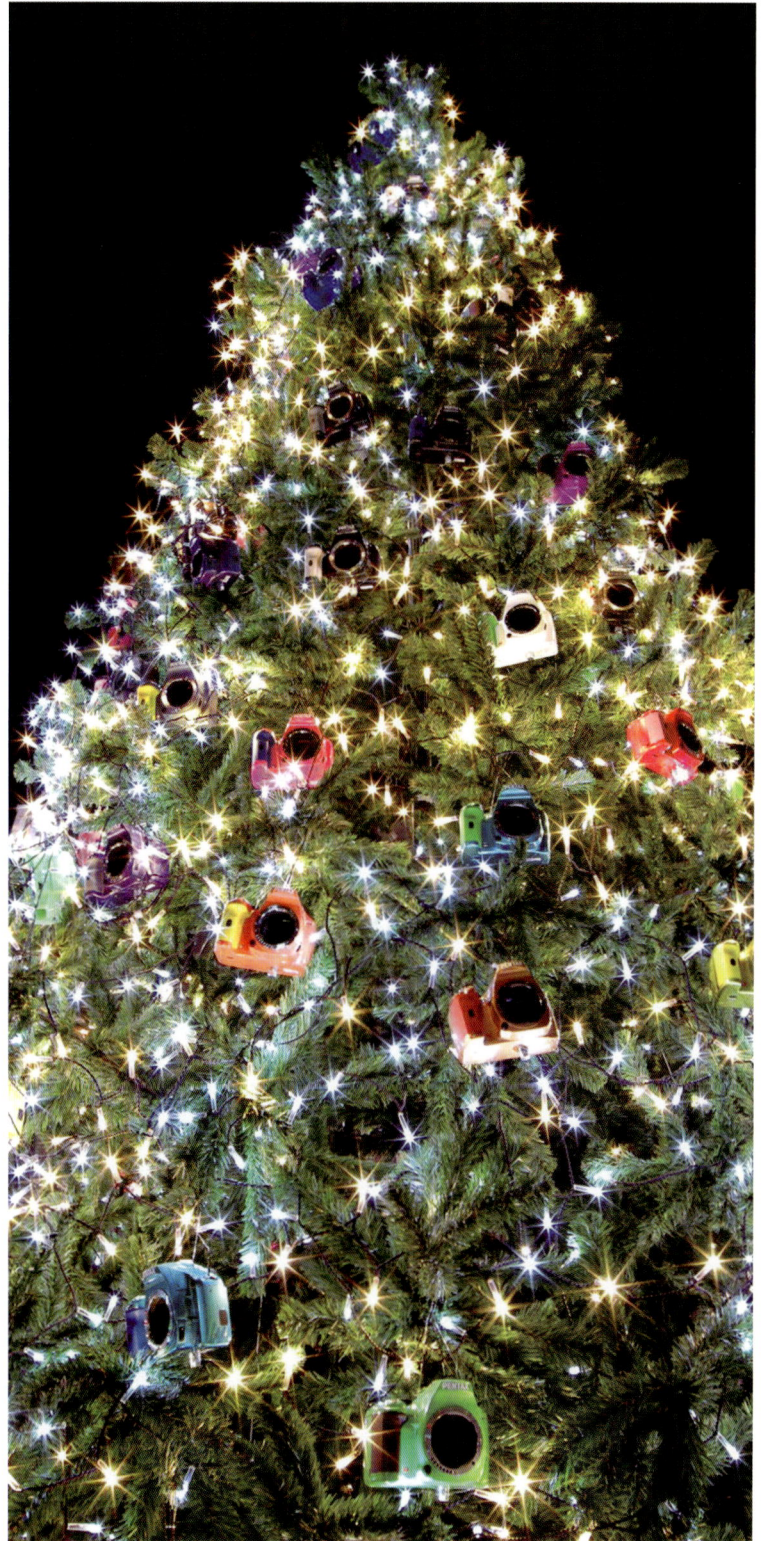

日本ビクター
JVC（Japan）

ハイビジョンムービー
COUNTER P.O.P.

ビデオカメラの最上位機種の展示台
ということで、上部のダイヤモンド
柄のアクリル素材で、商品の持つ「高
精細さ」を視覚的に表現しました。
全体はファミリー向けのテイストに
なっています。

As this stand was designed for
a top-of-the-range video
camera, the "high resolution"
of the product was visually
expressed with a diamond
pattern made from acrylic
material on the upper part of
the display, while the overall
image was a family-oriented
design.

P：スコープ・インターナショナル
MATERIAL：樹脂
W 300 × H 400 × D 200

ポータブルスピーカー
COUNTER P.O.P.

DAP プレーヤーをお風呂で楽しむス
ピーカーなので、お風呂の泡を左右
のパール紙で表現した展示台です。

This digital audio player is a
speaker for enjoying music
while in the bath, and paper
with a pearl finish is used on
both sides of the product to
simulate bath bubbles.

P：スコープ・インターナショナル
MATERIAL：紙
W 295 × H 140 × D 220

カシオ計算機
CASIO

EXILIM G

COUNTER P.O.P.

P：ベストプロジェクト
MATERIAL：プラスチック、紙
W 300 × H 220 × D 140

目的の為なら、環境は選ばない。目的の為なら、衝撃を恐れない。Endurance という開発コンセプトが生み出した未体験のタフネス・ボディ。過酷な環境で、過激なアクションを、如何に臨場感をもって記録するか。それに応える為に生まれたのが、Endurance です。これらの事柄を店頭等にてエンドユーザーへ適確に訴求するため、展示台には岩肌を用いて過酷な環境を表現し、商品と展示台のデザインコンセプトの一致を図っています。

When you set goals, you can't choose the environment and you can't be afraid of impact. The development concept "Endurance" gives rise to a new type of tough body. In the most rugged of environments, how would you record extreme action so it looks realistic? "Endurance" was developed in response to this. The rock face used for the display gives the feeling of a harsh environment to adequately express these conditions, establishing consistency between the product and design concept.

ぺんてる
Pentel

Shake

COUNTER P.O.P.

製品の最大の特徴である、シャープペンシルボディ中央の透明窓部分を拡大したモデルを中心に据え、これまでの筆記具ディスプレイに無い大胆な形状を採用しました。バックボードを廃することで、高さを出しつつも圧迫感の無い形状を実現しています。立体感に富んだ形状は、パーツの継ぎ目を見せないことで、なめらかな曲面を表現。紙製であることを感じさせない独特の素材感を持ち、製品ボディの全体像を美しく見せる陳列を可能としています。

This display showcases an enlarged model of the clear window on the central part of the mechanical pencil - the main feature of the product, adopting a bold new shape for writing tool displays. By eliminating the backing board, a feeling of height and openness was achieved. As this highly 3D shape has no seams, a smooth curve was created, and the unique feeling of the materials presents the product beautifully, giving the impression that a material other than paper was used.

P：菅屋
MATERIAL：紙、PP
W 300 × H 420 × D 200

P：菅屋
MATERIAL：紙類、PET
W 350 × H 420 × D 300

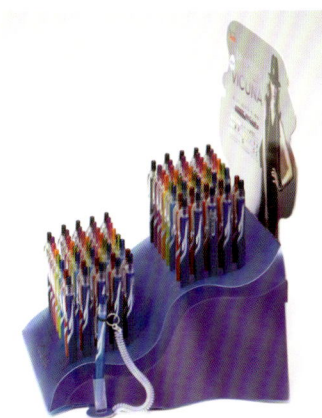

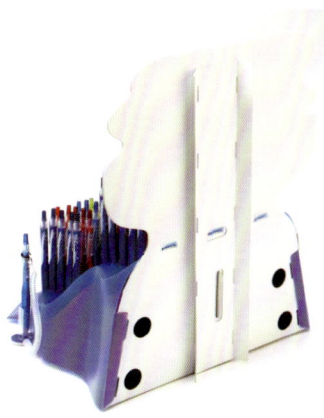

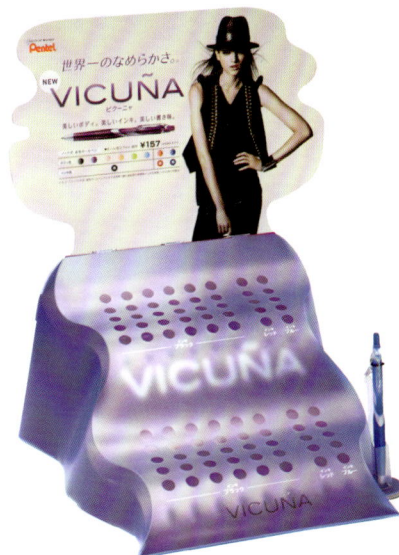

ぺんてる
Pentel

VICUÑA

COUNTER P.O.P.

美・美・美，ビクーニャ！というコンセプトで発売した新ジャンルの油性ボールペン「VICUÑA ビクーニャ」。徹底的に美を追求し、店頭用のディスプレイも化粧品のディスプレイのような雰囲気を醸し出せるように考慮しました。また、商品のレイヤードボディをイメージさせるため、ディスプレイも 2 重構造を採用し、美しさと奥行き感を出しています。文房具の売り場でこのディスプレイは大変インパクトのあるものに仕上がりました。また、キービジュアルはユニセックスなイメージを創出し、女性だけでなく若い男性層も視野に入れた提案をしています。

"VICUÑA" is a new type oil-based ballpoint pen. Here, beauty is comprehensively pursued, and the aim was to create an atmosphere similar to that of a cosmetics display. Additionally, a double-layer construction was adopted to imitate the layered body of the product, providing a sense of beauty and depth. As such, this display delivers an impact to any stationery counter. The key visuals create a unisex image in an attempt to attract the attention of young men as well as women.

ぺんてる
Pentel

ENERGEL EURO

COUNTER P.O.P.
SWING P.O.P.

国内に先駆けてヨーロッパで販売し、大好評を得た「ENERGEL EURO」はヤングビジネスマンをターゲットとしたゲルインキボールペン。「ENERGEL EURO」と凱旋門を合成したインパクトのあるメインビジュアルと特徴的なキャッチコピーを店頭で訴求することに重点を置きました。また、製品のデザイン性と4種のボール径を訴求するために、4つのステージに1本ずつ製品が並べられるように作成しました。

Pioneering the way in Japan and released in Europe, the highly popular "ENERGEL EURO" is a gel ink ballpoint pen targeting young businessmen. The main focus was appealing to customers through high-impact graphics that combine "ENERGEL EURO" and the Arc de Triomphe along with a characteristic catch phrase. Further, the display was designed so that the products could be arranged in four stages, highlighting the product design and 4 different ball sizes.

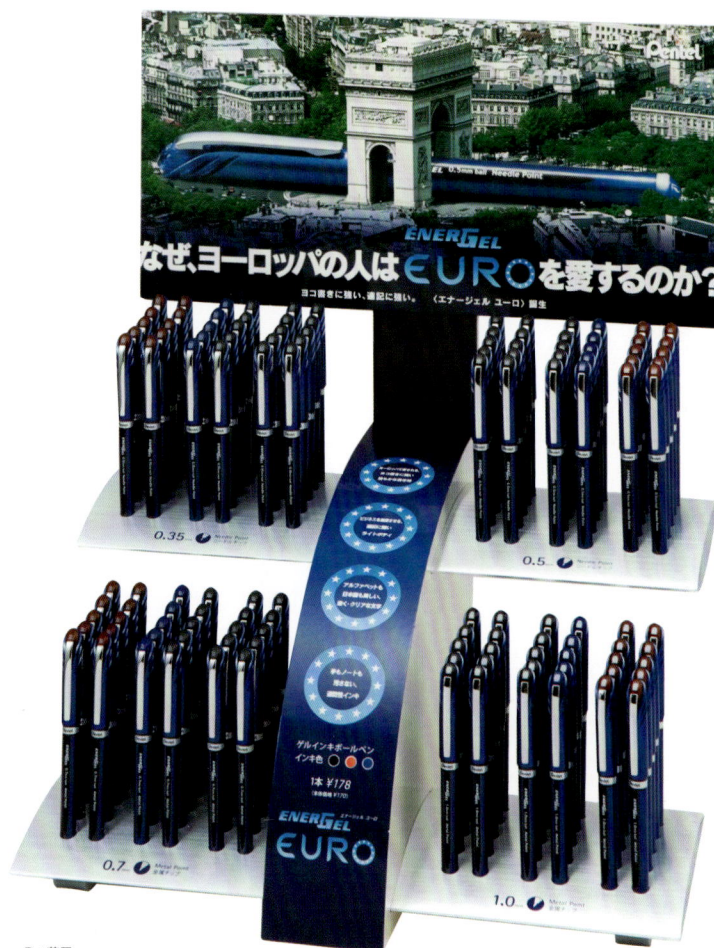

P：菅屋
MATERIAL：合紙
W 400 × H 505 × D 295

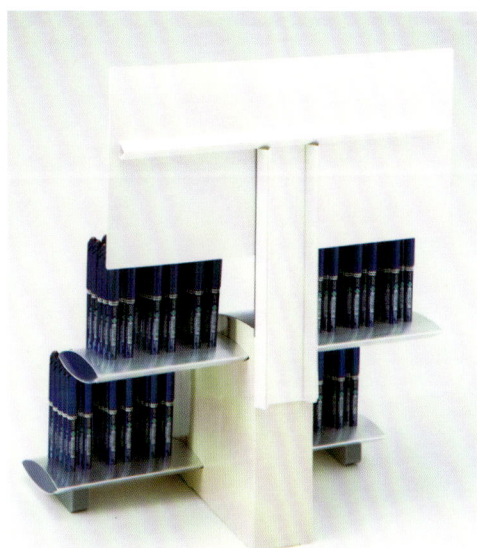

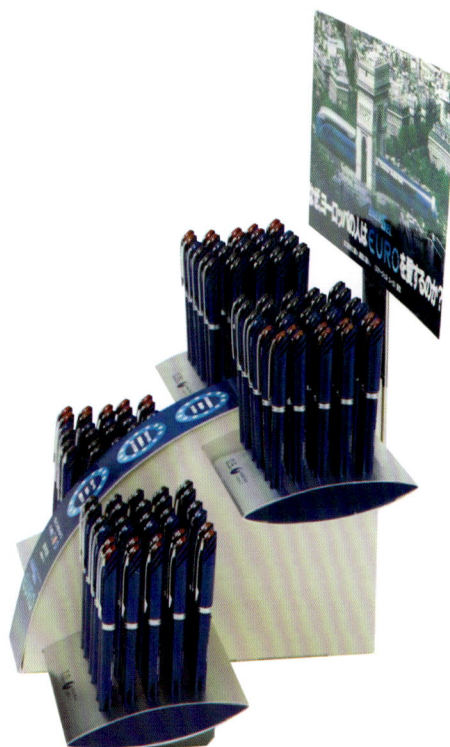

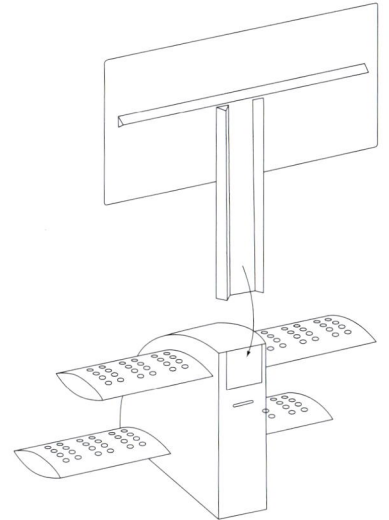

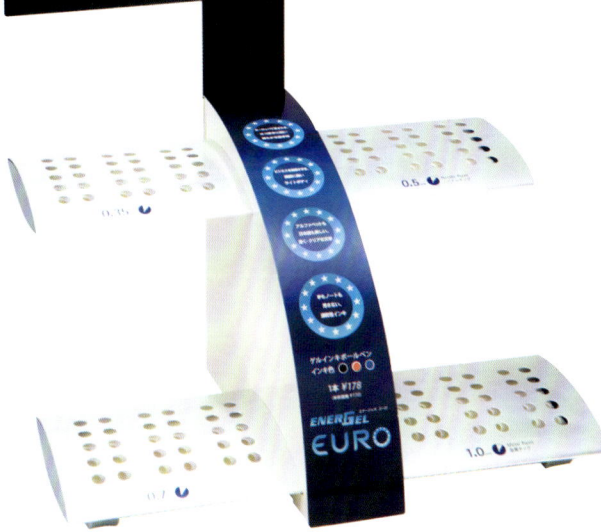

W 80 × H 100 × D 65

W 80 × H 80

W 95 × H 95

プラチナ万年筆
PLATINUM PEN

オ・レーヌ

COUNTER P.O.P.

新製品「耐芯構造」シャープペンシル、"オ・レーヌ"シリーズをボールペン、シャープ替芯を含めた全アイテムの総合ディスプレイセットです。表示看板に製品の特徴を説明しています。製品本数が多いため店頭で乱雑になりがちですが、製品がキレイに並ぶ様に底穴の形状を楕円にして工夫しました。(実用新案出願済)また、ディスプレイ本体前面傾斜でプライス別、アイテム別の区別をしています。

This is a general display set for items including the new "core strengthened" mechanical pencil in the "OLEeNU" series as well as ballpoint pens and mechanical pencil refills, with a display board featuring product characteristics. Although a variety of products often appears cluttered, an elliptical shape was adopted for the holes (utility model application filed) so that the products line up neatly. Further, the front sloping area features individual details.

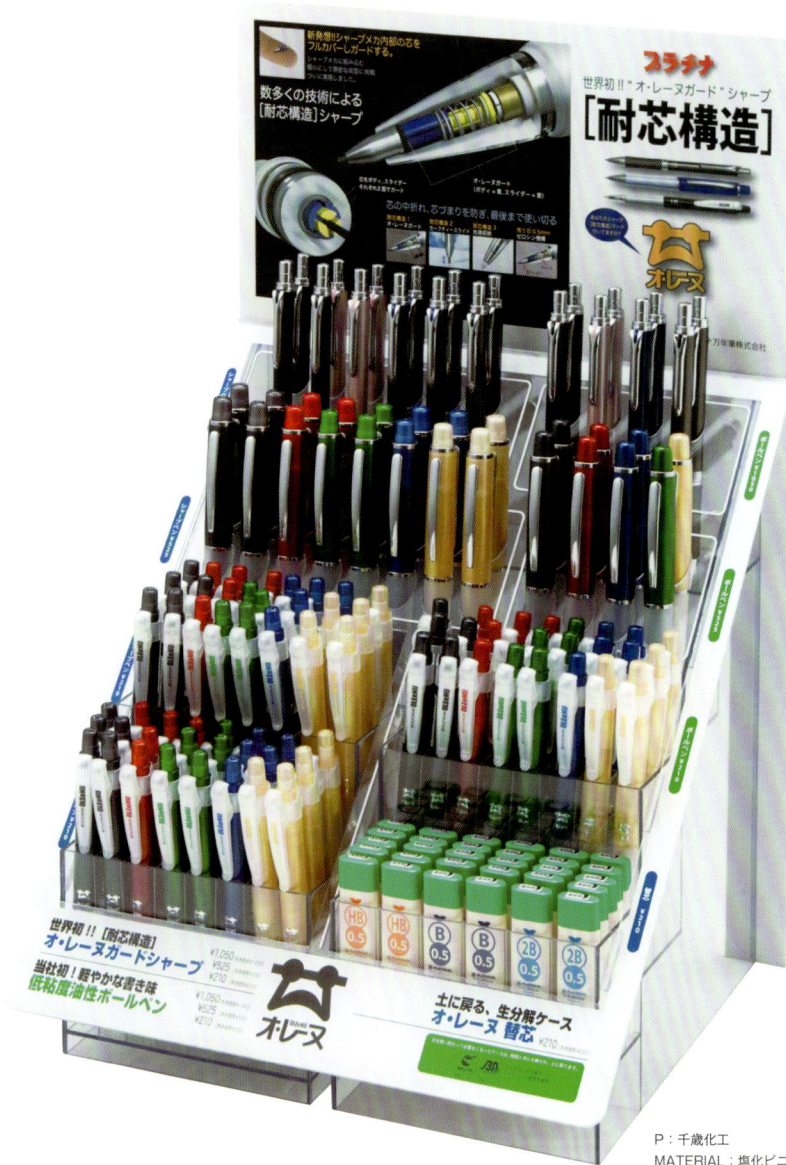

P：千歳化工
MATERIAL：塩化ビニル
W 290 × H 450 × D 255

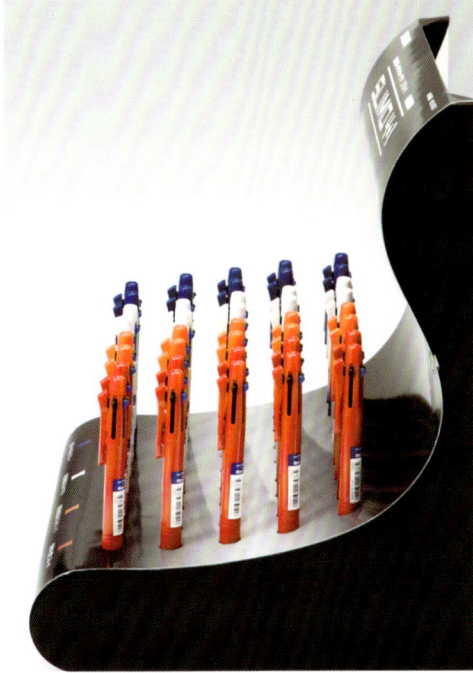

サクラクレパス
SAKURA COLOR PRODUCTS

SLIMO
COUNTER P.O.P.

ターゲットがビジネスマンなので落ち着きのあるディスプレイにするため、ベース色を黒にしました。また、商品の特徴が「軸が細い」ということで、軸が細いユーザーのベネフィットを具体的に挙げました。このベネフィットを「喜び」という言葉で表現し、ユーザーによりわかりやすく認識してもらうようにしました。

Since this product targets businessmen, black was used as the base color to create a display with a relaxed atmosphere. Further, as the main characteristic of the product is "a thin shaft," the display highlights the benefits of this. These are described as "delights," and the display aims to make this as easy as possible for customers to understand.

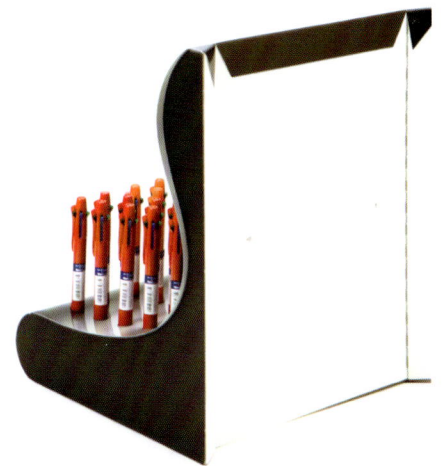

P：大昭和印刷紙業
MATERIAL：紙類
W 260 × H 350 × D 230

STATIONERY

サクラクレパス
SAKURA COLOR PRODUCTS

Plumie

COUNTER P.O.P.

什器の形状は、女性向け商品を意識し曲線的に仕上げました。グラフィックは、商品のカラフルな柄が陳列時にアイキャッチになるようシンプルなブラウンに統一しています。また、限られたスペース内でも筆記サンプルや配布用ミニチラシを配置し、ユーザーへの商品訴求ができるコンパクトな什器を意識し作成しました。

This display design used curved lines to target female consumers. The graphics were set against a simple brown background to make the colorful pattern of the products more eye-catching when displayed. Further, despite limited space, scribble paper and small-size leaflets for distribution were added. This compact display was designed to interest customers in the product.

P：マスパック
MATERIAL：紙類
W 300 × H 430 × D 250

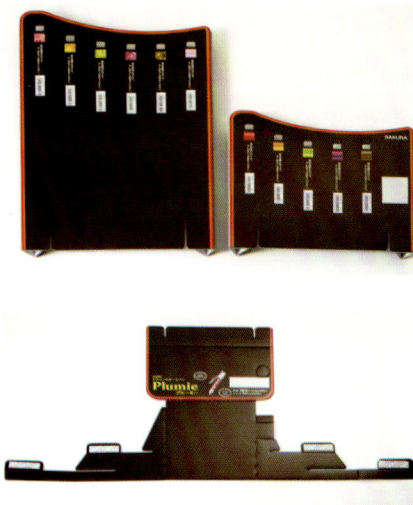

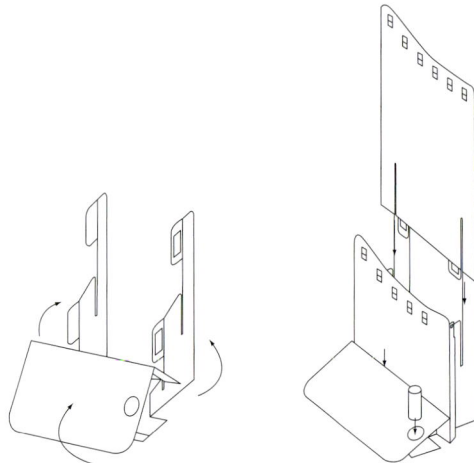

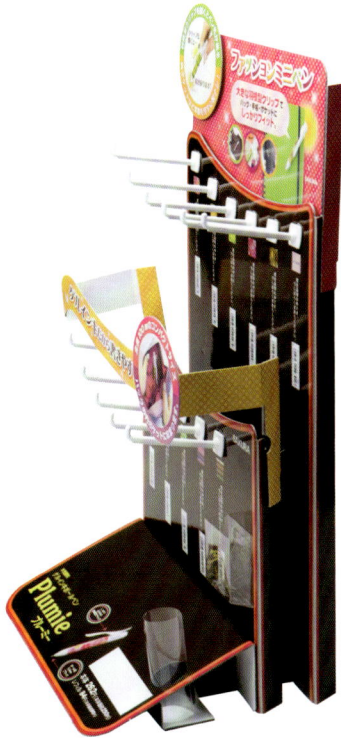

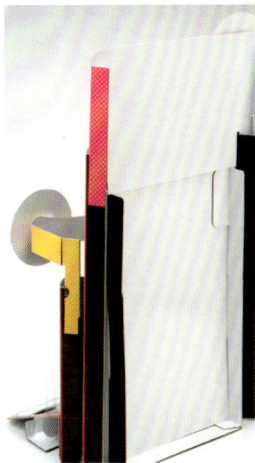

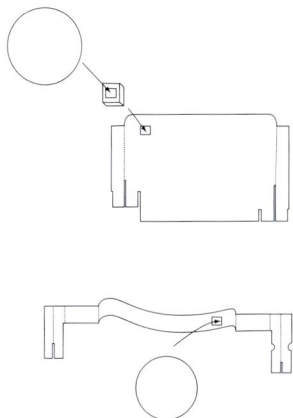

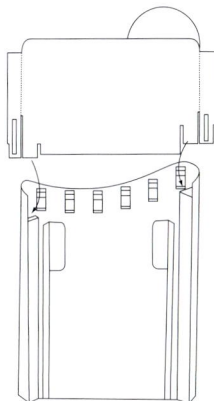

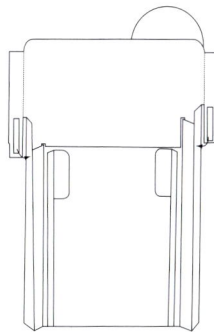

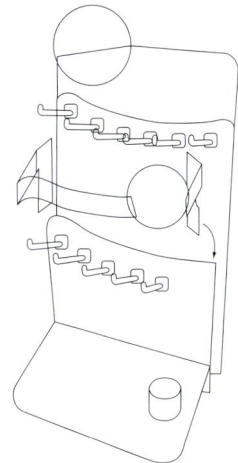

ゼネラル
General

PITATA32

COUNTER P.O.P.
HANGING P.O.P.

弊社はテープのりでは後発のため、ユーザーの認知度が低く、店頭に置いてもらうことが困難でした。そこで、様々な店舗に置いてもらうため、一般的なサイズの「ワイド壁掛けタイプ」「ワイドスタンドタイプ」と小スペースでも設置可能な「スリム壁掛けタイプ」「スリムスタンドタイプ」の1セットで4タイプの形を作成可能なディスプレイ什器になっています。

Since this company is a generic manufacturer of tape glue, customer recognition was low, making it difficult to get stores to display the product. As such, to ensure display at a variety of stores, a set enabling four different display formats was created. Display types included the normal size "wide wall hanging" and "wide stand," as well as the "slim wall hanging" and "slim stand" for smaller spaces.

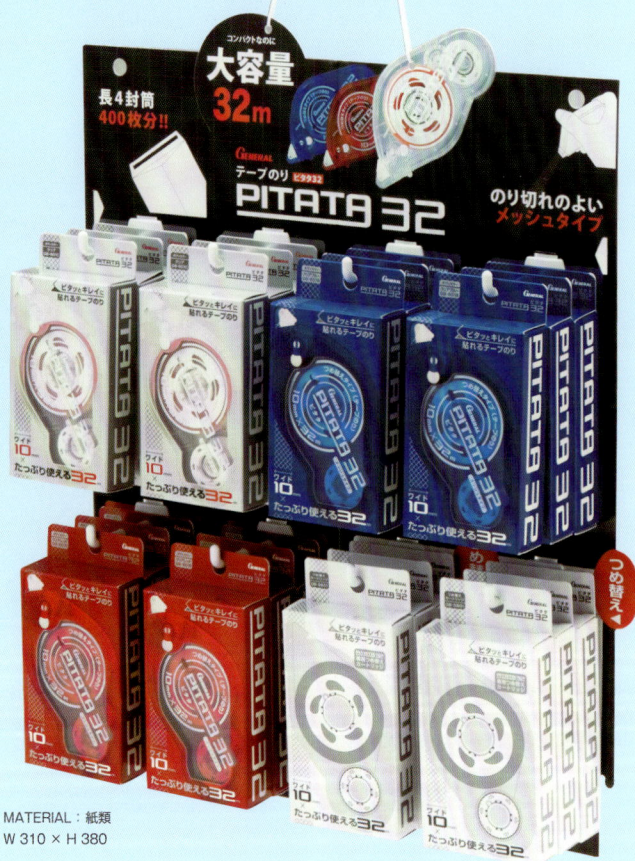

MATERIAL：紙類
W 310 × H 380

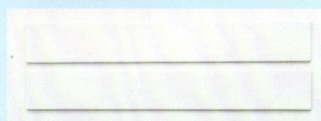

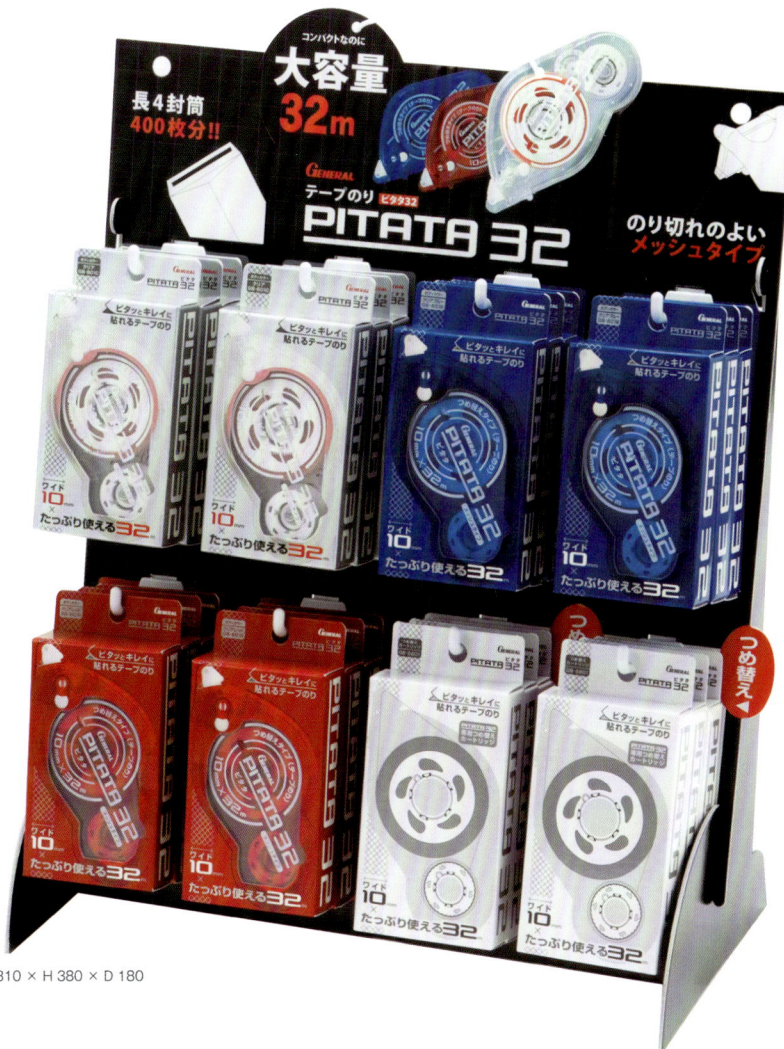

W 310 × H 380 × D 180

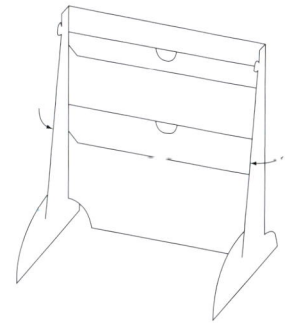

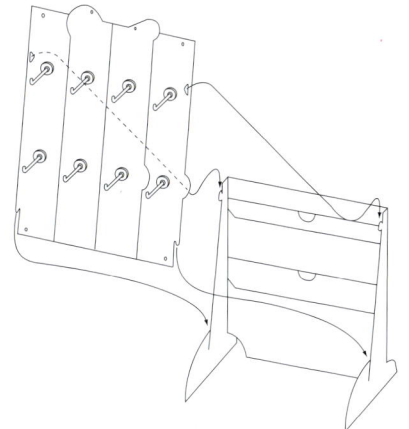

ゼネラル
General

PITATA32

COUNTER P.O.P.
HANGING P.O.P.

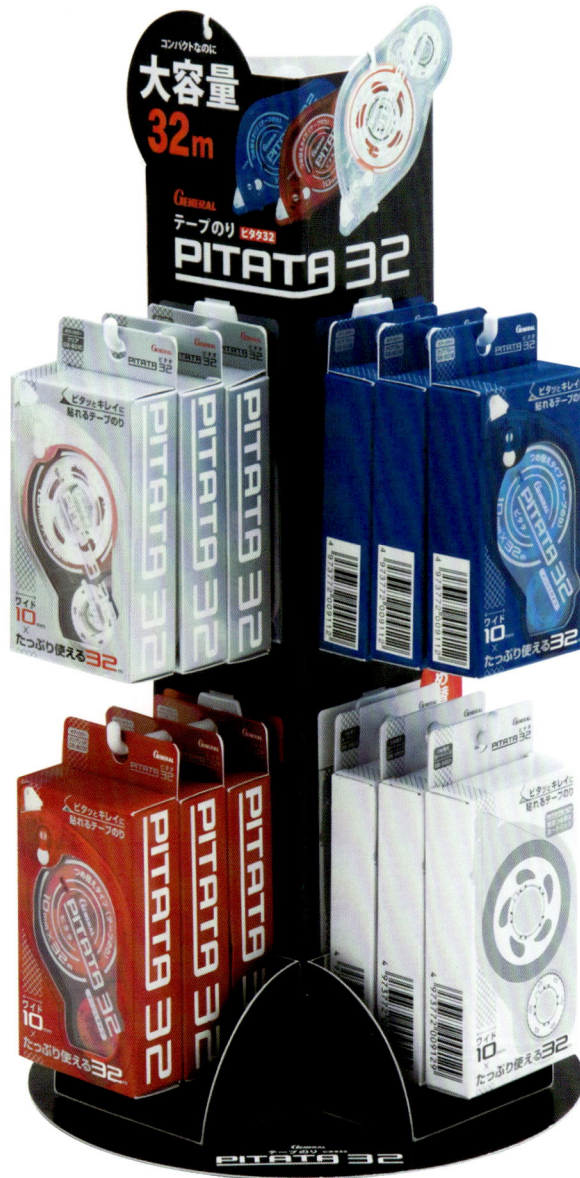

W 200 × H 380 × D 155

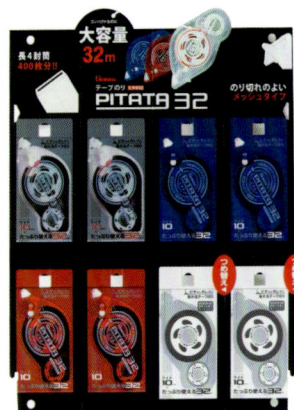

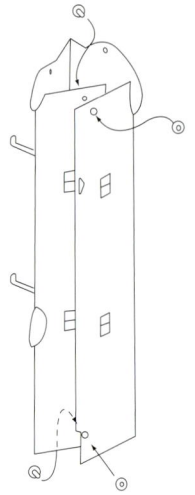

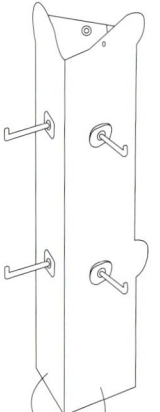

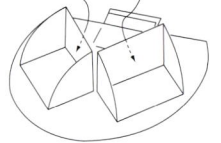

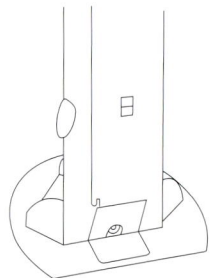

W 115 × H 380 × D 50

ゼネラル
General

PITATA Choice

COUNTER P.O.P.
HANGING P.O.P.

後発メーカーのため、とにかく「店頭で目立つように」という理由から原色を多用しました。実際に国内の文具什器にはあまり使用されない色合いのため、店頭で非常に目立つディスプレイ什器になっています。また、姉妹商品である「PITATA32」は組み立てが多少複雑なのに対して、壁掛けとスタンドの 2 タイプでありながら、取り出してすぐ使用できるという点を考慮しました。

As this product was produced by a generic manufacturer, a large amount of primary colors were used to make it "stand out." In fact, these tones are not often used for domestic stationery displays, so the display stood out considerably. Moreover, while a combination display with the sister product "PITATA32" posed difficulties, the dual-function display can either be hung against the wall or used as a stand, and consideration was given to simple and quick setup.

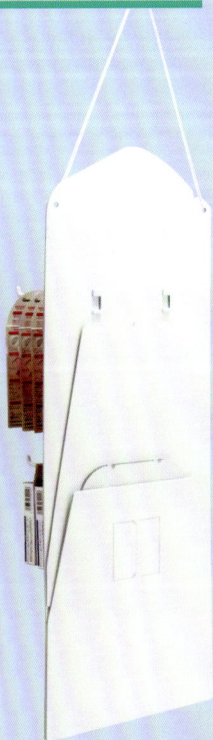

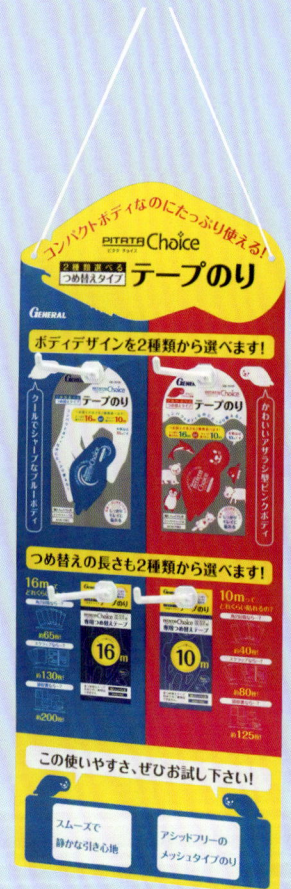

MATERIAL：紙類
W 250 × H 610

コンパクトボディなのにたっぷり使える!
PITATA Choice
ピタタ チョイス
2種類選べる
つめ替えタイプ **テープのり**

GENERAL

ボディデザインを2種類から選べます!

クールでシャープなブルーボディ

かわいいアザラシ型ピンクボディ

つめ替えの長さも2種類から選べます!

16m って どれくらい貼れるの?
10m

この使いやすさ、ぜひお試し下さい!

スムーズで 静かな引き心地

アシッドフリーの メッシュタイプのり

コンパクトボディなのにたっぷり使える!
PITATA Choice
ピタタ チョイス
2種類選べる
つめ替えタイプ **テープのり**

GENERAL

ボディデザインを2種類から選べます!

GENERAL
PITATA Choice
つめ替入タイプ
テープのり リリリ
16m 10m

しっかりキレイに貼れる

かわいいアザラシ型ピンクボディ

つめ替えの長さも2種類から選べます!

16m って どれくらい貼れるの?

GENERAL
PITATA Choice
専用つめ替えテープ
16m

PITATA Choice
専用つめ替えテープ
10m

10m って どれくらい貼れるの?
角2封筒なら…? 約40枚!
スクラップなら…? 約80枚!
便箋なら…? 約125枚!

この使いやすさ、ぜひお試し下さい!

スムーズで 静かな引き心地

アシッドフリーの メッシュタイプのり

W 250 × H 485 × D 245

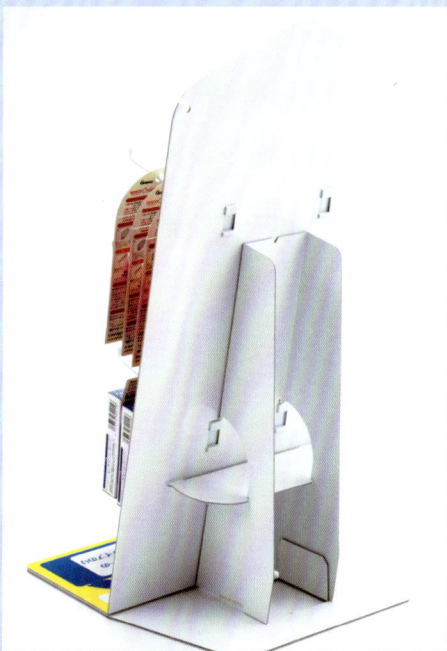

三菱鉛筆
MITSUBISHI PENCIL

Do! POSCA

COUNTER P.O.P.

Do！POSCA のカラフルさ、イラスト描きやデコリの楽しさがより伝わるよう、形状に丸みを持たせ、ピンク色をベースとしてファンシーさを意識しました。円柱の４分の１形状を１ユニットとし、縦並び、横並びのどちらでも組み合わせが可能です。更に複数ユニットを組み合わせすることで様々な形状を作ることができます。スペースや売り場の雰囲気に応じて形状変化ができることが、この什器の最大特長です。

The shape of the display was curved to emphasize the colorful, artistic and decorative nature of "Do! POSCA," and an element of fanciness was added by adopting pink as the base color. Each display is one quarter of a round column so that multiple displays can be combined vertically or horizontally to create a variety of shapes. The greatest feature of this fixture is the way the shape can be changed to suit the space or environment.

W 165 × H 555 × D 210

W 330 × H 310 × D 210

PL：三菱鉛筆
P：三協
MATERIAL：紙類、PET、塩化ビニル、ポリスチレン樹脂
W 165 × H 310 × D 210

STATIONERY

三菱鉛筆
MITSUBISHI PENCIL

uni COLOR 240 LIMITED EDITION

COUNTER P.O.P.

鉛筆「ユニ」誕生 50 周年を記念して、数量限定で発売された「ユニカラー240 リミテッドエディション」。日本の伝統色を加え、日本製にこだわり、色の選定・品質ともにパーフェクトをめざした渾身の 240 色の色鉛筆です。この製品の特別な質感や世界観を、店頭で端的に表現しお客様に訴求するために、製品の外観そのものを示す、クロス張り木製ケースを模したオブジェ型の小冊子BOX を中心に企画しました。

Celebrating 50 years since the birth of the pencil "Uni," the "Uni Color 240 Limited Edition" was released. In addition to traditional Japanese colors, this collection of 240 pencils showcases Japanese craftsmanship and aims to provide the perfect selection of colors and quality. The special texture and ideology of this product is expressed plainly via the display, and the simulation wooden case mimics the exterior of the product to appeal to customers, and is equipped with a pamphlet box.

PL：三菱鉛筆
P：中央工芸企画
MATERIAL：紙類、合紙
W 210 × H 185 × D 215

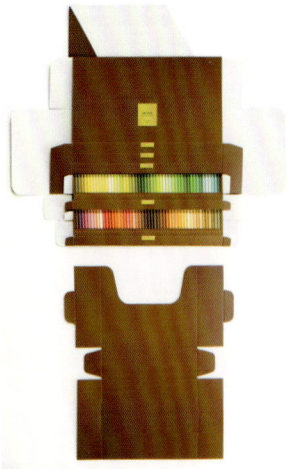

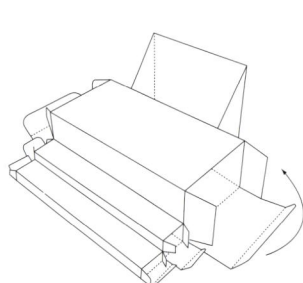

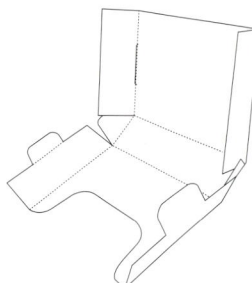

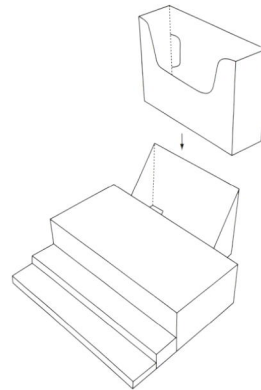

Poster

P：イデイ
MATERIAL：紙
W 450 × H 350 × D 300

トンボ鉛筆
Tombow Pencil

MONO

COUNTER P.O.P.

有名ブランドである MONO。ロゴとキーカラーをそのまま使用したブランドコーナーツールです。写真はツール全体を使用した例ですが、各パーツそれぞれバラバラで使用が可能で、売り場の状況に合わせてフレキシブルに対応できる設計になっています。

This display uses the logo and key color for the famous brand "MONO" to emphasize the brand image. Here, all the display parts are shown being used simultaneously, but each part can also be used individually, making this a flexible display that accommodates any situation.

トンボ鉛筆
Tombow Pencil

AirPress apro

COUNTER P.O.P.
HANGING P.O.P.

商品ターゲットに合わせ、女性を意識したデザインに仕上げました。ビジュアルでシーンをイメージしやすく表現しながら、機能面をしっかり訴求することで商品性をアピールしました。楕円形のやさしいフォルムとシンプルなホワイトを基調としたカラーリングで店頭での存在感や視認性を考慮しました。土台を取り外すことで簡単にハンガーディスプレイとしても使用できます。機能訴求POP は小スペース陳列になった場合にも対応できるクリップタイプです。

This display was designed to appeal to women in keeping with the product target base. While using graphics that encourage easy-to-visualize scenarios, product quality was advertised based on functionality. The gentle oval shape and simple white tones were used to create presence and visibility, and the base can be removed, turning this into a display that can easily be hung up. Highly versatile, it can also be used as a clip-on type display when space is limited.

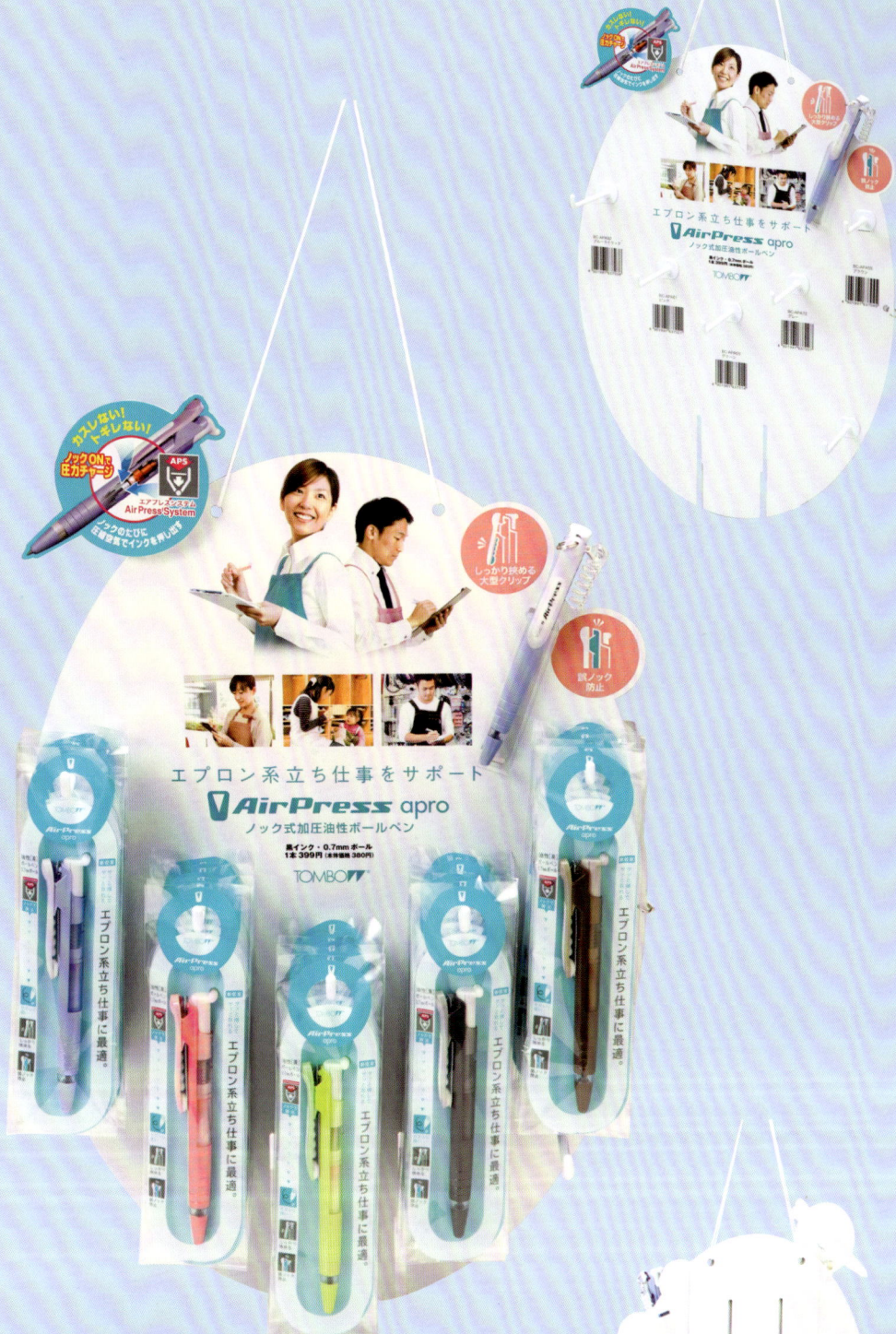

MATERIAL：紙類
W 315 × H 445

W 105 × H 150 × D 70

エプロン系立ち仕事をサポート

AirPress apro
ノック式加圧油性ボールペン

黒インク・0.7mmボール
1本 399円（本体価格380円）

TOMBOW

エプロン系立ち仕事に最適。

P：イデイ
MATERIAL：紙類
W 315 × H 480 × D 180

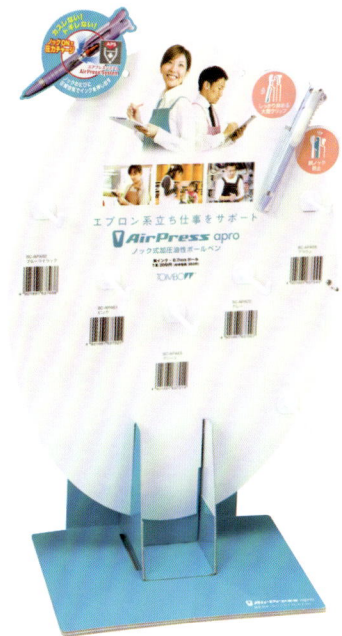

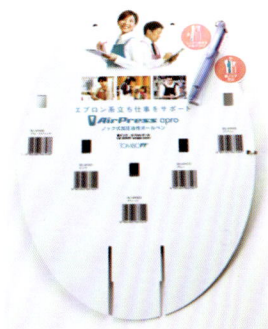

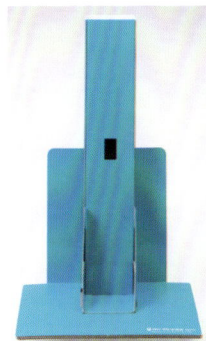

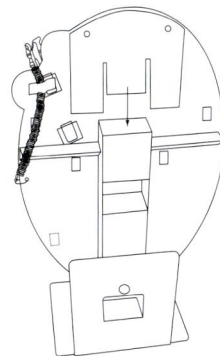

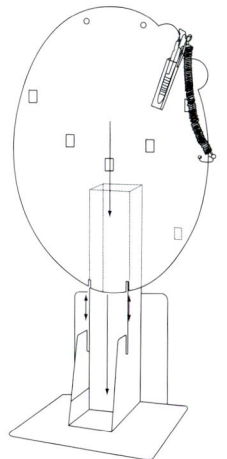

カスレない！トギレない！
ノックONで圧力チャージ
APS
エアプレスシステム
Air Press System
空気のたびに圧縮空気でインクを押し出す

FOOD
【食品】

SPORTS
【スポーツ】

CLOTHES
【衣類】

ENTERTAINMENT
【娯楽】

OTHER
【その他】

不二家
FUJIYA

milky

FLOOR P.O.P.

ロングセラー商品、ミルキー箱のデザインをそのまま什器にしました。内側の高さが2段階に調整できるので、商品が多い場合でも少ない場合でも高さを変えて美しく陳列することができます。また、背板を外し、天井やエンド最上段に飾れば、ミルキーのビッグパッケージのオブジェとしても使えます。

This display is a replica of the box design for the long-selling product "Milky." The internal height can be adjusted, with 2 different heights that allow the product to be attractively presented whether a small or large amount of product is featured. Further, if the rear backing is removed and the fixture displayed from the ceiling or the top of an end shelf, it can be used as a giant object.

MATERIAL：紙類
W 444 × H 744 × D 270

© FUJIYA CO.,LTD.

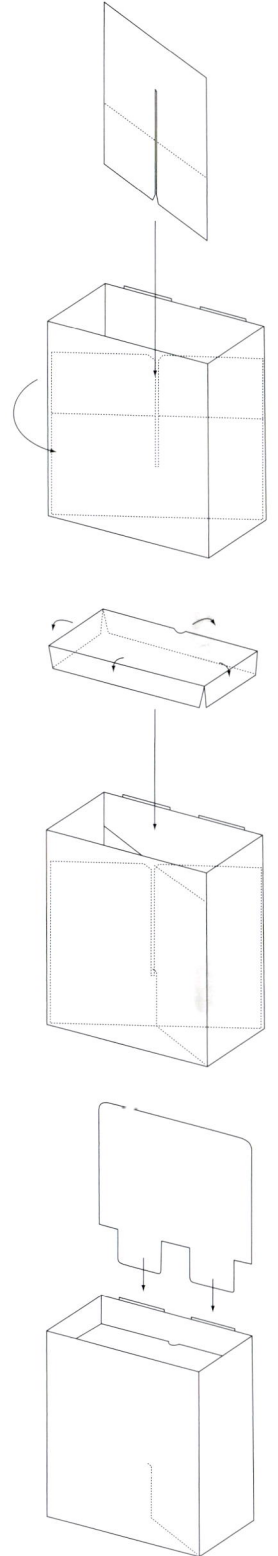

不二家
FUJIYA
LOOK A LA MODE CHOCOLATE
HANGING P.O.P.

ルックチョコレートが 1 段で 5 個、4 段で 20 個入ります。奥行きを取らないので、レジ前やエンド脇などあらゆる場所に陳列可能です。

Each rack holds 5 boxes of LOOK chocolate for a total of 20 boxes on all 4 racks. As the display is not very deep, it can be placed in a variety of locations including next to the register or on the end of shelves.

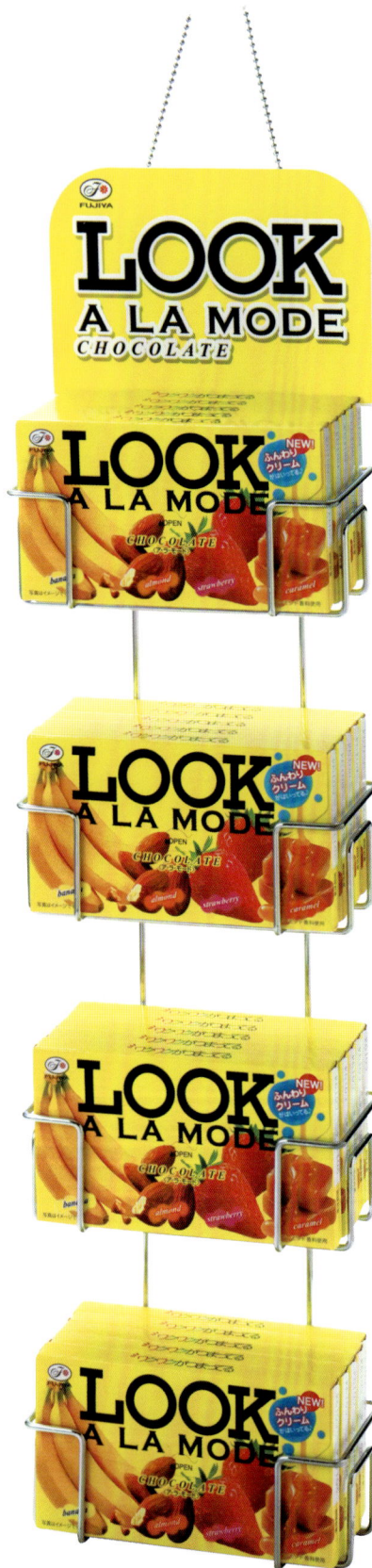

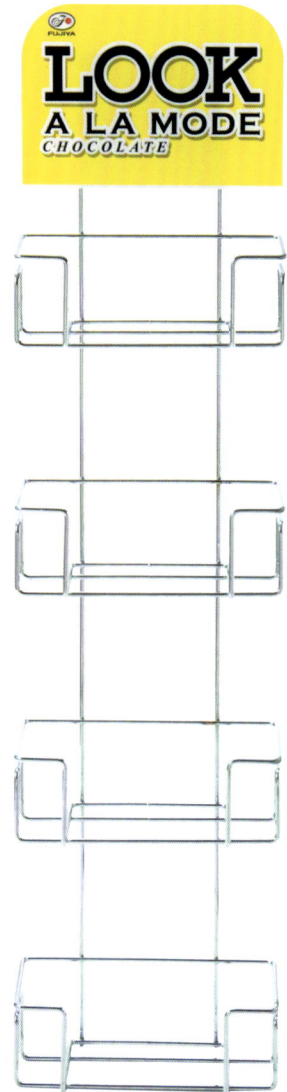

MATERIAL：プラスチック、鉄
W 140 × H 585 × D 73

FOOD

明治製菓
Meiji Seika

XYLISH

COUNTER P.O.P.

Wのミントの濃いーい奴、MINTZ登場。

気分スッキリ リフレッシュ!!

ガムとソフトキャンデーの濃厚スイーツ

XYLISH 息スッキリ&味長持ち

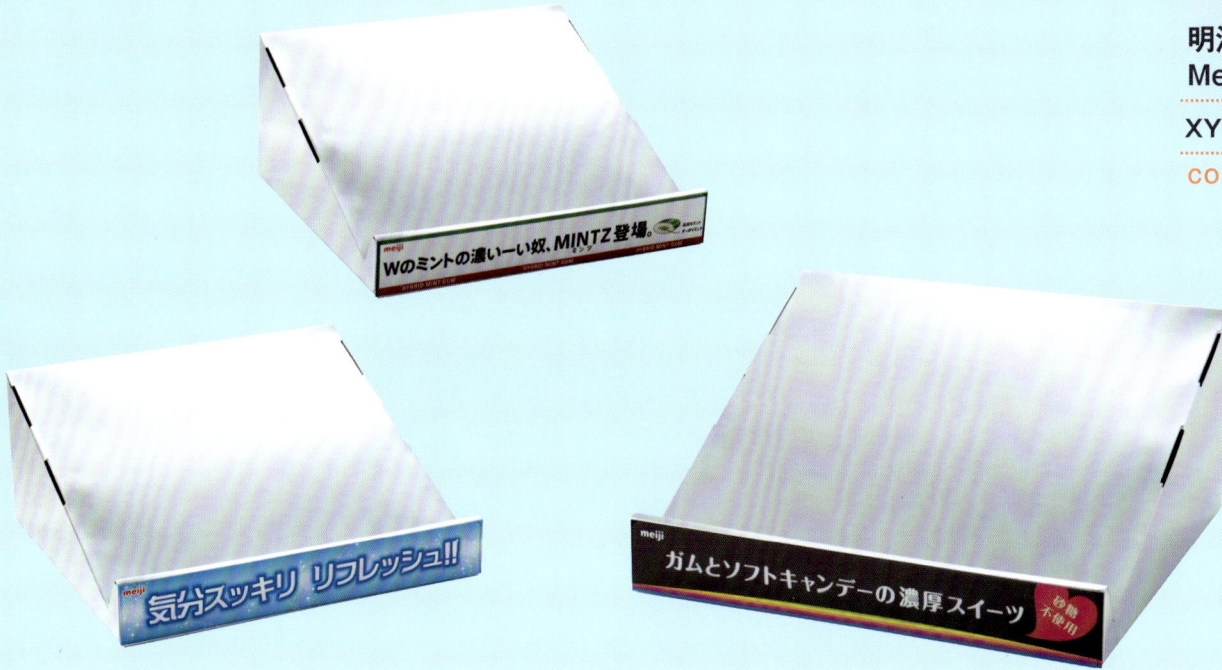

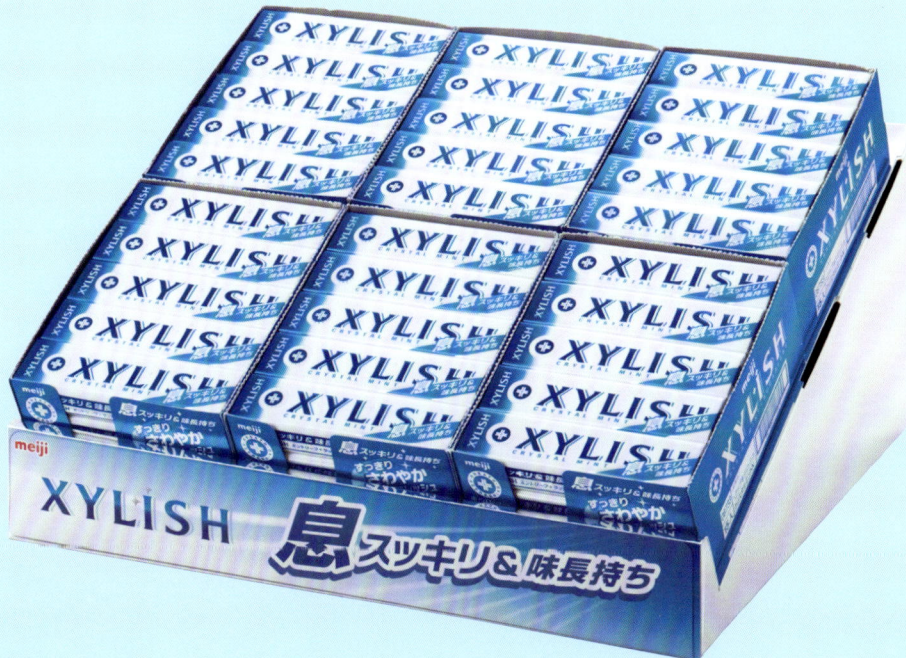

P：フロウ
MATERIAL：合紙
W 300 × H 130 × D 260

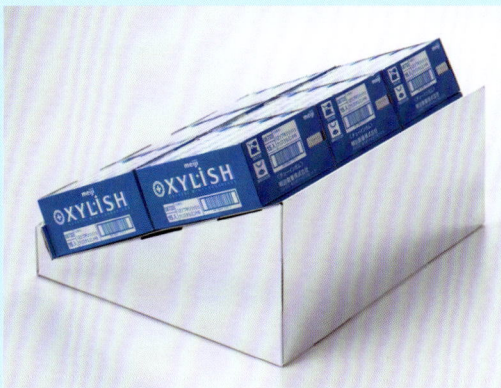

明治製菓
Meiji Seika

XYLISH

様々なサイズのボトルに対応できる
よう、デザインは個性を抑え、汎用
性を持たせた販売台です。

This display was designed to
be general-purpose with
subdued individuality to
accommodate various sizes of
bottles.

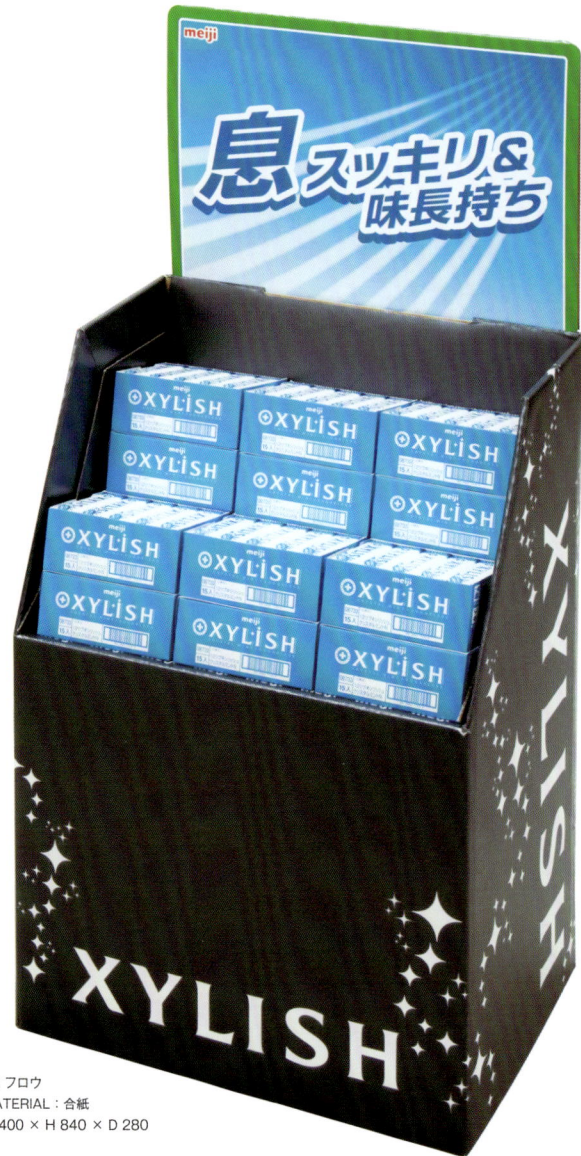

P：フロウ
MATERIAL：合紙
W 400 × H 840 × D 280

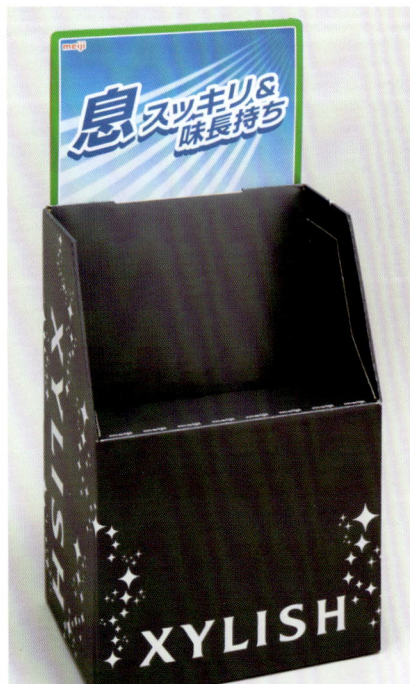

息スッキリ&味長持ち
XYLISH

気分スッキリ
リフレッシュ!!

Wのミントの濃いーい奴、
MINTZ登場。
HYBRID MINT GUM

ガムと
ソフトキャンデーの
濃厚スイーツ

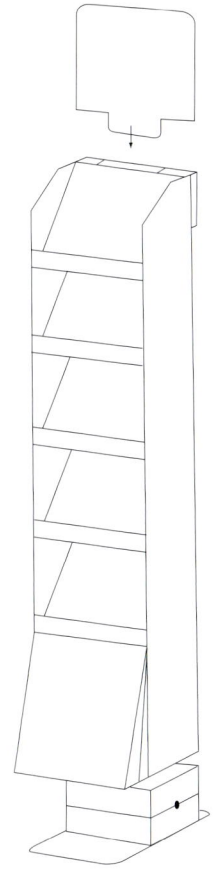

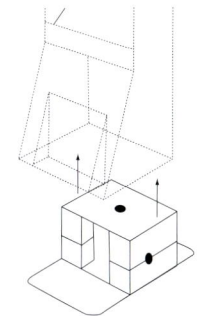

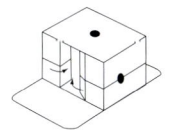

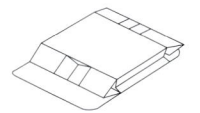

P：フロウ
MATERIAL：合紙
W 220 × H 1220 × D 360

193

カルビー
Calbee

Jagabee

FLOOR P.O.P.

容器をイメージできるようにカップ型にしました。店舗の柱まわりや隙間に配置できるように半円型になっており、エンドの最上段にディスプレイとして乗せると遠くからでも目立ちます。

This display was created in a cup shape to conjure up the image of a container. It is semicircular so it can be placed around a shop pillar or in a gap, and if it is placed on the top of an end shelf, it is visible from a great distance.

MATERIAL：紙類
W 520 × H 1060 × D 350

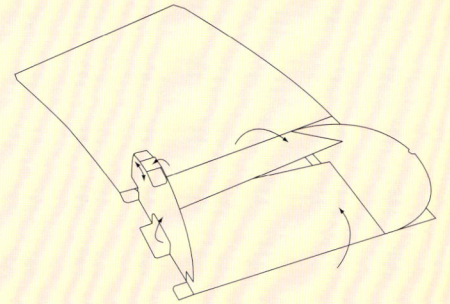

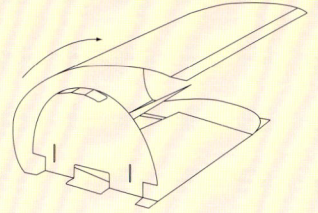

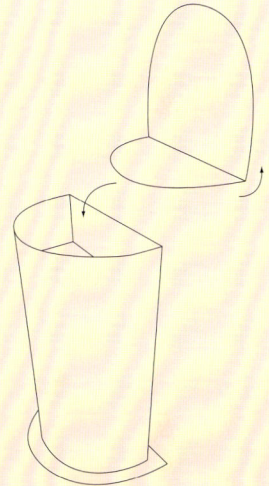

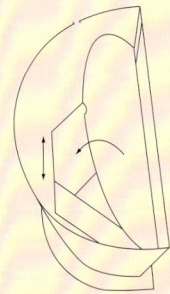

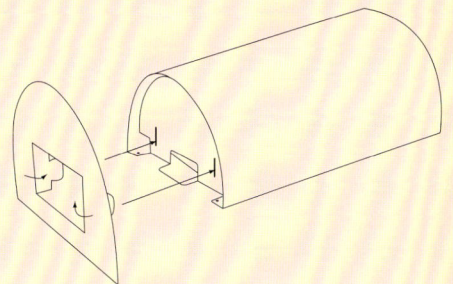

味の素
AJINOMOTO

クノール®

FLOOR P.O.P.

プライベートブランドの多いたまご
スープ市場に対し、ナショナルブラ
ンドならではの訴求を図りました。
商品の持つやさしさやあたたかさ、
「とれて3日以内のたまご使用」とい
う特徴を明快に伝達するため、にわ
とりが商品を抱えているようなデザ
インにしました。

This display was designed to
appeal to customers using a
national brand name in an egg
soup market packed with
private brands. To clearly
convey the characteristic
"Made using eggs no more than
3 days old" for this light and
warming soup, the design
features a chicken embracing
the products.

ピュアセレクト

FLOOR P.O.P.

作りたてのマヨネーズを店頭へお届
けする"直送感"をトラックで表現
しました。トラック後部は旬野菜
(じゃがいも)を陳列でき、生鮮と
連動した販売ができる仕組みです。
また、売り場の広さにあわせてサイ
ズを調整することが可能です。

This display uses a mock truck
to give the impression that
freshly-made mayonnaise is
delivered directly to the store.
The rear of the truck has
space for seasonal vegetables
(such as potatoes), allowing
sales to be combined with fresh
produce. Further, the display
size can be adjusted to suit the
available space.

P：味の素コミュニケーションズ
MATERIAL：紙類
W 610 × H 1020 × D 310

P：味の素コミュニケーションズ
MATERIAL：紙類
W 720 × H 850 × D 2140 (最大)

P：味の素コミュニケーションズ
MATERIAL：紙類、ABS樹脂
W 320 × H 1200 × D 260

P：味の素コミュニケーションズ
MATERIAL：紙類、PET樹脂
W 420 × H 900 × D 220

日本ケロッグ
KELLOGG（JAPAN）

オールブラン

FLOOR P.O.P.

（左）保管スペースを抑えるため組み立て式にしました。小袋・箱タイプの商品が同時陳列可能で、狭い場所でも正面だけでなく両サイドからも商品のフェイスが見えるよう左右に角度をつけたフックで対応しています。
（右）3種類の商品が混ざらないように、仕切りをセットして3分割できます。横からも商品が見えるよう透明樹脂を使用しました。保管時のスペース削減と組み立て時間短縮のため、簡単に組み立てられる構造になっています。

(Left) This display is ready-to-assemble to minimize storage space. Both small bags and boxes of the product can be displayed simultaneously, and the hooks were placed on an angle to the right and left to show the face of the product from all sides, even in narrow spaces.
(Right) So that the 3 products remain separate, the display is divided into 3 parts, and transparent plastic was used so that the products can be viewed from the side. The structure was designed for easy setup, reducing both storage space and assembly time.

P：味の素コミュニケーションズ
MATERIAL：合紙
W 1800 × H 1800 × D 900

カルピス
CALPIS

ウェルチ

FLOOR P.O.P.

11月〜年始にかけてボジョレー解禁・クリスマス・お正月と家族、友人が集うパーティイベントが多くなる時期に売り場での露出度アップを狙ったツールです。寒い季節の家庭内イベントをポップにサポートします。

In the party period from November through to the New Year when family and friends gather to celebrate the opening day of Beaujolais Nouveau, Christmas and New Year's, this tool aims to increase the degree of product exposure and support family events held throughout the cold season.

江崎グリコ
Ezaki Glico

GIANT Caplico

FLOOR P.O.P.

発売から 40 年以上のロングセラーブランド「カプリコ」のおいしさや楽しさを伝えるキャラクターとして 2005 年に誕生した『かぷすけ』。愛らしい表情のフロアジャンブル什器は華やか且つ印象的です。大量陳列が可能で、商品の PR に最適です。

"Capsuke" is a character developed in 2005 to convey the delicious taste and novelty of the long-selling brand "Caplico" released more than 40 years ago. This floor jumble display has an adorable expression, and is both bright and dramatic. Since it holds a large volume, it is perfect as an advertising tool.

P：美工
MATERIAL：紙、段ボール
W 480 × H 1080 × D 360

P：美工
MATERIAL：紙、段ボール
W 1010 × H 1350 × D 470

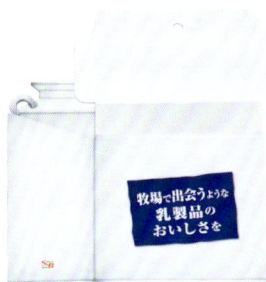

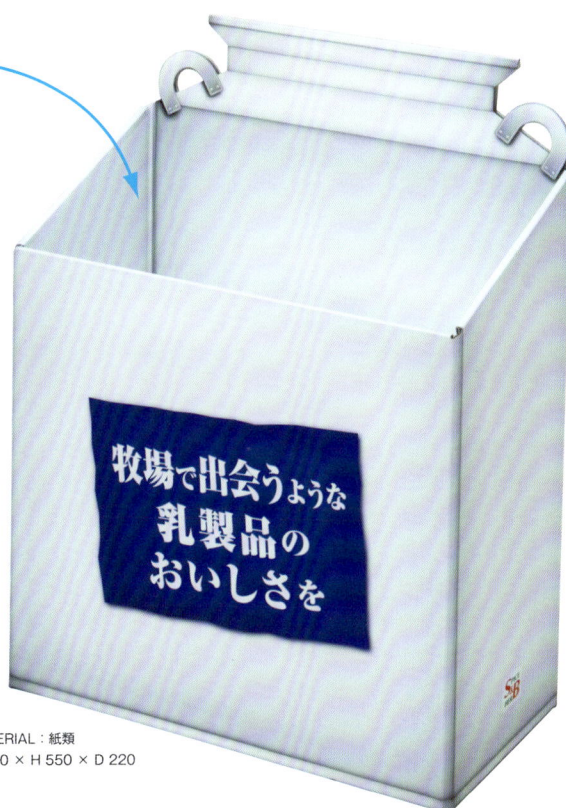

MATERIAL：紙類
W 420 × H 550 × D 220

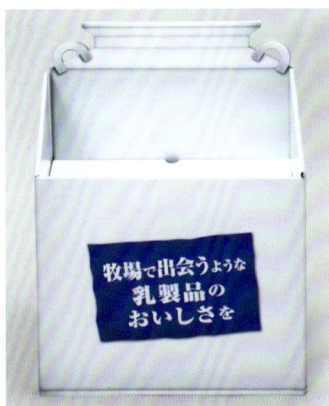

エスビー食品
S&B Foods

牧場しぼりシチュー

FLOOR P.O.P.
OTHERS P.O.P.

全体的に、「牧場しぼりシチュー」のコンセプトである、乳製品の素材感を白色や画像で表現し、お客様にアピールするようなデザインになっています。牧場で出会う乳製品のような「なめらかでふんわりとしたくちどけ感」、クリーム感をデザインに活かし、商品をレイアウトした時、パッケージのデザインと一体になって、北海道の牧場のイメージや乳製品の素材感を醸し出されるように色などを調整しています。

The color white and images that remind one of dairy products, the concept for "Bokujo Shibori Stew," are used throughout for a design that appeals to customers. The design is based on "a smooth and light melt-in-the-mouth sensation" that feels fresh from the dairy and "creaminess." When the product is set up, the display and product packaging blend together, and the colors, etc. were coordinated to conjure up images of Hokkaido farms and dairy products.

W 750 × H 300

Sticker

エスビー食品
S&B Foods

カレー屋さんのかくし味

COUNTER P.O.P.

2段でも1段でも使用できる汎用性のある形状のカウンターディスプレイです。

A versatile counter display that can be used as either two tiers or a single tier.

W 430 × H 255 × D 220

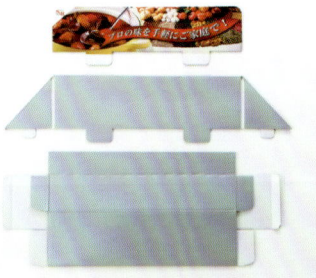

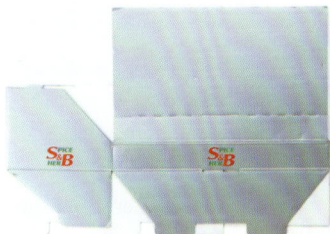

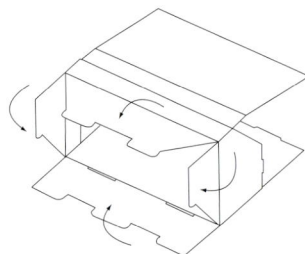

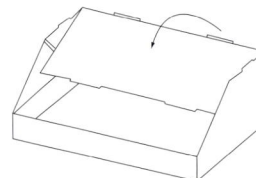

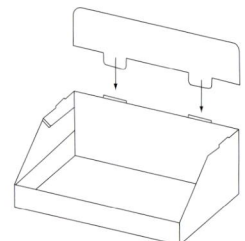

P：マスパック
MATERIAL：紙類
W 430 × H 375 × D 220

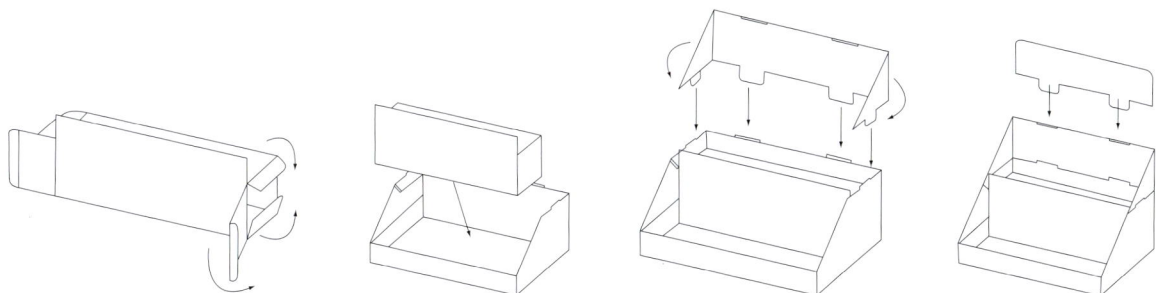

エースコック
ACECOOK

スープはるさめ プチパック

HANGING P.O.P.

スープはるさめの姉妹品である、袋タイプの「プチパック」を店頭でより露出度を上げていくために製作しました。通常並んでいる棚以外の、小スペースな場所であっても陳列出来るように、縦にぶら下げる事を工夫し、目に留まった時にも食シーンが明確に分かるように「マグで手軽に」というキャッチで印象付けるようにしたディスプレイです。

This display was designed to increase the level of exposure for the pouch type "Puchi Pack," the sister product to "Soup Harusame." It hangs vertically to allow for display in tight spaces, offering an alternative to the usual method of shelf display. The display makes an impression with the catch phrase "Convenience in a mug," providing a scenario for enjoying the product.

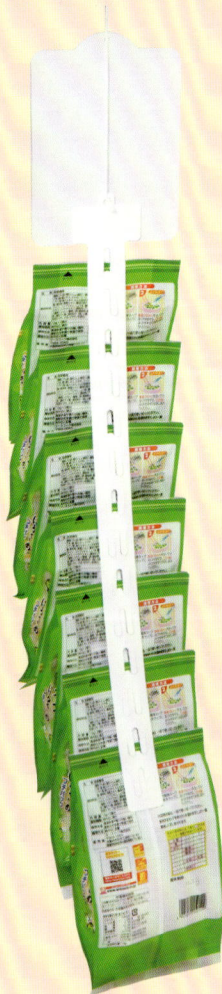

MATERIAL：紙類
W 150 × H 725

MATERIAL：紙類、金属
W 310 × H 925 × D 100

エースコック
ACECOOK

からだ食堂

HANGING P.O.P.

女性のライフサイクルに注目して考案した「からだ食堂」。数多くあるカップスープの中での陳列がなかなか目立ちにくい上、単品だけの陳列だと本来のコンセプトであるライフサイクルに合わせた食べ方、の訴求がしにくい状態になってしまいます。そこで壁掛け式什器に並べる事によって、からだ食堂というブランドイメージの醸成や世界観を演出しました。

The concept "Karada Shokudo" is a style of eating that compliments the lifestyle of women. It was difficult to come up with a display that stands out from the numerous other cup-of-soup displays, as well as hard to convey the product concept when only one of the brand's products was on display. As such, a wall hanging type display was selected so that the product could be lined up in rows, showing off the brand image of leadership and global ideology.

MATERIAL：紙類
W 210 × H 500

ヤマサ醤油
YAMASA

ワイワイ！鍋パーティー

OTHERS P.O.P.

鍋シーズンの店頭はどのお店に行っても同質化傾向です。長期のエンド大陳の中に、お客様参加型の POP があってもよいのでは？

During hot pot season in Japan, all shop displays tend to look alike. During this period, wouldn't it be nice to have a POP display on the edge of the shelf that customers can enjoy?

ヤマサ醤油
YAMASA

鮮度の一滴

HANGING P.O.P.
COUNTER P.O.P.

商品のコンセプトである、空気に触れないしょうゆ、ヤマサのしょうゆの特長である鮮やかな赤い色が持続できる新容器、この2つを売り場で目立たせるように販促物は赤を基調として商品の白いパウチ容器と対照的な物に仕立てました。

The concept here is vacuum-packed soy sauce in a new package that preserves the rich red color characteristic of Yamasa soy sauce. To showcase these two features, red is used for the advertising material, contrasting with the white pouch of the product.

A：システムコミュニケーションズ
MATERIAL：紙類、金属
W 300 × H 725 × D 120

W 800 × H 450

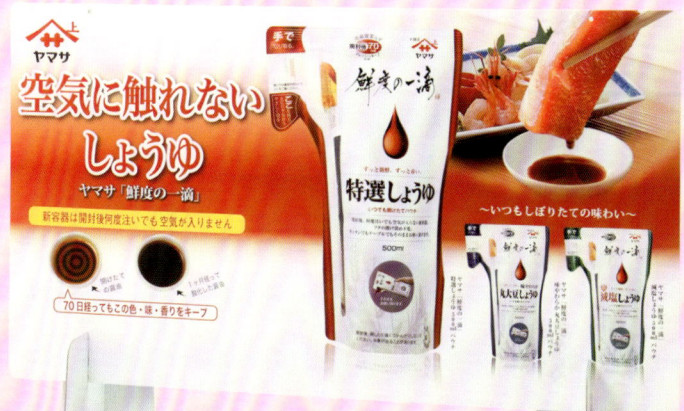

W 800 × H 710 × D 150

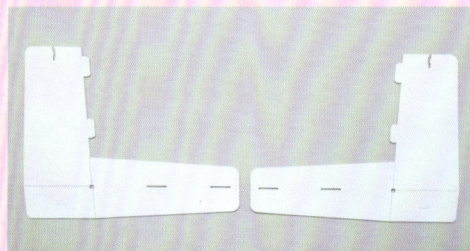

ヤマサ醤油
YAMASA

鮮度の一滴

COUNTER P.O.P.
OTHERS P.O.P.

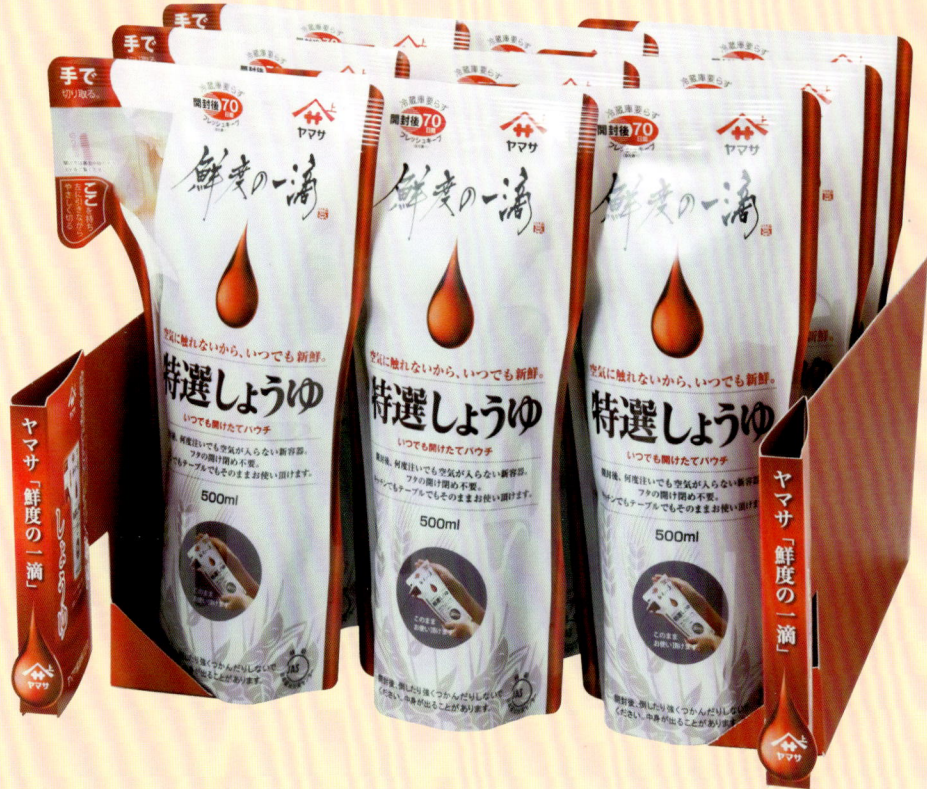

W 70 × H 140 × D 315

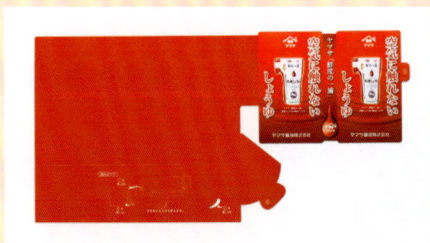

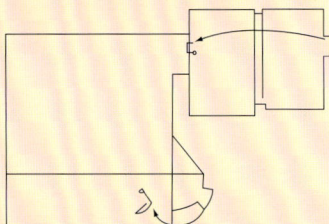

W 120 × H 390

ヤマサ醤油
YAMASA

昆布ぽん酢

COUNTER P.O.P.

夏場の需要が多くなるぽん酢。ゼラチンで固めたぽん酢ジュレをサラダにかけ、春夏のメニューを訴求、更に写真部分は 3D 加工して商品が浮かび上がる仕掛けにしました。

Ponzu is in high demand during the summer months. This display was designed to appeal with pictures of a spring/summer salad dressed with ponzu jelly, using pop-outs for the photos to give the product greater presence.

A：システムコミュニケーションズ
MATERIAL：紙類
W 900 × H 655 × D 150

W 135 × H 135 × D 250

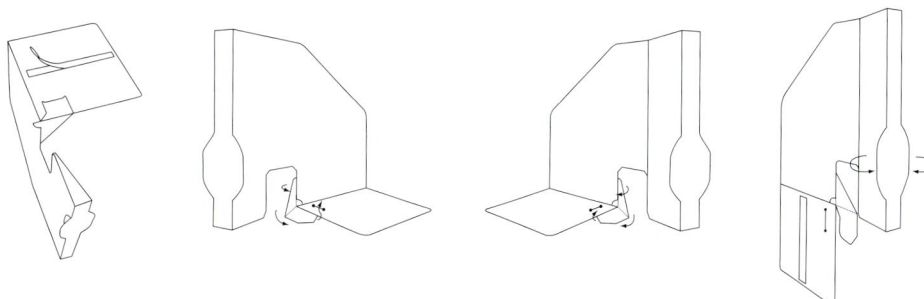

エバラ食品工業
EBARA FOODS INDUSTRY

黄金の味

担々ごま鍋の素

FLOOR P.O.P.

消費者に対して『商品認知と購入を同時に訴求できる販促物』をポイントに製作しました。消費者が遠くから見てもわかるように、商品をそのまま拡大したようなデザインに製作し、売り場での存在感と同時に、商品認知にも繋がるように工夫しました。スーパーのエンドや島陳に使用できるサイズと、商品の重量に耐えられる設計にしました。

Based on the concept "simultaneously promoting product recognition and purchasing" amongst consumers, this display uses an enlarged version of the product so that it is visible from a distance as well as create a greater sense of instore presence and promote product recognition. In addition to a compact size enabling use next to shelving or as an island display, it has a large capacity.

A / P：横浜エージェンシー
MATERIAL：紙類
W 530 × H 1130 × D 400

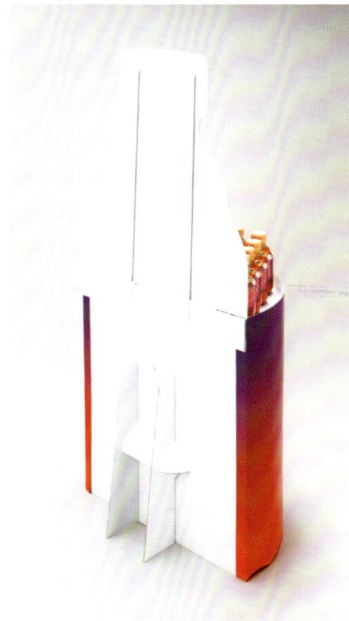

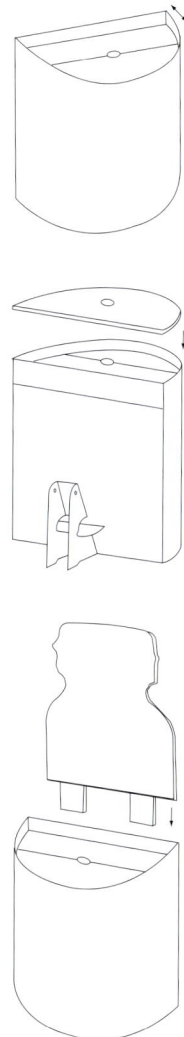

エバラ食品工業
EBARA FOODS INDUSTRY

コラーゲン鍋の素

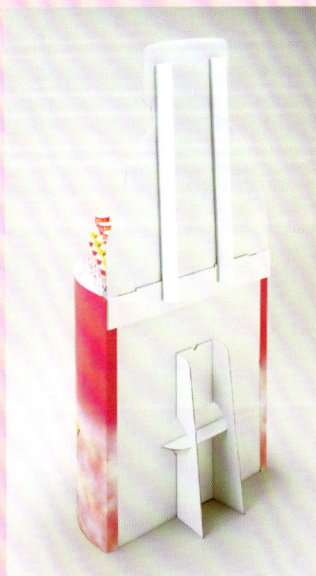

A／P：横浜エージェンシー
MATERIAL：紙類
W 220 × H 540 × D 70

FOOD

エバラ食品工業
EBARA FOODS INDUSTRY

料理にポン！コラーゲン

HANGING P.O.P.

『さまざまな料理に使えること』が
商品特徴なので、商品の特徴を活か
せる販促物としてカレンダー什器を
製作しました。カレンダー什器にす
ることで、スーパーのエンドや定番
棚・冷ケースなど商品の利用シーン
に合わせた売り場に陳列でき、売り
場での商品露出を高めました。

The product's main feature is
the way it "can be used in a
variety of foods," and to take
full advantage of this, a
calendar design was adopted.
Doing so allows the display to
be placed in various locations -
at the end of shelves, on
shelves, beside chill cases - to
suit each scenario, leading to
greater instore product
exposure.

211

エバラ食品工業
EBARA FOODS INDUSTRY

コラーゲン鍋の素

OTHERS P.O.P.

新規性・トレンドの高い商品であり、商品認知が低いことから『コラーゲン川柳キャンペーン』を絡めた販促物にすることで、商品認知と話題性を高め、より商品を身近に感じてもらい、購入に繋がるように製作しました。

A highly novel and trendy product. As product recognition was low, this display was used to promote the "Collagen Haiku Campaign." The aim was to increase product recognition and interest as well as create familiarity to encourage shoppers to purchase the product.

A / P：横浜エージェンシー
MATERIAL：紙類

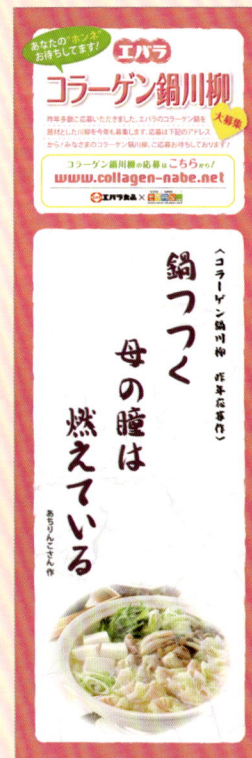

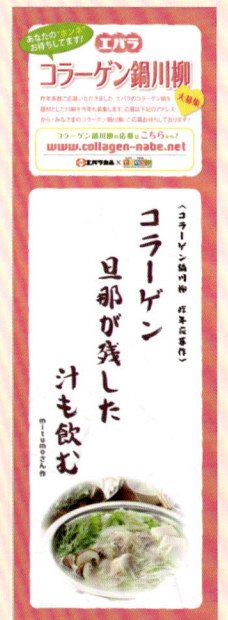

食べた後 お腹満足 肌満足♪
主婦集い "食べるエステ"と 鍋囲む!
エステより 簡単美味しい エバラで美
コラーゲン その文字だけで 効いた気に
起き抜けに 鏡へ直行 プルるんルン
我先に 潤いチャージ スープ飲む
食べ過ぎも 翌朝うれし コラーゲン
冷え性や お肌に嬉しい コラーゲン鍋
色気より 食気で綺麗に 鍋食べて
コラーゲン 旦那が残した 汁も飲む
翌朝の ハリを想って つつく鍋
美肌鍋 今日は私が 鍋奉行
ハリの素 一滴残さず たいらげた
肌のため 残さずさらう 鍋の底
鍋のシメ うどんも肌も ツ～ルツル♪
頬なでる コラーゲン鍋 食べながら
コラーゲン 聞いて飛びつく 五十代
エバラ コラーゲン鍋川柳 大募集
コラーゲン鍋川柳の応募はこちらから!
www.collagen-nabe.net
エバラ食品 ×
鍋つつき つついて平気の 肌目指す
明日合コン コラーゲン鍋で 勝負肌
食べるだけ 美人になれる 鍋の素
開けるだけ 簡単なのに ぷる肌さ
食欲と 美容がセット お得鍋
いつもより ツヤツヤ顔の 鍋奉行
鍋囲む 家族は笑顔 母美肌
鍋つつく 母の瞳は 燃えている
この鍋は 隣の女(ヨ)には 教えない
光る肌 美人の秘密は 鍋の元
ぷるぷるの 肌を夢見て 鍋つくる
コラーゲン! 残りつゆまで 顔に塗る
コラーゲン 食べるエステに イッテキマ～ス(^o^)
娘言う 汁は母さん 具は私
コラーゲン 美味しく摂るなら エバラ鍋
サプリより お鍋で摂ろう コラーゲン
肌ぷるん 美食同源 コラ鍋で
つるつるは 娘の肌と 我が顔
肌ぷるる ナベで差が出る 三十路かな
コラーゲン 肌の色かわる 鍋パーティ
朝起きて プルプルしてる? と父が言う

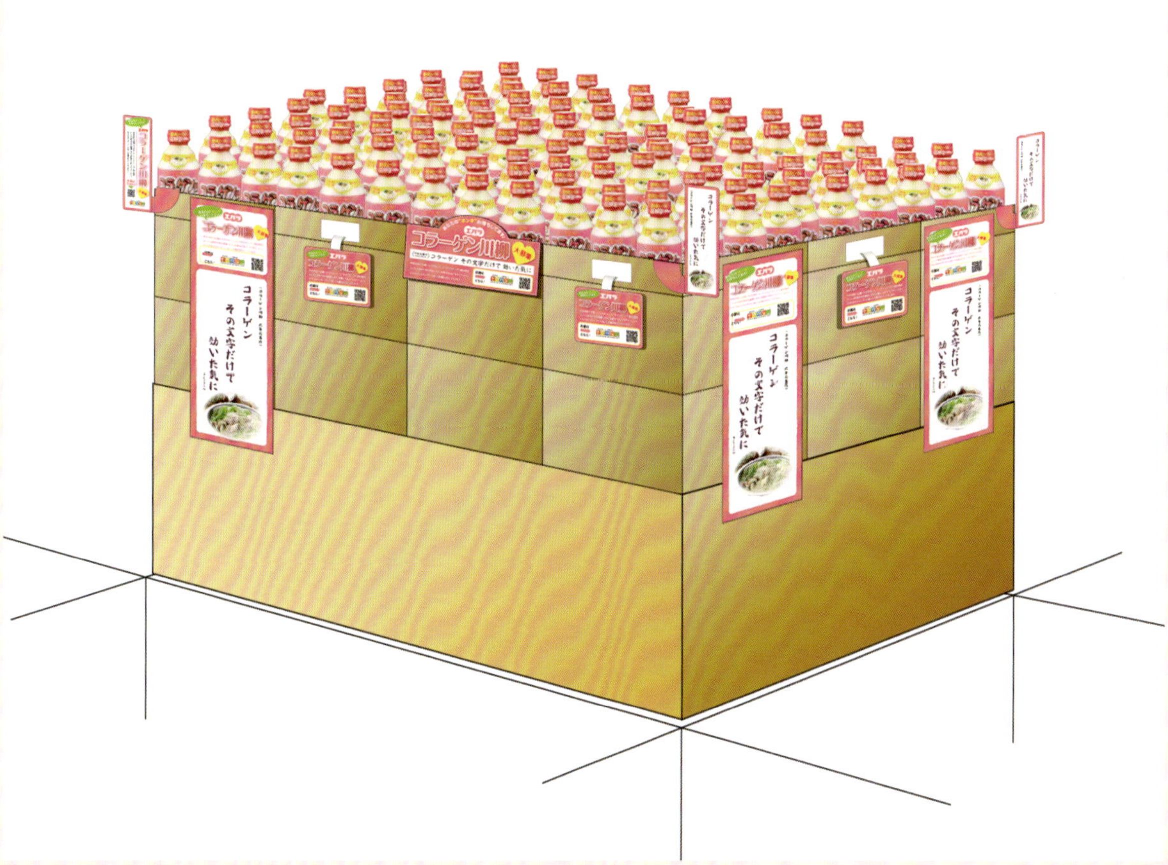

敷島製パン
SHIKISHIMA BAKING

Pasco 超熟® イングリッシュマフィン

COUNTER P.O.P.
HANGING P.O.P.

超熟イングリッシュマフィン発売に伴い、商品の認知を上げるためにパッケージをそのままエア POP にし、店頭での注目度を高めました。よりリアリティを出していくために、パンとパッケージを分けた構造になっています。また、このエア POP は自立することも、吊り下げることもできるので、店頭で幅広く使用できます。

In conjunction with the release of these Top-selling English Muffins, the packaging was used as a balloon POP to increase product awareness, leading to a higher product profile. To better simulate the real product, separate structures were used for the bread and packaging. Further, as this balloon POP can be used freely or hung from above, it opens up shop floor space.

A / P：ベストプロジェクト
MATERIAL：ポリスチレン樹脂
W 300 × H 750 × D 200

P：アルファ
MATERIAL：アクリル、スチール
W 270 × H 800 × D 100

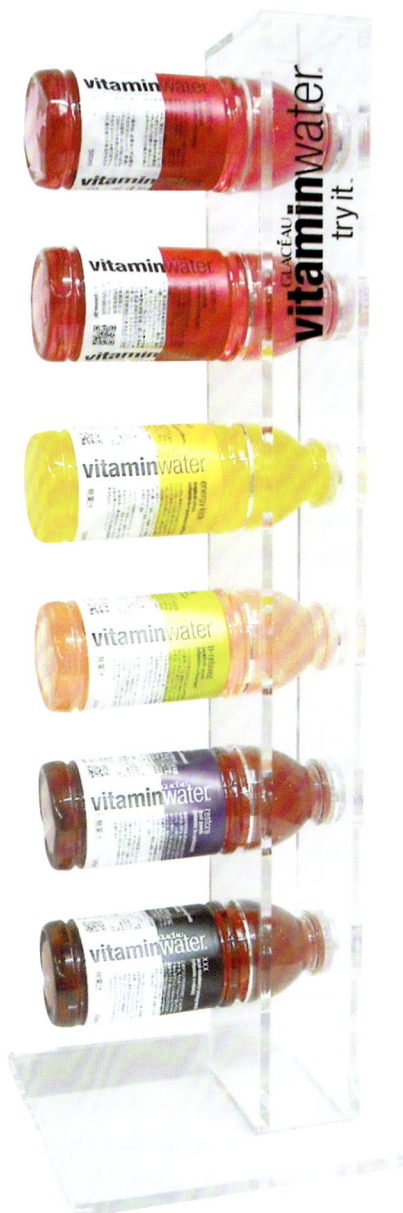

P：河淳
MATERIAL：アクリル
W 220 × H 670 × D 220

中国醸造
CHUGOKU JOZO

真っ赤ップ

HANGING P.O.P.

広島地域で販売している広島東洋カープ応援商品の清酒 200ml カップ拡売のために開発したハンガータイプのディスプレイです。カープの赤を基調に"上昇、勝利"をイメージし、スーパーなど量販店のエンドで消費者の目を引き、手に取りやすく、好位置のスペースを獲得するためにインパクトのあるデザインにしています。

This hanging type display was developed to expand sales of the 200ml sake cup sold in support of the Hiroshima Toyo Carp baseball team in the district of Hiroshima. Based on the theme "rise and conquer" in the Carp's team color of red, the display attracts attention as an end display in supermarkets, etc., enticing customers to pick up the product, and was designed for maximum impact so that it would be placed in a good location.

日本コカ・コーラ
Coca-Cola（Japan）

glacéau vitaminwater®

COUNTER P.O.P.

ワインラックのような形状・素材にすることでプレミアム感を演出し、グラソーブランドならではのスタイリッシュなイメージをより引き立たせています。またグラソー ビタミンウォーターのレインボーカラー戦略に則って、製品特徴の 1 つでもあるカラフルかつ鮮やかな液色を店頭で消費者に効果的にアピールできるよう、縦 1 列に製品を並べられる形状にして、カラーバリエーションをひと目で見て消費者の目に留まるよう工夫しています。

This display provides an expensive feel through a design and materials that resemble a wine rack, taking full advantage of the stylish image inherent to Glaceau. Strategically arranged so that the display effectively appeals to consumers with the bright and colorful tones characteristic of this product, the bottles of rainbow-colored Glaceau Vitamin Water are set vertically in a single row for a color variation that draws instant attention.

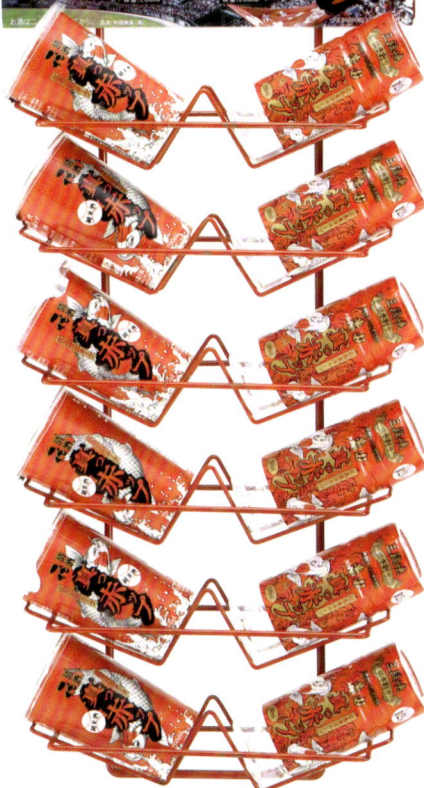

アディダス ジャパン
adidas Japan

2010 FIFA ワールドカップ 南アフリカ大会
adidas Every Team Needs a Shirt with a Story
キャンペーン

FLOOR P.O.P.

遠い南アフリカの地で、大いなる目標に挑む我が SAMURAI BLUE。「世界ベスト 4」、それは日本のサッカー史に「革命」を起こすこと。彼らと共に新たな歴史を創るべく、革命へ導く羽をまとえ。日本国民よ。「革命ヲ起コセ。」リアルコミック調のクリエイティブを生かし、店頭でのプレゼンスを最大化させるため、立体のジオラマ構造にて作成しました。

Japan's "Samurai Blue" national soccer team took on the monumental challenge of trying to "revolutionize" Japanese soccer history by gaining a place in the "world's top 4" in distant South Africa. This creative display uses realistic cartoon images to make customers feel like they are standing next to the players as they set about this challenge under the catch cry "Start a revolution!" A 3D diorama type construction was used to maximize presence.

EVERY TEAM NEEDS A SHIRT WITH A STORY

すべての個性を団結させ、革命を起こせ。

革命ヲ起コセ。
adidas.co.jp/JFA
IMPOSSIBLE IS NOTHING

adidas

P：プロスパーグラフ
MATERIAL：紙類、合紙
W 1500 × H 2280 × D 630

アディダス ジャパン
adidas Japan

2010 FIFA ワールドカップ 南アフリカ大会
adidas Every Team Needs a Shirt with a Story
キャンペーン

FLOOR P.O.P.

2010 アディダスのグローバルキャンペーンテーマは、"Every Team Needs..." それは 2010FIFA ワールドカップ南アフリカ大会を戦うチームに必要なもの、を展開していくキャンペーン。サッカー日本代表を初めとする各国代表に必要なもの …それは歴史と伝統が込められたユニフォーム。"Every Team Needs a Shirt with a Story" というテーマの元、各国の代表ユニフォームをリアルコミック調のクリエイティブを生かし、店頭でのプレゼンスを最大化させるため、立体のジオラマ構造にて作成しました。

The 2010 international campaign theme for adidas was "Every Team Needs … ," a campaign outlining what every team needs when competing for the 2010 FIFA World Cup in South Africa. And what does each of these national teams need? A uniform steeped in history and tradition. Based on the theme "Every Team Needs a Shirt with a Story," this creative display uses realistic cartoon images to depict the uniform for each team. A 3D diorama type construction was used to maximize presence.

P：プロスバーグラフ
MATERIAL：紙類、合紙
W 1500 × H 2280 × D 630

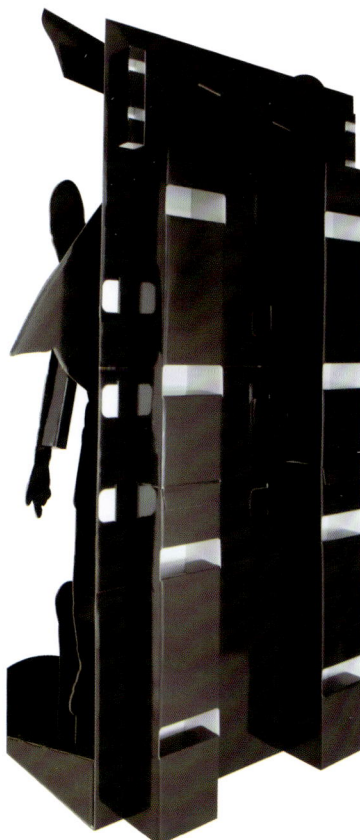

SRIスポーツ
SRI Sports

SRIXON Z-STAR シリーズ

FLOOR P.O.P.

陳列什器の本体及び背面にPRスペースを多くとることと、商品を多く陳列できるように開発しました。新商品の発売を、背面POPと本体の側面でPRすると同時に、商品を大量に陳列し、購入者の注意と購入促進を図りました。

This display was designed with ample PR space on both the main body and backing as well as a large area for displaying the product. While the rear pop-up and sides provide advertising about the release, the display holds numerous items, attracting the attention of consumers and promoting sales.

MATERIAL：紙類
W 400 × H 1640 × D 470

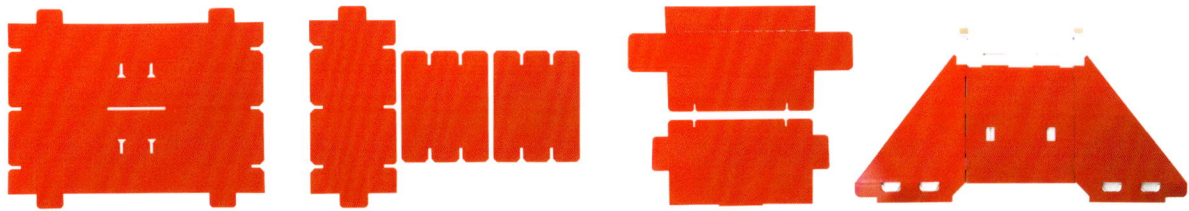
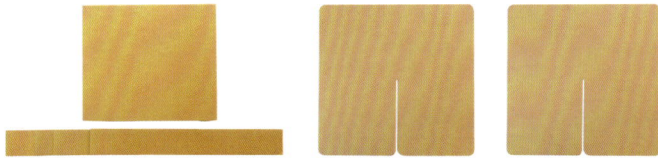
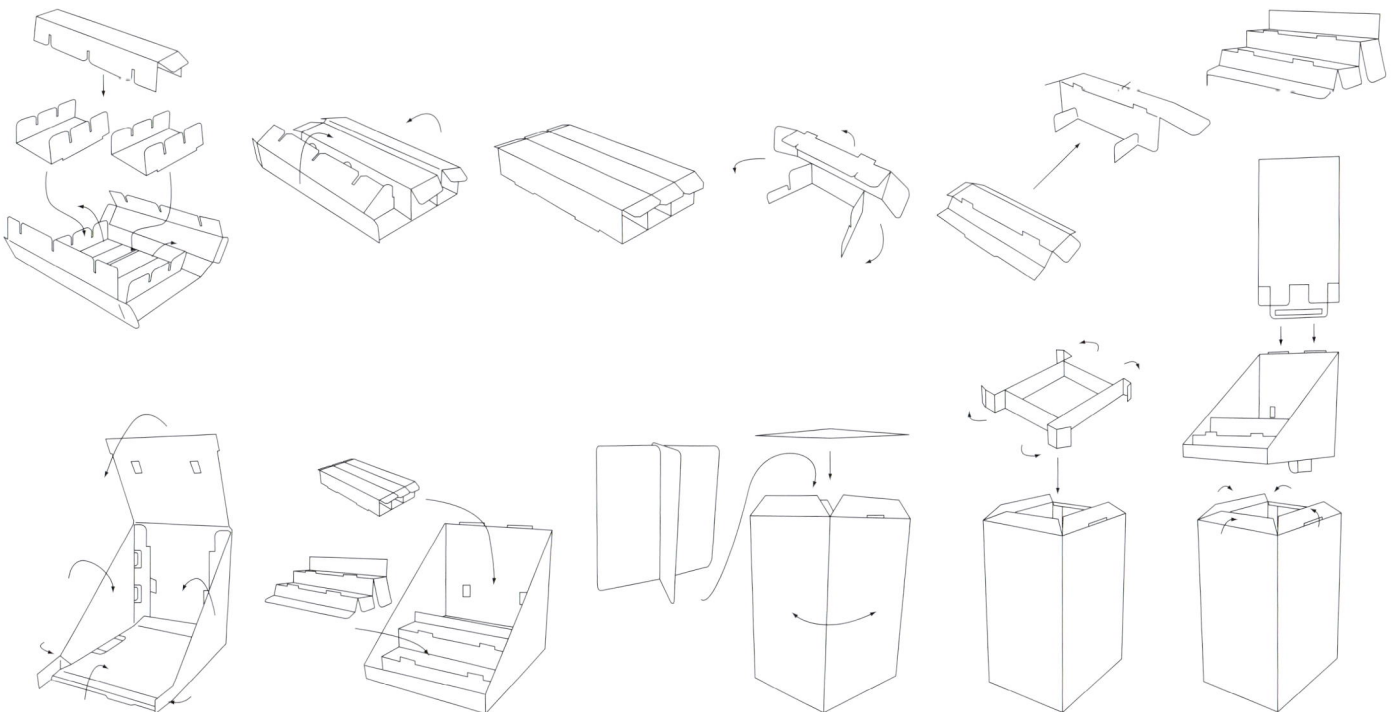

ヨネックス
YONEX

VERY COOL

運動時にクーリングと衣服の吸汗速乾技術を高め、衣服内温度を約 3℃低く保つ「ベリークールウェア」。石川遼プロ着用のポロシャツにも採用されているベリークール機能を、より多くのお客様へ知って頂きたく、涼感を感じられる POP を作成しました。メタリック素材のブルーから涼しさが感じられる仕様となっています。

"Very Cool Wear" lowers body heat by around 3°C during exercise using advanced technology to produce a cooling effect as well as improve the sweat absorption and drying properties of clothing. The polo shirt worn by pro golfer Ryo Ishikawa is made from Very Cool material, and the display aims to convey the product features to a wider audience through a "cooling" image pop-up. The cooling effect is enhanced through the use of metallic blue materials.

P：ワヨー
MATERIAL：紙類、PET
W 550 × H 400 × D 50

MATERIAL：紙類
W 110 × H 90 × D 60

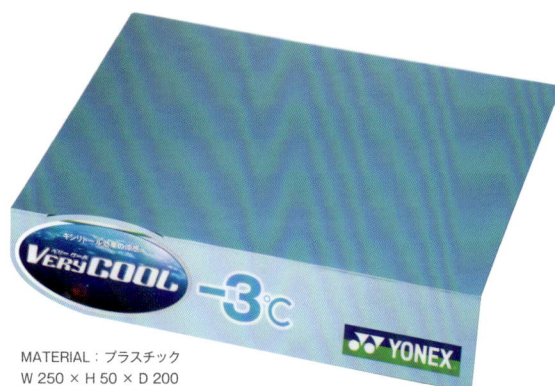

MATERIAL：プラスチック
W 250 × H 50 × D 200

W 110 × H 330 × D 60

ヨネックス
YONEX

春のラケットまつり

COUNTER P.O.P.
HANGING P.O.P.

毎年恒例となった春のラケットまつり。2010 年はヨネックスのラケットをお買い上げして頂いた方へ、オリジナルスポーツバッグをプレゼント。さらに抽選で 1,500 名の方へオリジナルラケットバッグをプレゼントするというキャンペーン内容にて開催致しました。ディスプレイは、新入生や新チームを対象とし、春の新緑のさわやかさ、祭りの賑やかさを表現。メインとなる POP は、天井からの吊り下げと床置きの 2 通りのディスプレイができる仕様とし、様々な店舗で賑やかな雰囲気を演出できるようにしました。

Every year, Yonex holds its customary Spring Racket Festival. In 2010, this display was used to announce a campaign offering a free original sports bag to customers who purchase a Yonex racket as well as the chance to go into a special draw to win one of 1,500 original racket bags. The display targeted newcomers and new teams, combining the refreshing green of spring with festival cheer. The main POP display was designed either to be hung from the ceiling or placed on the floor, and helped to brighten up the instore atmosphere.

P：小田急エージェンシー
MATERIAL：紙類、PET
W 620 × H 670 × D 80

W 620 × H 420 × D 100

MATERIAL：紙類
W 150 × H 210 × D 110

ヨネックス
YONEX

DISNEY SPORT
produced by YONEX

COUNTER P.O.P.
SWING P.O.P.

ヨネックスとディズニースポーツの
コラボレーションが実現しました。
キャラクターの可愛らしさを活用
し、お客様が楽しく買い物ができる
ように POP を作成しました。カタ
ログ立てにはミッキーをモチーフに
した形状とするなど、ディズニーの
世界観を表現しました。

This POP display was used to
announce a collaboration
between Yonex and Disney
Sports, and capitalizes on the
cuteness of the characters to
make shopping more enjoyable
for customers. A Disney theme
is established by using Mickey
as the motif on the catalog
holder, etc.

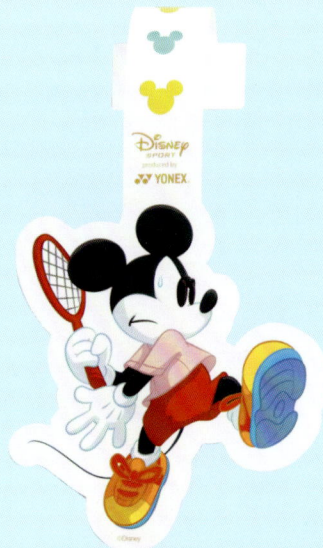

W 90 × H 95

W 105 × H 65

W 450 × H 165 × D 80

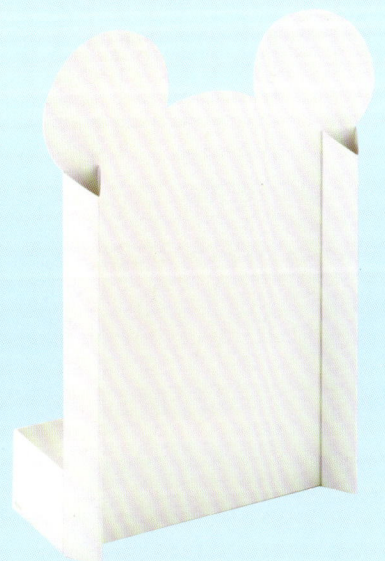

P：ロア・アドバタイジング
MATERIAL：紙類
W 250 × H 370 × D 110

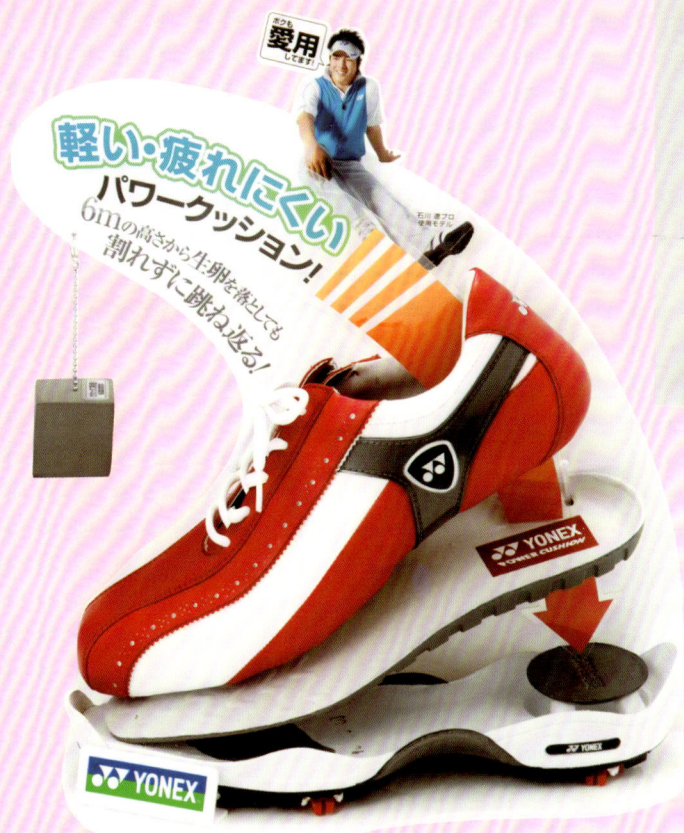

P：ワヨー
MATERIAL：樹脂
W 750 × H 380 × D 250

P：ランドマーク
MATERIAL：紙類

ヨネックス
YONEX

パワークッション
COUNTER P.O.P.

衝撃を吸収するのに反発する衝撃吸収素材「パワークッション」。6m の高さから生卵を落としても割れずに 3m 跳ね返るパワークッションを採用した、石川遼プロも愛用するゴルフシューズの機能を、より多くの方へ興味を持って頂きたく作成しました。シューズの構造はお客様の目に触れる機会が少ないので、店頭で直接手に触れている方が多く見受けられました。

"Power Cushion" is an absorbing material that protects from the shock of impact. The display was designed to attract more product interest from people by using the favorite golf shoes of pro golfer Ryo Ishikawa, claiming that if a raw egg were dropped onto the fitted "Power Cushion" from a height of 6m, that without breaking, the egg would be projected for 3m. As this shoe construction is not a common sight, many customers were seen touching the display.

第 100 回ヨネックス
全英選手権記念フェア
COUNTER P.O.P.
OTHERS P.O.P.

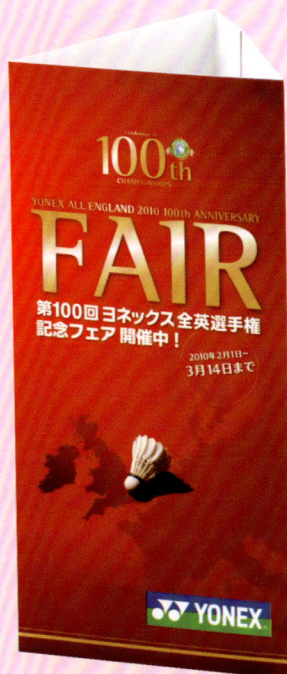

毎年トップ選手が集結するヨネックス全英選手権の 100 回大会を記念し、店頭販売企画としてフェアを開催致しました。三角柱型の形状を採用し、組み立てやすくどの方向からでも目に触れることをテーマとして作成しました。その他、店頭ポスター・バトミントンラケットシャフト POP・100 回記念リーフレットとセット組みし、統一したイメージを店頭にてコーナー展開を実施しました。

In commemoration of the 100th Yonex All England Open, an annual event that attracts top athletes, an instore fair was organized to promote sales. The triangular prism shape was adopted because it is easy to assemble and can be viewed from any angle. This was distributed along with a poster, badminton racket shaft POP display and 100th anniversary leaflet so that a theme-corner could be established in stores.

ワコール
WACOAL

夏キャンペーン

COUNTER P.O.P.
FLOOR P.O.P.

「汗に強い夏のワコール」をテーマに単品商品ではなくブラジャーを中心に肌着や機能ボトムを集約し、太陽のマークとブルーのカラーを共通カラーとして展開しました。機能をわかりやすく印象づけるためにインパクトのある体感ツールや POP を開発しています。

Based on the theme "Summer Wacoal: Sweat Resistant," this display is comprised of not individual products, but a collection of undergarments focusing on bras and functional bottoms, and was developed using a sun-like symbol with blue as the main color. To make the product functions easy to understand, this POP display was developed in combination with sensory tools that deliver an impact.

とっても軽い!!
新「スゴ衣」登場

汗に強い夏のワコール

吸汗速乾性にすぐれた
新「スゴ衣」。

スゴ衣®薄軽爽（シンプル）
CLA-140 キャミソール（サイズ M）の場合
約 **35g**

クールクリスタ NUDY®
CLA-181 キャミソール（サイズ M）の場合
約 **51g**

クールクリスタ
NUDY®

薄軽爽
スゴ衣

スゴ
薄　　スゴ
軽　　スゴ
爽　　新 スゴ衣

wacoal

MATERIAL：スチレンボード、紙類、金属
W 210 × H 345 × D 80

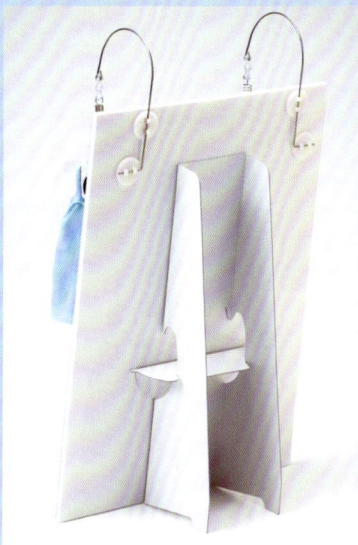

227

ワコール
WACOAL

夏キャンペーン
OTHERS P.O.P.

汗に強い夏のワコール
本日の
ムレムレ指数
90
ひどく
ムレムレ

MATERIAL：スチレンボード、PET
W 295 × H 180 × D 15

汗に強い夏のワコール
本日の
ムレムレ指数
70
かなり
ムレムレ

10 ムレムレ しにくい

30 ムレムレ しにくい

20 ムレムレ しにくい

40

50 すこし ムレムレ

W 240 × H 75

ワコール
WACOAL

夏キャンペーン

OTHERS P.O.P.

MATERIAL：スチレンボード
W 295 × H 180

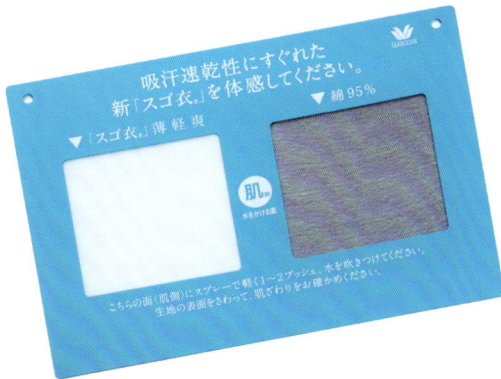

MATERIAL：プラスチック、布
W 265 × H 185

MATERIAL：プラスチック
W 105 × H 105

ワコール
WACOAL

夏キャンペーン

OTHERS P.O.P.

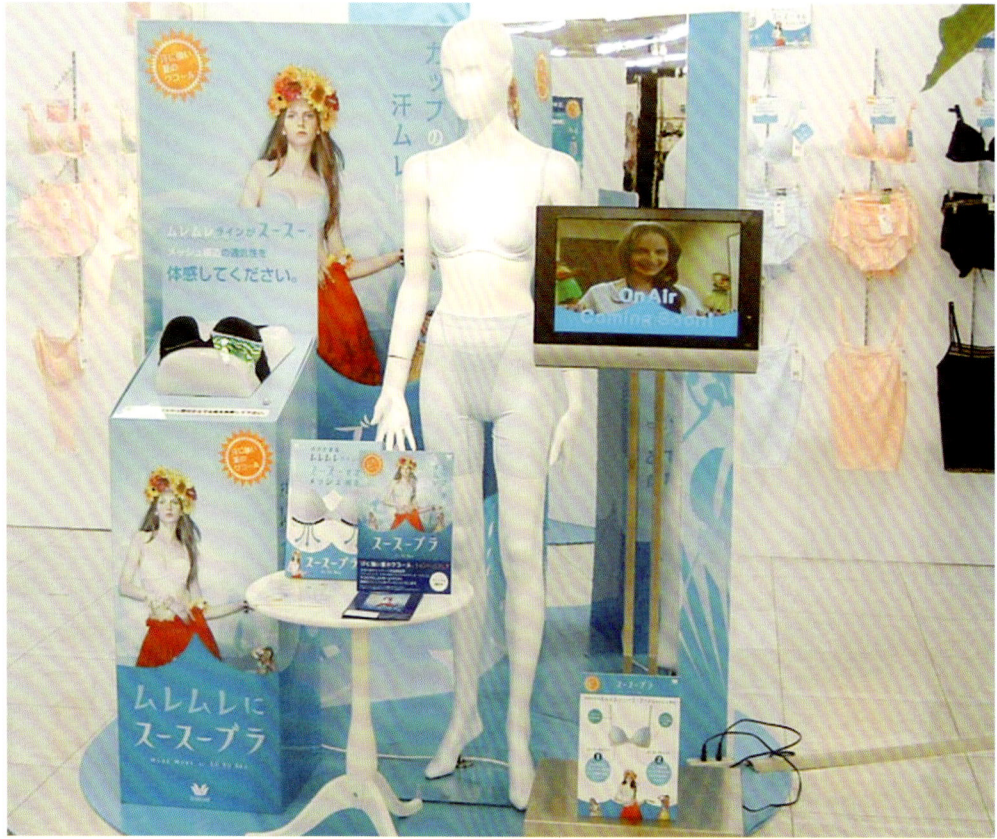

MATERIAL：スチレンボード
W 295 × H 180

MATERIAL：プラスチック
W 105 × H 105

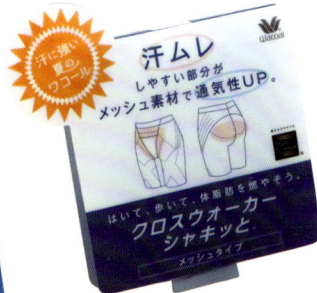

ワコール
WACOAL

ララン春キャンペーン
OTHERS P.O.P.

ブラジャーの商品特徴のリボンをア
イコンに春らしいピンクのカラーで
売り場を統一しました。素材に高級
感を持たせた POP や什器でター
ゲットの女性を意識した、かわいら
しく上品でわかりやすい演出で展開
しています。

Employing the product's
characteristic bow as the main
motif, this display was unified
with the rest of the store using
the spring color of pink. POP
displays and fixtures were used
to create a high-class feel, and
the result is a cute, elegant and
easy-to-understand display
targeting women.

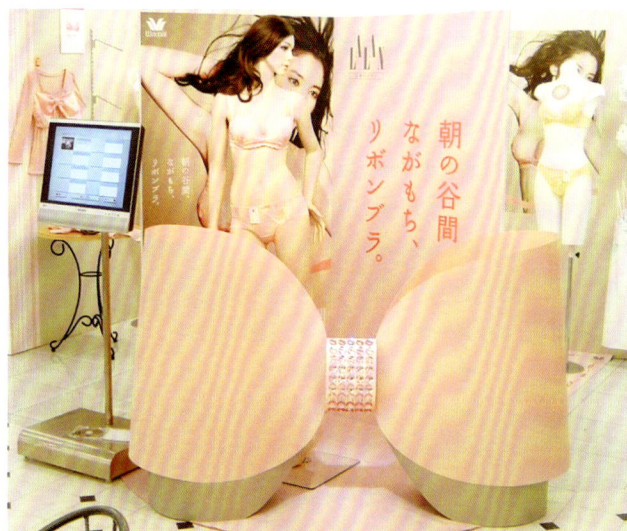

朝の谷間、
ながもち、
リボンブラ。

MATERIAL：プラスチック
W 100 × H 100

谷間ながもちの秘密
新開発「キープリボン」が
バストの動きにしっかりフィット。

新開発「キープリボン」

MATERIAL：紙類
W 295 × H 170

トリンプ・インターナショナル・ジャパン
Triumph International Japan

絶対恋するブラ

COUNTER P.O.P.
FLOOR P.O.P.
OTHERS P.O.P.

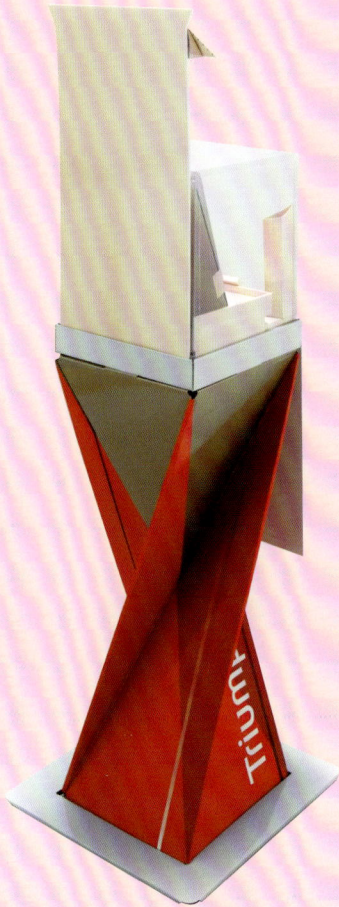

MATERIAL：紙類、アクリル、樹脂
W 450 × H 1420 × D 450

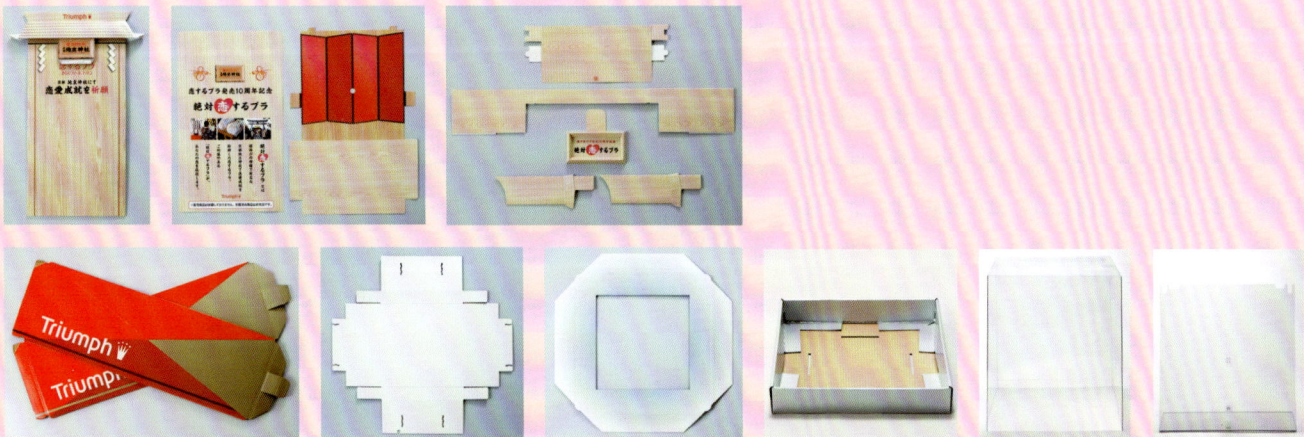

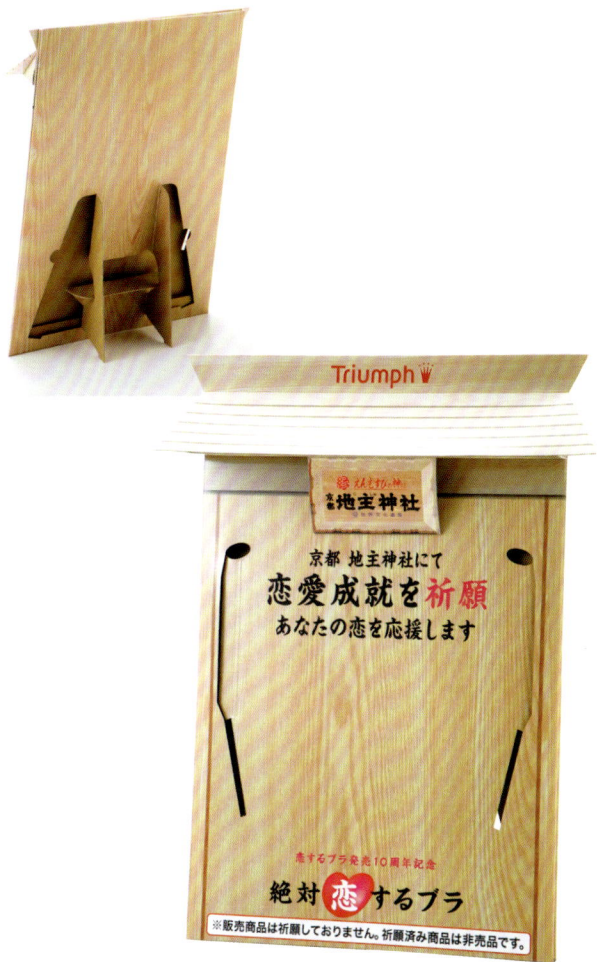

W360 × H 460 × D 90

W335 × H 245 × D 55

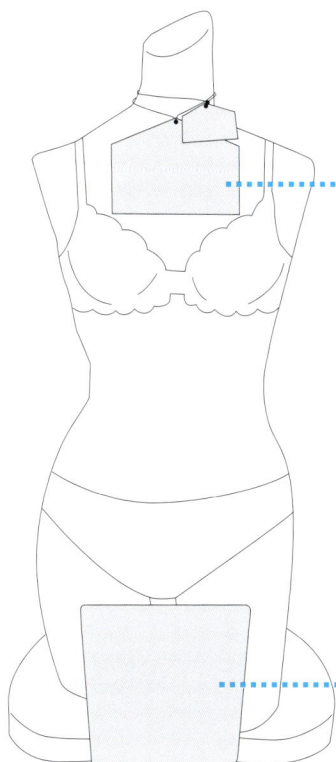

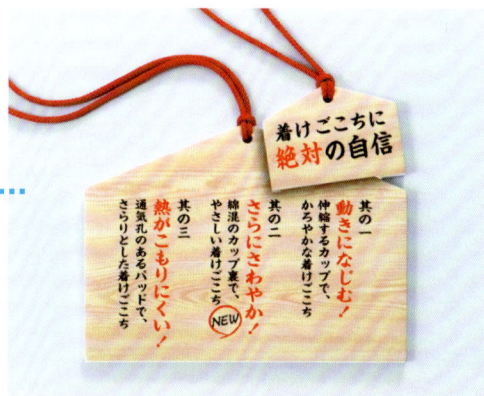

トリンプ・インターナショナル・ジャパン
Triumph International Japan

YoseAgeha

天使のブラ

恋するブラ

SWING P.O.P.
OTHERS P.O.P.

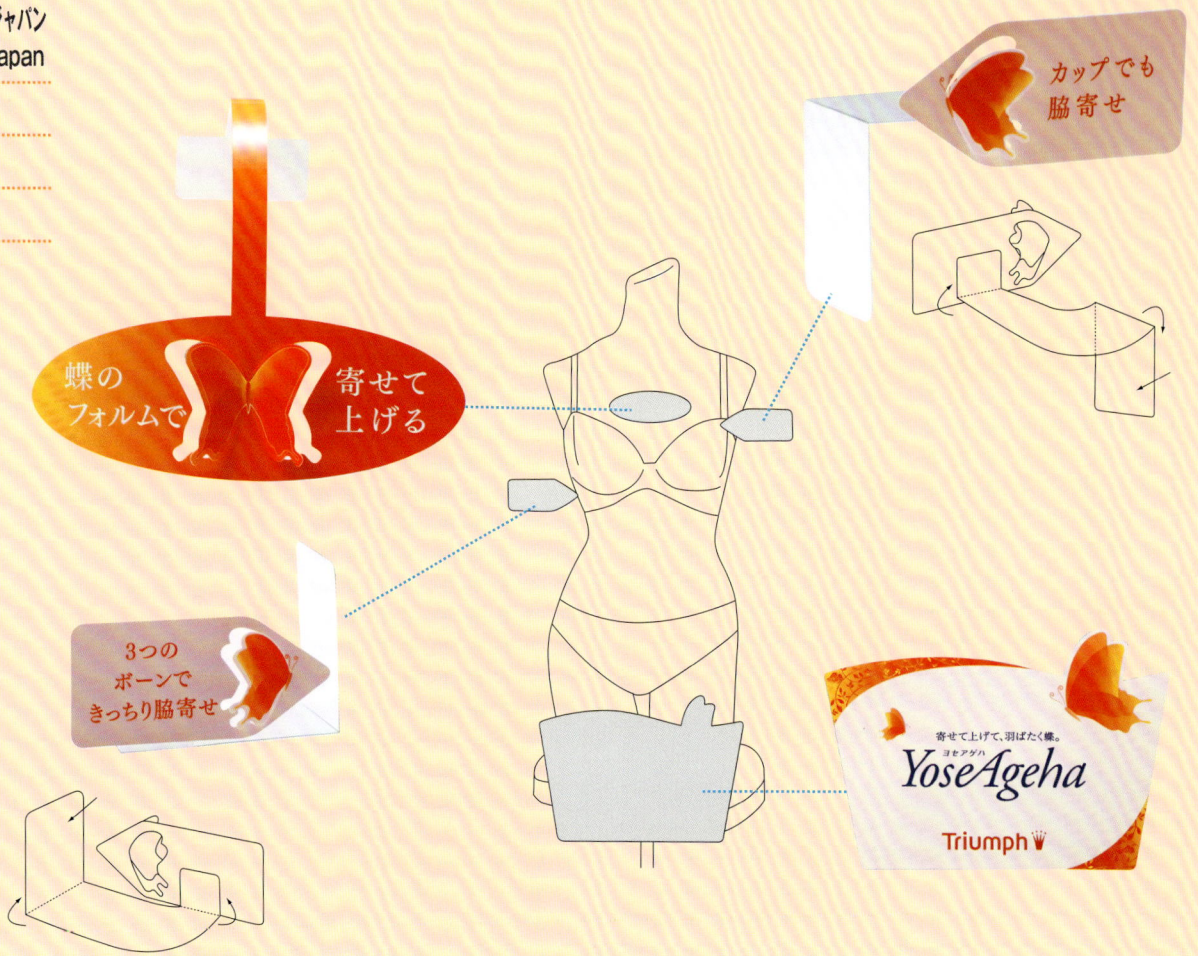

蝶の
フォルムで
寄せて
上げる

カップでも
脇寄せ

3つの
ボーンで
きっちり脇寄せ

寄せて上げて、羽ばたく蝶。
YoseAgeha
ヨセアゲハ
Triumph

谷間
くっきり

通気性
2.3倍
アップ！

谷間くっきり
天使のブラ
冷感エアー

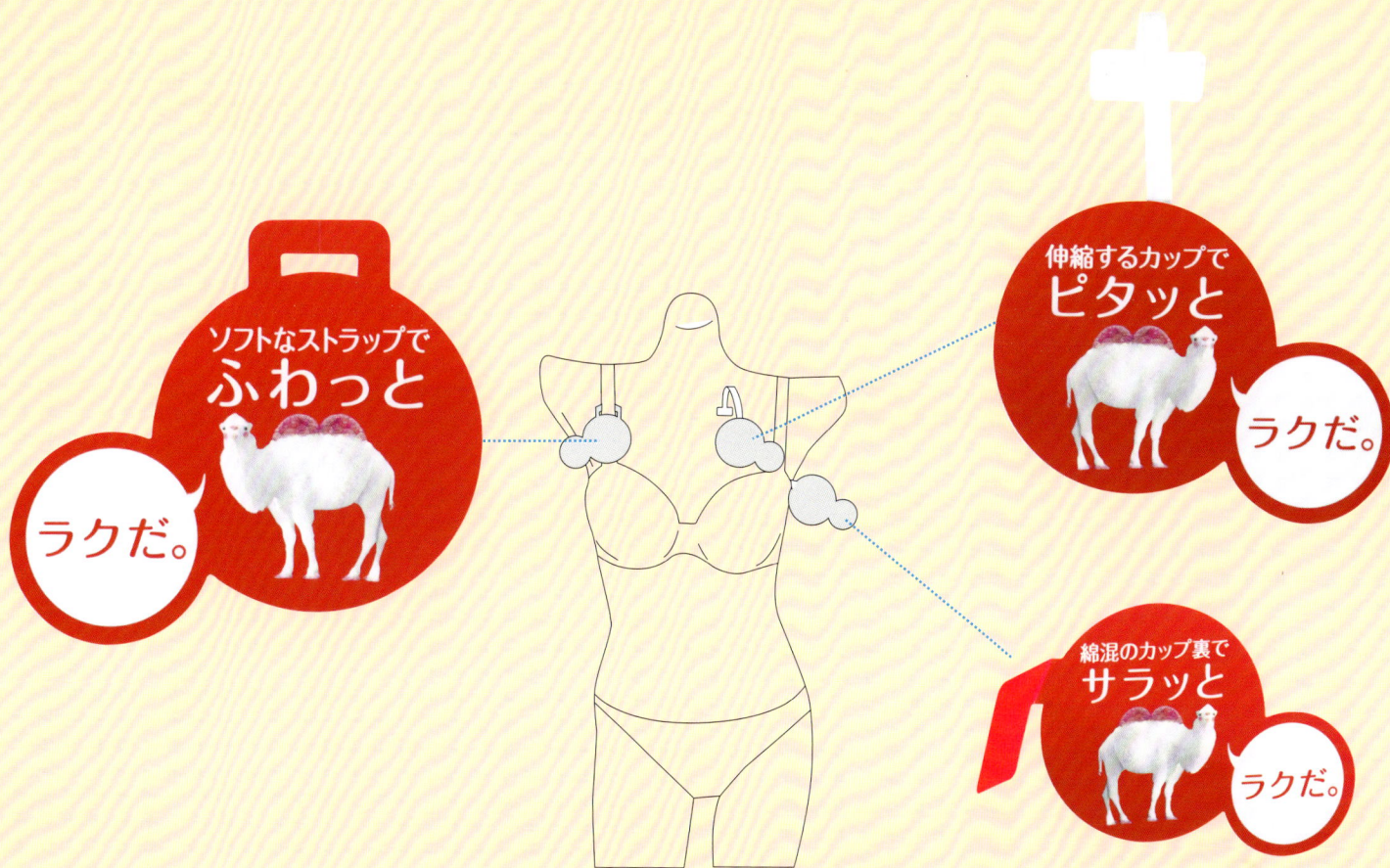

ワーナー エンターテイメント ジャパン
WARNER ENTERTAINMENT JAPAN

劇場版 銀魂 新訳紅桜篇

FLOOR P.O.P.

ターゲットとなる小中学生に対し、少しでも興味を持ってもらえるよう簡単に参加できるルーレット型フロアディスプレイを作成しました。ルーレットを回して、当たったキャラクターにその日1日なりきって！というコメントを入れ、一層楽しく参加してもらえるよう工夫しました。

To attract even a slight amount of interest from elementary and junior high students targeted by this campaign, an easy-to-use free-standing roulette wheel was adopted. Making it more fun for the children, the display asks them to spin the wheel and assume the role of the character it lands on for the whole day!

© 空知英秋／劇場版銀魂製作委員会
P：スパイス
MATERIAL：紙、ABS
W 1670 × H 2230 × D 450

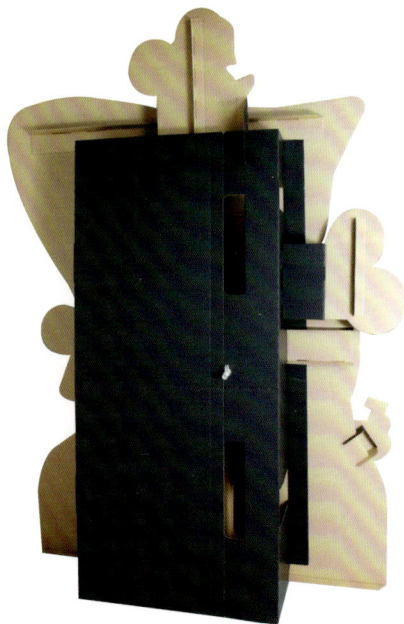

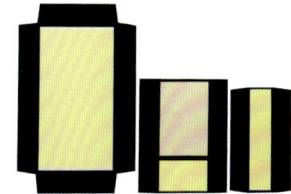

アスミック・エース エンタテインメント
ASMIK ACE ENTERTAINMENT

SAW6

FLOOR P.O.P.

映画館内でのディスプレイとして作成しました。劇中でキーとなる箱を立体的に表現し、その中にキャンペーンサイトへアクセスする QR コードを入れることで、思わず開けてみたくなるような参加型のディスプレイです。

This display was designed for use at movie theaters. The main feature is a 3D box containing the QR code customers need to access the campaign site, enticing them to open the box and look inside without hesitating.

P：スパイス
MATERIAL：紙
W 915 × H 1900 × D 550

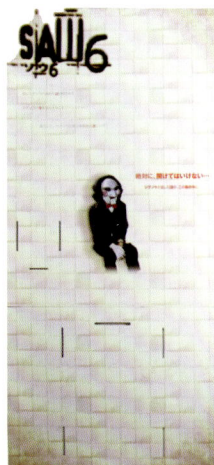

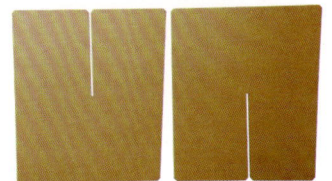

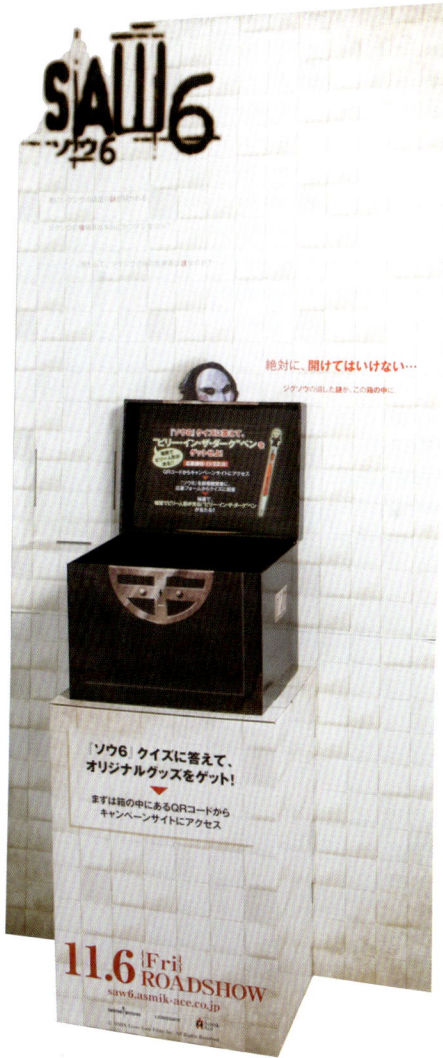

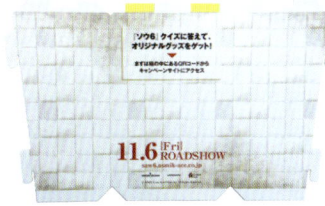

スクウェア・エニックス
SQUARE ENIX

FINAL FANTASY XIII

FLOOR P.O.P.

ファイナルファンタジーシリーズ発売をユーザーにアピールするためのアイテムです。作成コンセプトは「発売告知と大型タイトルとしての存在感」。主人公をメインビジュアルに使い、商品アピールを最大限に生かす為に大きさも等身大としました。発売近くで使用する立看板では、より目立ちより大胆にアピールする為にどこからでも見てわかる立看板にしました。特にキャラクター背面にはミラー紙を使い、ミラー部分にもキャラクターが写りこみ存在感を大きくしています。

This item was designed to advertise the release of the Final Fantasy Series. The development concept was "presence through release information and a large-size title." A life size image of the heroine was used for the main visual to maximize product appeal, and as a standing advertisement for use prior to release, was designed to attract attention from every viewing angle. In particular, mirror paper was used behind the character, with the reflection providing increased presence.

PS3

2009.12.17
発売

FINAL FANTASY XIII
ファイナルファンタジーⅩⅢ

SQUARE ENIX.

P：ソニー・ミュージックコミュニケーションズ
MATERIAL：紙類
W 760 × H 1770 × D 320

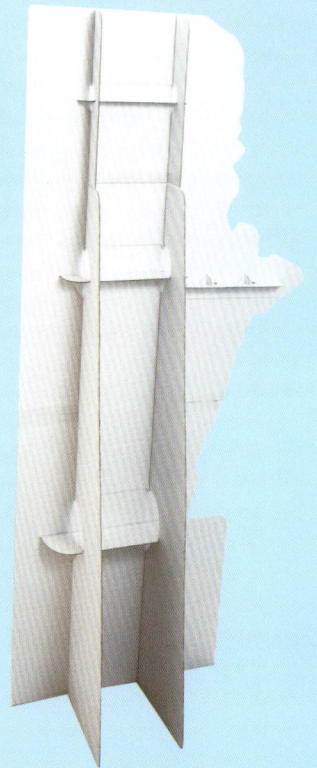

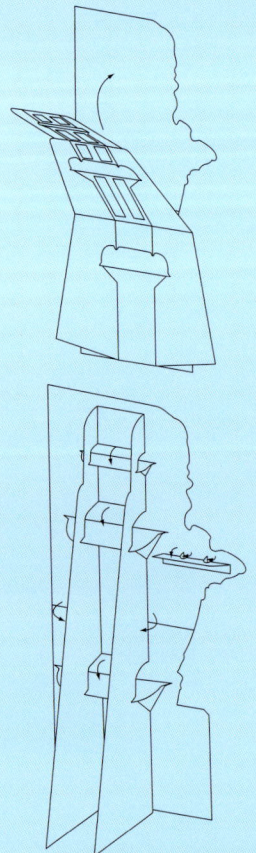

双対する世界の真実に触れた時、
人は定められし宿命と対峙する。

FINAL FANTASY XIII
ファイナルファンタジーXIII

2009.12.17 発売

P：ソニー・ミュージックコミュニケーションズ
MATERIAL：紙類
W 600 × H 1860 × D 280

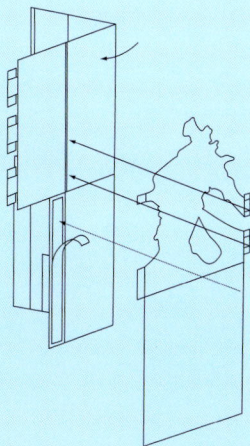

スクウェア・エニックス
SQUARE ENIX

FINAL FANTASY XIII

COUNTER P.O.P.
OTHERS P.O.P.

ゲーム登場キャラクターと各キャラ
クターに付随する召喚獣を紹介する
ためのアイテムです。作成コンセプ
トは「キャラクターイメージを購入
者へ伝達する販促物」。キャラクター
立看板は約１ｍ近くの大きさで作成
し、どこからでもキャラクターが分
かる事をを目指しました。さらに各
キャラクターのイメージ作りを画面
写真やキャラクターのワンシーンを
取り入れることでゲームソフト購入
前に、購入者がキャラクターへの愛
着をより持っていただけるようなア
イテムとして作成しました。

These items were designed to introduce the game's characters and the beasts associated with each character. The development concept was "items that convey the character images to consumers." The standing characters were approx. 1m high, and aimed for easy recognition of the character from any angle. Further, the items were designed to better familiarize consumers with the characters before they purchased the game software by using images such as screen shots and scenes of each character in action.

W 270 × H 900 × D 160

W 410 × H 870 × D 160

W 520 × H 850 × D 160

W 360 × H 580 × D 160

W 330 × H 880 × D 160

W 600 × H 760 × D 160

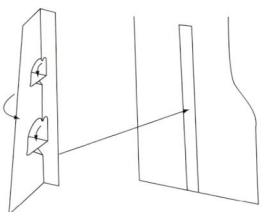

W 360 × H 200 × D 50

W 360 × H 200 × D 50

W 330 × H 190 × D 50

W 280 × H 165 × D 50

W 280 × H 180 × D 50

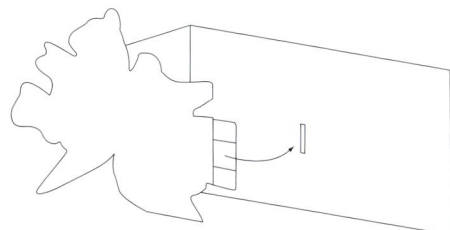

スクウェア・エニックス
SQUARE ENIX

FINAL FANTASY XIII

OTHERS P.O.P.

店頭棚や映像モニター周りで商品をア
ピールするためのアイテムです。作成コ
ンセプトは「タイトルアピールとゲーム
世界のイメージ作り」。人気タイトルで
あるファイナルファンタジーというタイ
トルを前面に出し、イメージカラーであ
る白背景と一目で分かるタイトルロゴを
前面に押し出しました。告知ポスターで
は3種類作成し、「ゲーム主人公＋発売
日告知」、「ゲーム世界感の表現」、「ゲー
ムの全体像の表現」と徐々にゲームタイ
トルの世界を表現していきました。店頭
で購入者は様々なビジュアルを目にし、
発売への期待感を作りました。

These items were designed to draw attention to the product by using them around the shelves and image monitors, and were based on the development concept "title appeal and gaming world images." The popular game title "Final Fantasy" was displayed across the front, and the title logo was emphasized by using it against a white background. 3 different advertisement posters were created to advertise the world inside the game: "game heroes + release information," "a scene from the game," and "a general image." Consumers were exposed to a wide range of instore visuals, creating a feeling of anticipation for the upcoming release.

W 900 × H 500

W 720 × H 490

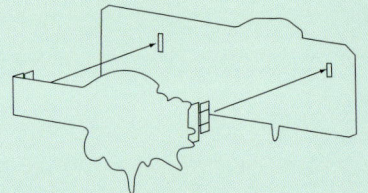

W 600 × H 280 × D 25

Poster

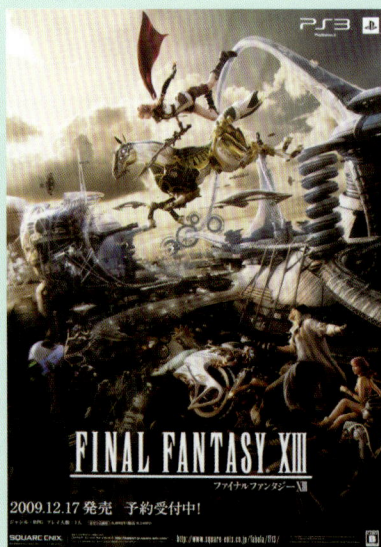

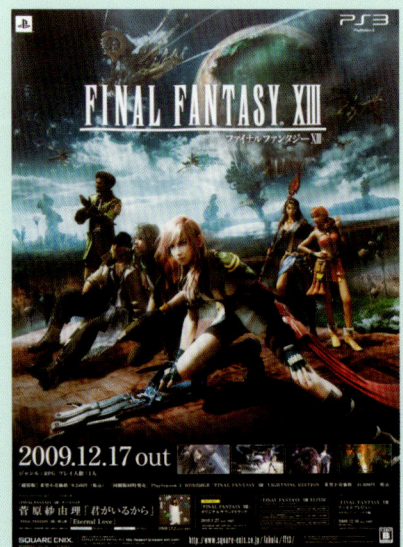

東映
TOEI

劔岳 点の記

COUNTER P.O.P.

タイトルの剣岳の険しさを、折りによって立体的に表現しました。また、豪華俳優人を並べてデザインし、作品の大作感を訴求しています。

A 3D effect was created by folding and modeling the material, adding to the sense of precipitousness indicated by the title. Further, a "big hit" feel was achieved by including a lineup of the all-star cast.

P：スパイス
MATERIAL：紙
W 270 × H 170 × D 130

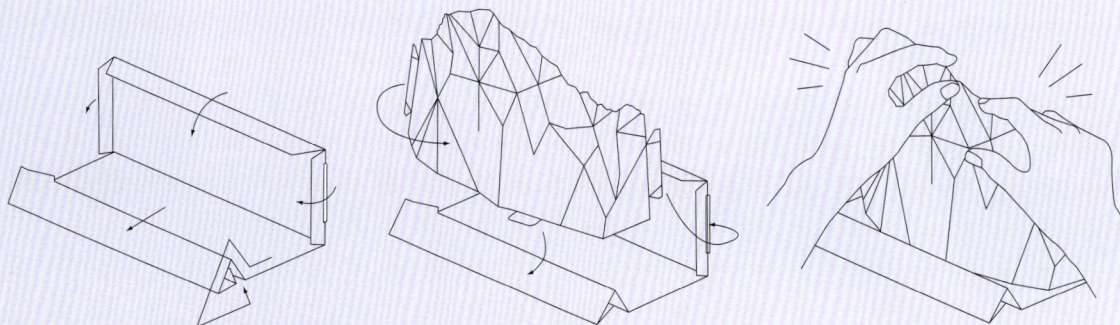

エクシング
XING

CROSSO

COUNTER P.O.P.
OTHERS P.O.P.

CROSSO 小冊子ケースは、お店で
のオペレーションを簡素化すること
を考え、梱包ケースがそのままディ
スプレイケースになる仕様となって
います。ドア POP は、カラオケ店
のルームに掲示し、設置機種とサー
ビス内容を訴求するものです。お客
様が店内を移動する際にも、設置機
種が一目でわかるような販促 POP
です。階段ステッカーは、カラオケ
店内の共有スペースを有効活用した
販促 POP です。表裏両面にデザイ
ンを施し、ガラス面に貼り付けて両
面から訴求することが可能です。ま
た、後ではがしやすいよう、弱粘着
シールを採用しています。

Simplified instore setup was a
consideration when designing
this CROSSO leaflet case, and
as such, the shipping case
itself was used as the display
case. The door POP display
was designed for use on the
doors of karaoke rooms to
inform customers of the
equipment model and available
services when they enter the
room. The sticker was
designed as effective common
area advertising for karaoke
establishments. A design is
featured on both the front and
back so that the sticker can be
attached to glass and viewed
from both sides. Further, it uses
a gentle adhesive to make is
easy to remove later on.

P：セブロ
MATERIAL：合紙、塩化ビニル
W 105 × H 150 × D 40

P：セブロ
MATERIAL：合紙、塩化ビニル
W 100 × H 200 × D 50

W 620 × H 120

Sticker

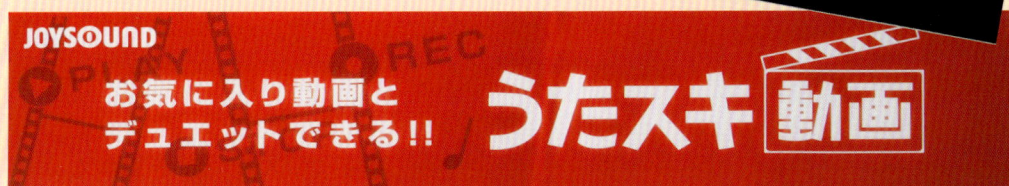

日本たばこ産業
JT

Winston

FLOOR P.O.P.
HANGING P.O.P.
OTHERS P.O.P.

いかに商品に興味を持ってもらう
か。さらに手にとってもらえるか。
商品広告の永遠の課題に挑むため
に、今までに無い超個性派キャラク
ターを起用しています。自販機など
中距離から視認できる買い場では無
視できない存在感と登場感に注力し
ました。気になる視線、誰なんだ、
どういうシチュエーションなのか
等。謎の存在感と記号性は、隙のあ
る表現により、ちょっぴりユーモア
を持たせています。CVC 店内など
の買い場では、限られたスペース、
情報過多な環境であるが故に、記号
性をより強調した表現、形状を追求
しました。

How interested are you in
products? Do you pick them
up? Original and highly
distinctive characters were
used to confront the age-old
topic of product advertising.
Efforts focused on creating
displays with a presence and
appearance that could not be
ignored and which attracted
attention from afar such as
vending machines. The
displays aimed to evoke
curiosity and responses like
"Who is that?" and "What's
going on over there?" An air of
secrecy and symbolism is
achieved through vague
expressions, adding a light
touch. As displays at CVC and
the like provide an abundance
of information within a limited
space, the aim was to create
emphatic expressions and
shapes through symbolism.

W 155 × H 280 × D 33

W 210 × H 400 × D 120

A：博報堂
P：ハックルベリー
MATERIAL：紙類
W 600 × H 790 × D 250

日清ペットフード
Nisshin Pet Food

JP-Style

OTHERS P.O.P.

他社よりワンランク上のイメージを演出するべく、メタル紙を使い、色調も黒を基調にした落ち着いたデザインにしました。正面だけでなく、左右のサイドボードをつけることによって、より一体感のあるエンドディスプレイに仕上げました。

This subdued display was designed to outdo the displays of its competitors using metallic paper based on a black theme. In addition to the board on the front, the display is made more complete by attaching side boards at the right and left.

A：リクエスト
P：スバル
MATERIAL：紙類、合紙、PET
W 1300 × H 2300 × D 450

プロクター・アンド・ギャンブル・ジャパン
P&G

IAMS

FLOOR P.O.P.

大きく高さのあるポストサインとして、ペットフード売り場の場所を店内で目立たせること、ブランドのキービジュアルを大きく配し、ブランドのイメージを創出しつつ、製品便益を同時に訴求すること、をコンセプトにしたフロア POP に仕上げています。

The concept behind this free-standing POP display was to make it stand out as a pet food display using post type signs of considerable height and recreate the brand image using oversized key visuals for the brand, while simultaneously highlighting the merits of the product.

MATERIAL：紙類
W 1000 × H 1800 × D 210

くらコーポレーション
Kura Corporation

回転むてん丸
FLOOR P.O.P.

「無添くら寿司」が展開するオリジナルストーリー〝回転むてん丸〟に登場するキャラクターを使用し、店頭で子どもたちの目を楽しませ、憩いの空間を作り出すよう制作したフロア什器です。

The characters appearing in the original story "Kaiten Muten Maru" developed by "Additive-free Kura Sushi" were used to delight children customers, and the result is a floor fixture that creates a relaxed space.

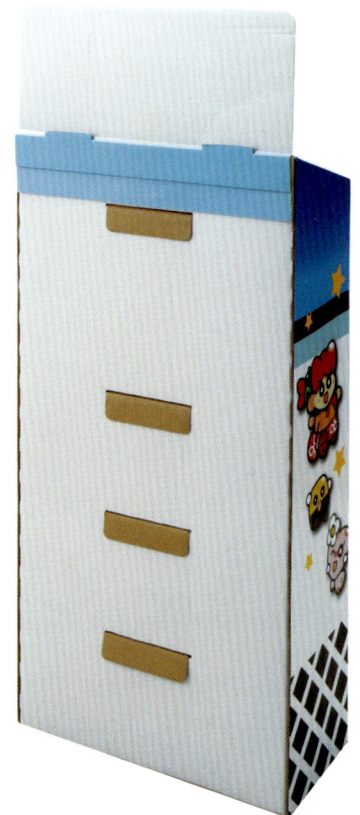

P：マスパック
MATERIAL：紙類
W 460 × H 1130 × D 210

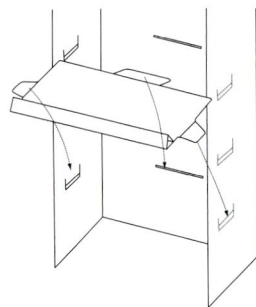

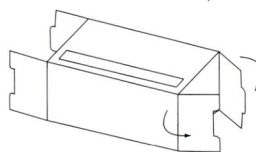

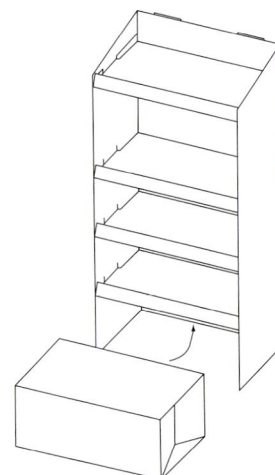

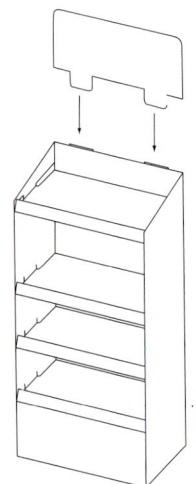

プラザクリエイト
PLAZA CREATE

MACARON カメラポーチ

FLOOR P.O.P.

自立式のフック什器は、幅をコンパクトにして、店頭に置きやすい仕様になっています。

The narrowness of this self-standing hook type display makes it easy to use.

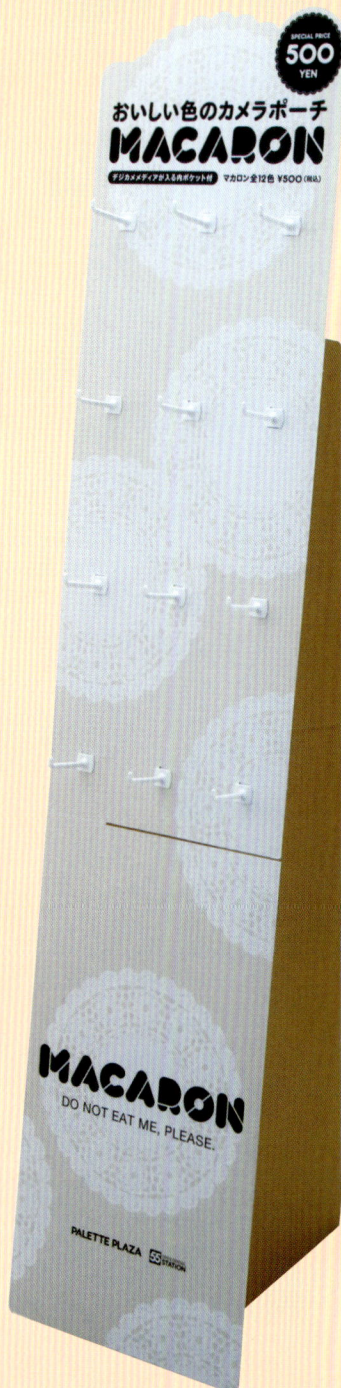

おいしい色のカメラポーチ
MACARON
デジカメメディアが入る内ポケット付　マカロン全12色 ¥500（税込）

SPECIAL PRICE
500 YEN

MACARON
DO NOT EAT ME, PLEASE.

PALETTE PLAZA 55 STATION

P：マスパック
MATERIAL：紙類、プラスチック
W 300 × H 1380 × D 350

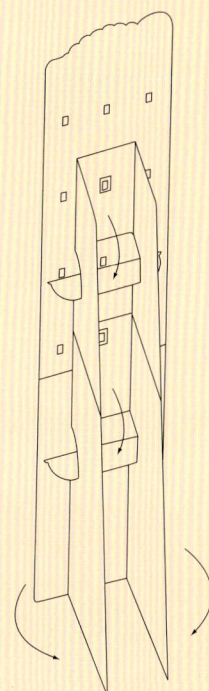